MW00623245

Carrier of Intention in 49 Jewish Prayers

Editors: Elizabeth W Goldstein
and Kimberly Burnham with
Forward by Shefa Gold

Creating Calm Network
Publishing Group

Music, Carrier of Intention in 49 Jewish Prayers published by The Creating Calm Network Publishing Group, Spokane, Washington

ISBN-10: 1937207137
ISBN-13: 978-1-937207-13-7

For reprint permissions and author presentations
Contact us at
Creating Calm Network Publishing
CCNPublishingGroup@Gmail.com or
Kimberly Burnham TheBurnhamReview@juno.com
(860) 221-8510
or contact the authors directly.

http://JewishMusic.CreatingCalmNetworkPublishingGroup.com

Co-editors, Rabbi Elizabeth W. Goldstein and Kimberly Burnham share the pages of this Jewish music anthology with 40 other authors including: Shefa Gold, Kimberly Burnham, Ann J White, Elizabeth W. Goldstein, Serene Victor, Natalie Young, Sheila Pearl, Susan Colin, Judy Caplan Ginsburgh, Joy Katzen-Guthrie, Rosalie Boxt, Beth Hamon, Shawn Israel Zevit, Robbi Sherwin, Jeff Gold, Hannah Seidel, Marci Vitkus, Rebekah Giangreco, Lisa Doob, Shira Wolosky, Sheldon Low, Saul Kaye, P. Faith Hayflich, Victoria Carmona, Brian Yosef Schachter-Brooks, Dahlia Topolosky, Mindy Sandler, Jack Kessler, Eric Komar, Rami Shapiro, Shira Kline, George Henschel, Diane J. Schmidt, Ruth Anne Faust, Aaron H. Tornberg, Arnie Davidson, Rebecca Schwartz, Shelly Aronson, Steve Dropkin, Ter Lieberstein, and Michael Gurian.

Gratitude

There is a saying, "A rising tide lifts all ships." An anthology lifts all spirits. This book is no exception and our gratitude goes out to all who made it possible including of course, the authors for sharing their stories, spiritual heart, wisdom, and expertise. We thank our families, our friends and all who have helped us grow and learn how to engage with our community and the universe around us. We give a special thank you to Ann J. White and Barbara Bolich for help with editing; and to all who read advanced copies and gave feedback to make this a better book.

"What would happen if one woman told the truth about her life? The world would split open." —Muriel Rukeyser.

We hope with these stories we open up new perspectives on the world and our place in the universe.

—Editors, Elizabeth W. Goldstein and Kimberly Burnham

What people are saying about *Music Carrier of Intention in 49 Jewish Prayers*...

"The book is so beautiful, I love everything I see." —Joy Katzen-Guthrie, co-author of *Music, Carrier of Intention in 49 Jewish Prayers*.

"The author's bios were riveting. I love reading about the journeys people take and the choices they make to get to a certain place in their life. Each person is unique and each of the authors has done such interesting things." — Mindy Sandler, co-author of *Music, Carrier of Intention in 49 Jewish Prayers*.

"Amazing to take one concept and have 49 different conceptions of it." — Shelly Aronson, co-author of *Music, Carrier of Intention in 49 Jewish Prayers*.

"Few of us walk into *shul* prepared to be stripped naked; prepared to be torn open; prepared to meet God in, with, and as ourselves and our neighbors. We come with the week's stories, triumphs, and tragedies, and may have no intention of dropping them. We don't come in order to be free. We must be coaxed toward liberation, and it is the music that does this." —Rabbi Rami Shapiro, co-author of *Music, Carrier of Intention in 49 Jewish Prayers*.

"Stellar work! So honored to be a part of this project." — Arnie Davidson, co-author of *Music, Carrier of Intention in 49 Jewish Prayers*.

Table of Contents

Sacred Relationships
Shefa Gold

For as long as I can remember, it was music that helped me to open the doors to mystery, meaning, love, connection, integration, transformation and the infinite realms. And yet, I grew up into a world where the work of the artist seemed marginalized ... as if the world would be built by more serious people. And then the artist might decorate that world, make it palatable or pretty, or entertain us with her fanciful flights of imagination and color. The making of beauty was seen as an afterthought or a luxury ... at best—something nice; at worst—a distraction from the real thing.

Nothing could be further from the truth.

In *Music, Carrier of Intention in 49 Jewish Prayers,* we find articulate proof of this truth: The vast treasures of liturgy and sacred text that we have inherited will remain locked-up, mute, and useless, until the yearning, radiant heart of the artist touches them.

The voices that you will hear in this book will inspire you to receive the gifts of sacred text and make those gifts your own. With music, we can bring dead words on a flat page to vibrant and astounding life. In addition, we can take those living words into the depths of our own hearts, where they will illuminate our own vast inner resources.

The power of intention activates those inner resources. And those inner dimensions can in turn transform our liturgy into a wondrously useful vehicle for transformation.

What all of these artists know is that we can't just look at a sacred text and "put it to music." It just doesn't work that way.

I must come into sacred relationship with that text—which means becoming vulnerable to its power or medicine. The music emerges from that place of vulnerability, from the delicate space of possibility between my deepest most passionate yearning and these ancient words. I must enter the mystery of that space, but I will bring with me everything that I know about melody, harmony, rhythm and breath. I bring my enthusiasm and all my strength and talent. I also bring my raw intention, which will be refined in the fires of the creative process, purified by the living waters of inspiration, blown open by the *Ruach HaKodesh* (The Holy Spirit) and grounded in the Tradition that I have inherited.

In *Music, Carrier of Intention in 49 Jewish Prayers* you will meet a fabulous array of explorers and adventurers who have had the courage to step into the wilderness in order to have a direct encounter with God/Truth. Emerging from that encounter, each of these explorers has been willing to make a joyful sound with exquisite faith in the power of that sound to unite us in love, heal our broken hearts and send the world to its dance.

—**Rabbi Shefa Gold**, author of *The Magic of Hebrew Chant: Healing the Spirit, Transforming the Mind, Deepening Love* published by Jewish Lights. September, 2014, Jemez Springs, New Mexico.

The Journey Begins
Kimberly Burnham

During the *Selichot*, 2013 services in Boulder, Colorado tears ran down my face. The music and words of the prayers touched my heart. *Selichot* is a service with penitential poems and prayers, especially those said in the period leading up to the High Holidays of *Rosh Hashana* and *Yom Kippur*.

2013 was the first year I started my journey towards the High Holy Days at *Tisha B'Av*—a day commemorating the tragedies that have befallen the Jewish people. In the middle of the United States on Hazon's Cross USA bicycle ride, at a campground; I sat on the rustic floor of a cabin as Hannah Seidel chanted Lamentations (*Eikhah* in Hebrew). I didn't understand the Hebrew words, but the feelings—the loss, the destruction, the sadness—traveled through the ages in her voice. Through the vibration, I felt the brokenness. I knew I had to step up and contribute in a bigger way to *Tikkun Olam*, healing of the world.

The Hazon's 2013 Cross USA ride was also an opportunity to visit, pray and worship with 20 or so communities from Seattle to Washington, DC. These included Jewish Renewal, Reform and Reconstructionist, Conservative and Orthodox communities, from big East coast cities to tiny Western communities, which rarely even have a *minyan*—the 10 Jews needed to, have a formal Torah service. Every Shabbat, Hannah Seidel, the other bicyclists, and I learned in new communities. I saw strength in diversity. I felt the way I was similar and different from the people I met. I connected deeply in some places and felt still the stranger in others, but in every community, I learned something about Torah, about sustainable environments, about people and most of all about myself. I learned what I need to connect to that higher power surrounding me. This book grew out of my experiences.

Music, Carrier of Intention in 49 Jewish Prayers is a look into the very heart of a Jewish prayer community. It is a way for each of us to learn, grow and find stronger ways to connect. It is a way to heal our world and ourselves.

I hope that you enjoy the wisdom, the inspiration and the intention of each of the authors as much as I do. You will find the words and heart-felt emotions of Rabbis and Cantors, talented musicians and gifted writers, liberals and conservatives, people from vastly different communities from your own. You will find ways to connect and learn from the differences as you read individually or study in a book group or other community setting.

I hope you will think about your stories and the songs you connect with most deeply. The Jewish-American poet, Muriel Rukeyser (1913-1980) said in her poems, *The Speed of Darkness*, "The Universe is made of stories, not of atoms."

Each chapter ends with a set of questions for you to consider. Our promise is that as you read the stories and feel the dance of the words, you will experience more ways to engage in magical and breathtaking relationships. Let the journey continue...

—**Kimberly Burnham**, PhD (Integrative Medicine), Co-owner of the Creating Calm Network Publishing Group. September, 2014. Spokane, Washington.

Bringing the Liturgy to Life, Notes to Congregations, Communities and Book Clubs
Ann J. White

When I had a congregation, I marveled at their hunger for knowledge. What is the story behind this song? What are its biblical ties? What was life like at the time of the song's creation? And most importantly, how can we bring the message to life in our world and day-to-day living?

Music, Carrier of Intention in 49 Jewish Prayers is a powerful teaching tool. It can breathe life and personal meaning into liturgy. It is a treasure trove of wisdom.

Some of the chapters describe the history of the song; others reflect on personal remembrances invoked by the music; and still others open doors to transformation.

There are many ways congregations can use this inspiring book to expand their knowledge of the liturgy and thereby enhance their *kavanah* or intention as part of a Jewish life experience.

One way to engage is a weekly study where the group looks at one chapter, one song per meeting. If a cantor is present, the song could be sung—perhaps shining light on the various melodies. Having the congregation's *siddur* or prayer books would also be important so the group can discuss their memories and feelings when the song is chanted or sung. Each chapter can be shared, with the discussion questions used to fuel group ideas and comments.

Another way to read could be to have a monthly study Shabbat service and during that service, one chapter could be presented, the song chanted, and the questions discussed as a way of enhancing the ritual or liturgical experience.

Rabbis can use various chapters as seeds for sermons and discussion while at the same time sharing his or her personal experience of the song.

A congregation might use this book as a resource for possible scholar-in-residence opportunities by asking various authors to visit with them and share their magic. Technology is such that perhaps one or two of the authors could visit your group via Skype or a Google hangout.

Individuals and groups can also imagine what they would write with an invitation to be in this book. What would you have written in your chapter? Would you have written a song, a poem, or an essay? Would your piece have shared a glimpse of your inner landscape or your experience of a particular song in your community?

Contact us if you would like to participate in Volume Two, or if you would like one or more of the authors to speak to your community in person or via phone or skype.

There is no end to the teaching this delightful, thoughtful, and poignant book offers. The myriad ways it can be used to uplift and breathe meaning into your Jewish experience are rich and powerful.

—**Ann J. White**, Rabbi and Publisher, Creating Calm Network Publishing Group. September, 2014. Sheboygan, Wisconsin.

Openings

"There are gates in heaven that cannot be opened except by melody and song." —Attributed to Rabbi Shneur Zalman of Liady, founder of Chabad.

Meditation on Birchot Hashahar—Morning Blessings
Elizabeth W. Goldstein

As I prepared for the 2013 Hazon Cross Country ride in which I planned to bicycle across the state of Washington, I was incredibly fearful that I would be unprepared. Serene Victor bicycled across the US with Hazon the previous year, in 2012. I had met this energetic, 65 year old woman briefly, in Spokane a week into her ride. Almost a year later, I noticed on Facebook that she was in town (across the country from her own home) and I reached out to her. I had so many questions about riding long distances. She invited me to ride with her the next day on the beautiful Trail of the Coeur d'Alenes in Harrison, Idaho. I accepted and another friendship was born. She reminded me of her blog which she had written the year before during the 2012 summer. Using bits of liturgy, her words give new meaning to our prayers. Here is one example:

Blessed is Adonai our God, who rules the universe, and has given the rooster understanding to distinguish between day and night. (Birchot hashachar, Morning Blessings)

July 9, 2012: "It is human to strive for mastery of the universe. In fact, the biblical story of creation describes this as a central task of humans. We are created in the image of God, the Creator, and thus we create ways to control and order our lives. As moderns, we are consumed by this striving and have been able to exercise so much control over our environment that we feel like masters of the universe but for extraordinary acts of nature that pull us back to a realization of our vulnerability. But there are regular, everyday moments, too, that can pull us back into alignment.

We are now regularly waking with the sun and going to sleep with the moon. It struck me that the first of the *"birchot hashahar"* quoted above acknowledges this clear distinction of night and day that we are experiencing on this ride. There was no artificial extension of light into the night, no pulling the shade to keep a room dark to extend sleep. In this biking community, we are in harmony with the rhythms of the universe. When I recite this blessing, I now mean what I say." —Serene Victor, Newton, Massachusetts, SereneBikes.Blogspot.com.

http://SereneVictor.CreatingCalmNetworkPublishingGroup.com

Growing Your Spiritual Community

1. Do you have some kind of morning ritual or practice?

Harmonizing a New Journey
Natalie Young

Adonai s'fatai tiftach ufi yagid t'hilatecha
Eternal God, open my lips,
that my mouth may declare Your glory.

As long as I can remember, my life has been filled with music. I take in the world through this lens and hear music as the wind blows through the trees, or in the ocean as the waves lap against the shores. My conversations with God are filled with music. I feel blessed to have music as a creative outlet, where melodies fill me and penetrate my soul. For me it is the way I can express the deepest parts of myself. The words I seek to share what I am feeling don't always come so easily. Sometimes I let music speak for me.

Anyone who has sat through a movie without a soundtrack can attest to the awkwardness of the experience. Music is a tool to help guide the emotions and reactions of an audience, from setting up suspense, or fear, to a moment of the hero's triumph. Much as music is used for the screen or the stage, the music created for our Jewish services is quite similar.

As a composer of Jewish music, I have sought to create music that can connect me to our liturgy. Music is born out of intense emotion...out of tragedy and great joy; out of questions, longing, healing and hopefulness. Music is our way of connecting to the deepest most hidden parts of ourselves. Through song, we can move from a place of solitude to a place of belonging and community. We can move from quiet meditation and personal contemplation to a place of joy and celebration. It helps tell our story and helps us remember who we are.

In crafting a service, I see my role, as a cantor, as the director of a sacred drama. I want to bring my congregation on a journey of spirit, so that each person is elevated and changed by the end of their experience. I want people to feel empowered to find their voice and to connect in a personal and meaningful way for them. Music can serve as a thread to tie one element of a service to the next so that each prayer flows one to another in some kind of context, rather than our prayers feeling random and superfluous.

As a prayer leader, I have learned that a congregation reflects the energy and commitment that is put out by those leading services. We act as a mirror. If we ourselves are withdrawn or not spiritually invested in what we are doing; if we passively sit back and don't engage when someone else is at the helm, our congregants will often take that as permission to do the same. We must be present at all times, in body, mind, and spirit. To be part of a sacred community is not for the leadership alone to manage. And to be part of a sacred drama with that community means that the congregation needs to know that they are part of the cast and that they need to actively engage. While the words of our prayers can seem inaccessible for some, through music, texts can rise off the page in a more meaningful way. They connect to us through our emotions.

Open Up My Lips

"Adonai s'fatai tiftach, ufi yagid t'hilatecha."

*"Oh God, open my lips
that my mouth may declare your glory."*

This opening meditation to the *Amidah,* our standing prayer which leads us into our personal time to talk to God, is central to the message that I hope to share with my congregants. We don't all have the words we need when we seek them. For me this prayer acknowledges our humanity and has us turn to something beyond ourselves, to God, to help us find our voices.

"Open my lips" we ask God to help us actively engage and find the proper words to praise God. For me, the most personal way is through song. After all, it is music that gives wings to our words and frees them from the recesses of our mind and heart, allowing them to ascend outward and upward. The words of this prayer are personal and will mean something different for each person who prays them. As we prepare to turn inward and have that private conversation with God, the text invites a quieter and more reflective melody. We must consider what mood will be set by the particular musical setting of a prayer. More importantly, how does each prayer flow from the previous prayer and on into the next?

Harmonizing

My first year of cantorial school was spent in Jerusalem learning with colleagues and friends and gathering inspiration from our rich Jewish culture. I remember sitting on the balcony of a friend's apartment with my guitar, experimenting with a new chord progression, when this haunting melody flowed though me. I sang it over and over until it stuck and became my new setting for *"Adonai S'fatai."* I created two more parts that afternoon and had the blessing of two cantorial friends and colleagues there to try it out with me. Each voice seemed to add a greater depth to the piece, layering upon the previous voice until the three parts wrapped around each other in rich harmony.

There is something magical that happens when voices come together to create harmonies. In order for those harmonies to work, people have to listen to each other and make room for one another. If one voice tries to overpower another, the balance is off and it all falls flat. It takes finesse and sensitivity to create balanced harmony and positively focused energy in music. As a cantor who works with other vocalists and instrumentalists, we are constantly striving to recreate those moments in rehearsals so that when we come together for services, we can focus our energy on bringing the congregation in on what we have created. It is an amazing experience to have the entire congregation singing with us in harmony. When people open themselves up to the experience of singing, adding their voice to the chorus of voices in the congregation, they become an integral part of creating that sacred space for everyone else. It is a shared accomplishment that everyone recognizes and can enjoy. This is what it is to be part of a healthy and vibrant community where all can trust their prayer experience will be one where they can let go and be safe. There are no judgments.

Beginning a New Journey

While harmonies can add new dimensions to a piece of music, a strong melody should be able to stand on its own. The power of a beautiful melodic line sung in unison has the ability to unite a people as well. Its impact can be felt within the first few notes. I have used my voice without any instrumentation to cut through the sound of people talking and getting settled in their seats as a way to alert congregants that services are starting.

How one sets the tone at the beginning of a service and how one transitions from one element of the service to the next are both important considerations. These considerations affect how the congregation will receive what we are offering them. We must be mindful of the fact that we are about to interrupt a conversation, and if we want people to respond positively, it must be done with care. To have someone get on a microphone to quiet people down can feel cold and uninviting. It is different however, if people hear singing, a gentle but audible voice over the talking that does not fight against the conversation, but eases into it. They are more likely to allow themselves to be moved in a new direction. The introduction of a new sound, singing instead of talking, alerts people that something is happening, that services are starting, that it's time to stop talking and change the focus in the room. It also allows us as services leaders to decide how we want our sacred drama to begin.

Whatever journey we prepare ourselves for, the use of music to guide our way will only make the journey sweeter. Our rich musical heritage, filled with songs both old and new, have always been there to accompany our joys and sorrows. No matter the lifecycle event or service that fills our homes and sanctuaries; music has been and always will be an important part of our Jewish identity and personal self-expression. May we be open to the new voices and creativity of those who bring the music and our traditions to life.

Natalie Young

An award-winning composer, whose music is sung by communities all over the world, Cantor Natalie Young has a gift for writing beautiful and memorable melodies. She has made prayer experiences accessible for worshippers young and old. The power of music is something she takes seriously, not just in her writing of music, but in how she connects with people and crafts each service as a cantor. Sharing her musical gifts and teachings as a cantor/composer-in-residence throughout the year, Natalie proudly serves as the cantor at Temple Beth El in Aliso Viejo, California. She lives with her husband, Rabbi David Young, their three children: Gabriel, Alex, and Bella, and their puppy, Orion.

Natalie's work can be found in *Shirei Ha-T'fillot* by the Movement for Reform Judaism, the *Ruach Songbook*, and the *Shalshelet Festival Songbook*. She has been commissioned to compose a piece for the upcoming *Shirei Mishkan HaNefesh Anthology*. Her songs have been featured at *URJ Biennials*, the *Shalshelet Music Festival*, *Hava Nashira*, *American Conference of Cantors* conventions, *North American Jewish Choral Festival*, HUC-DFSSM, and various concerts around the country. Many of her songs have been recorded by other artists and her own recording projects include the *WRJ Centennial CD*, *Stacey Beyer's Candle Blessing Project*, *Noam Katz's Mirembe*, *The*

Soul Within, and *Kol HaLev V'Kol HaNeshama.* You can enjoy Natalie's two solo albums of original music; *Carry Me* and *Natalie Young: Standing on the Shoulders.*

http://NatalieYoung.CreatingCalmNetworkPublishingGroup.com

Growing Your Spiritual Community

1. Does your community have a formal cantor? If not who serves in that role?

2. If you wrote a job description for a cantor in your community what would it look like?

3. If you wrote a job description for a congregant in your community what would it look like?

4. Think about the *Amidah,* or central prayer in your spiritual practice. What relevance does this phrase have, "Open my lips…?"

5. Do you agree that "music gives wings to our words and frees them from the recesses of our mind and heart?" Why or why not? Is there anything else that "gives wings" to the words of your prayers?

6. Are there people in your community who harmonize during services? What does that feel like?

7. In your community is there a specific way the rabbi or cantor gets people's attention or signals a transition to another part of the service?

Here I Stand: What It Means To Sing on Behalf of You
Sheila Pearl

How does a former opera singer and a Jew by Choice evolve into a "Sweet Singer of Israel" whose central role is to stand before *Adonai* and the congregation in a state of humility and surrender, naked and vulnerable? That was my question, as I began to learn about the role of *kavanah* or intention for the cantor. In my early years of training as a singer of art songs and operatic roles, my challenge was to literally step inside the intention of the text, the poetry, the character in the opera. It was my goal to become one with the music and the text, bringing into my body and psyche the full import of the artistic composition. Yes, for me the metaphor was clear: it was a love song in the best sense of that phrase. It was a form of intimacy which can best be understood when we talk about "making love" — the ultimate metaphor for two becoming one, for the unity of all.

Intimacy

As a developing cantor, I studied Jewish text and allowed the music to make its way into my senses. It occurred to me to treat the relationship between myself and the prayerful song as a love song between my soul and *Adonai*. I began with that intention and allowed a sense of sweet intimacy to form the texture of the music I would offer as cantor. My practice of mindfulness meditation became my essential partner on the *bimah* (raised platform in a synagogue). Meditation grounded me and helped me create my intention at the beginning of each and every prayer service to sing in that inner space I recognized as "intimacy" or a sense of being seen or "into-me-see." Meditation allows total transparency. Meditation was my tool for creating the ongoing intention of vulnerability; it kept me centered so that I could choose the emotional container of courageous compassion for myself and my congregation, opening my heart and soul with utter nakedness.

From the time I was in college, exploring the world's religions and later choosing Judaism as my new spiritual home, I was a student of both philosophy and religion and a seeker of wisdom. Among some of the more obscure sources, which would become my companions was the Gnostic Gospel of Thomas in which I found a text which became a centerpiece of my spiritual compass: *If you bring forth what is within you, it will save you; if you do not bring forth what is within you, it will destroy you.*

What this text inspired me to see decades before I ever thought of becoming a cantor was that if I was not willing or able to be totally vulnerable and to risk digging deep within myself for who and what I am, I would spiritually perish. However, in being willing to do the work of "getting naked" before *Adonai* and my congregation, I would save myself and – as a representative of my congregation—my *Kehilah: If you bring forth what is within you, it will save you; if you do not bring forth what is within you, it will destroy you.*

It was *Rosh Hashana*, September 17, 2001 – six days after 9/11 in New York City. The world was still in shock; those of us living in New York were numb, many of our own beloved friends and family had been lost in this nightmarish terrorist attack. During that week, I was

26

called to serve as a social worker/grief counselor at ground zero, while also preparing myself and my choir for the services of *Rosh Hashana*. My exhaustion was profound. How could I properly serve my congregation as its cantor, its *sheliach tzibor*, and be the representative on behalf of my people? I felt stripped of all ego, defenses, and elements of pride. I felt totally naked as I approached the eve of *Rosh Hashana*.

Being at ground zero that week shifted my perspective on life, on what is important, and my feelings about whether I could be in a position of leadership in any way. I felt humbled. There were times I was so numb I couldn't feel my body. As a singer, that is a big problem. As a singer of the liturgy for *Rosh Hashana* in a Reform temple, that is a disaster – at least for me, since the music I had been singing for over 20 years and would be singing during these holidays was demanding physically and emotionally.

Each year, the preparation for the *Rosh Hashana* and *Yom Kippur* services for the cantor is like preparing for a marathon as a runner. It is about preparing the body, the mind and the spirit in concert with one another. It is a mind-body-spirit exercise in balance and intention. As a cantor, I am required to be totally present to my body, to my sensuality as a singer, as well as to my spiritual container for being present, mindful and grounded in pure intention (*kavanah*).

For *Rosh Hashana* 2001, my challenge was even greater than in previous years: I knew that for this *Rosh Hashana*, as with none other in my career, my intention to be naked, present, and entirely humbled before Divine Spirit (*Shechinah*) would be what would carry me through the challenges of the music and demands upon me as a singer. I knew that I would need to be willing to totally surrender to that inner nakedness (vulnerability) in order to fulfill my role as cantor. With the pressures of that week leading up to *Rosh Hashana*, I did not have the luxury as in previous years, to rest and prepare my singer's body for the challenges of the music. Unlike regular weekly prayer services, the music for *Rosh Hashana* and Yom Kippur is for the cantor like singing two operas back-to-back – a grueling test of stamina and vocal technique. In 2001, I had to be willing to be defenseless and fragile, yet dig deeper into my inner resources than I had ever before.

What could I use as my guide? Looking through my resources, I found my old friend, that seminal quote which had captured my attention years earlier: *If you bring forth what is within you, it will save you; if you do not bring forth what is within you, it will destroy you.*

My guidance was to reach deep within my own well of inner resources and trust that all that I need is there, and if I did not bring forth what was deep within me, it would destroy me. I had learned that everything is energy and that the energy I bring forth from deep within myself is an energy which is contagious. It was my responsibility to choose an intention which would bring forth the highest vibration on behalf of my congregation. If I did not allow myself to be fully naked to myself, to *Adonai* and, to my congregants, it would destroy me – and perhaps all of us.

At the beginning of the *Rosh Hashana* evening service, the first major portion of the liturgy recited is the "*Hineni*" prayer ("Here I am"). A colleague of mine, Rabbi Rachel Barenblat "The Velveteen Rabbi", has composed a paraphrase of the text, included here:

Hineni

Here I stand
painfully aware of my flaws
quaking in my canvas shoes
and in my heart.
I'm here on behalf of this kahal
even though the part of me
that's quick to knock myself
says I'm not worthy to lead them....
....Accept
my prayer
as though I were exactly the leader
this community needs in this moment,
as though my voice never faltered.
Free me from my own baggage
that might get in the way.....

...Transform our suffering into gladness.
Dear One, may my prayer reach You...

It has always been important to me to understand the texts: In my study of the word *Hineni*, I discovered that it is repeated 22 times in the Hebrew Bible. It reflects our ancestor's readiness to do God's work, to take up whatever task was theirs. The word *"Hineni"* appears four times in the story of the Binding of Isaac and five more times in the stories of Jacob, Esau and Joseph. In each instance, the word constitutes something more than mere physical presence. *"Hineni"* means that "I am here with all my being, physically and spiritually, ready to do what I need to do and fully present in the moment."

At some point in our lives, we have each been Abraham; we have faced tremendous challenges and difficult choices. The week of 9/11 was our collective wake-up call; and we were awakened from our complacency.

For us, as for Abraham, something happened to shake us up. Our plans are changed. Our path takes an unexpected turn. We face challenges we could not have imagined.

Saying *Hineni* for ourselves is the first step. As Rabbi Hillel said, "If I am not for myself, who will be for me?" Yet, the next question follows: "If I am only for myself, what am I?" Life gains meaning only when we begin living for something larger than ourselves. Reaching this state takes time. Some people may never get there. Yet, we must try. Abraham does. On their journey up the mountain Isaac turns to his father and says, "*Abah*, Father," and Abraham answers, "*Hineni Beni*, here I am my son." I am with you. Things may not seem right. I am frustrated and afraid. Our future looks uncertain. But *Hineni*, I am here with you.

For me, the *Hineni* prayer has been, and remains, my greatest challenge to integrate my physical, sensual singer's body with my spiritual presence and emotional balance; to set aside my ego, my pride, my illusions of self-importance, while still balancing my vocal technique, my physical stamina and sensual presence to serve the highest level of prayer. To stand before the ark—before *Adonai* and my congregation on *Rosh Hashana*, I am challenged to open every sensual channel to be present with intention to allow myself to be an open vessel of spiritual and energetic expression. It is the defining moment when I reach deep inside for support of the high notes which express the drama and pathos of this poignant text: *"Transform our suffering into gladness..."*

During *Rosh Hashana* 2001, I experienced a turning point in my own spiritual development as a cantor. The challenge had always been to choose the intention and to be vulnerable, energetically and spiritually. In 2001, I rose to a higher and more intense level, as I allowed my body to become the instrument of poetic and spiritual presence. I brought to life the vibrations of the text and pulled forth the sense of the music composer blended with the feeling from the author of the liturgical text. At that turning point, I appreciated how essential it was to become the weaver and midwife of the new life coming through my entire body and spirit as I sang *Hineni,*

Here I am
standing before you
painfully aware of my flaws
Free me from my own baggage
that might get in the way.

Once I was able to stand before my congregation in a state of total vulnerability, I understood the power of liberating myself from any need to protect myself from perceived slings and arrows. As a "representative of my congregation" I was able to offer the energetic gift of liberation. Once any of us opens ourselves to the ultimate act of love, we have touched the Divine. To love without reserve and to receive love without apology is truly an act of "making love." As a cantor, I have felt a deep humility in knowing I have become the facilitator of dialogue between *Adonai* and The People of Israel, between our Creator and Us. It is the ultimate intimacy: "into-me-see." Love.

Sheila Pearl

Finding her own way to use her singing voice and counseling skills, Sheila Pearl, M.S.W. embraced the opportunity to serve The Barnert Temple in Franklin Lakes, New Jersey as cantorial soloist for 13 years and Temple Beth Jacob in Newburgh, New York for five years. A graduate of Hebrew Union College's Certification Program for Cantors, Sheila developed adult and children's choirs and instrumental ensembles, created curricula for Hebrew schools, as well as a concert series of Jewish music.

In 2004, Sheila retired from congregational life and reinvented her professional niche. She is currently a Keynote Speaker, Author and full-time Relationship Coach, with a private practice in Newburgh, New York.

Sheila is a graduate of the University of California at Berkeley with seven B.A. Degrees including English Literature and Philosophy. She received her Master's degree in Clinical Social Work from Yeshiva University's Wurzweiler School of Social Work.

Sheila is the author and co-author of several books, including *Still Life: A Spiritual Handbook for Family Caregivers of Alzheimer's Patients and other Difficult Challenges*; and co-author with Jack Canfield and Kimberly Burnham in *Pearls of Wisdom: 30 Inspirational Ideas to Live Your Best Life Now*.

http://SheilaPearl.CreatingCalmNetworkPublishingGroup.com

Growing Your Spiritual Community

1. What does it mean to be *Hineni* or present?

2. What does this statement mean to you? "If you bring forth what is within you, it will save you; if you do not bring forth what is within you, it will destroy you." What do you have within you that you want to bring forth in a greater way?

3. What was the impact of 9/11 on your community? If you were not a part of your current community at the time of 9/11 have you spoken to anyone in your community about the events of that day and the impact on your community? Are there any new customs in prayer that emerged in your community during the time after 9/11?

4. If you attend, what are the most challenging or thought provoking parts of the *Rosh Hashana* services?

Balancing Ritual and Novelty Each New Day
Susan Colin

There is wisdom in the Jewish ritual process and every day is a new day. The rituals and worship structures in Judaism continually prove this. That we have lifecycle rituals like *Shiva* (mourning) and *B'nai Mitzvah* is evidence that people do well with some structured acknowledgment of the processes we go through during our lives.

Music is there for all these moments, from the landmarks to the every day. Jewish life is varied. Our levels of observance and our extraordinary repertoire of melodic settings for text embrace our basic need for individual expression, while connecting us to the larger community. While we may all be familiar with the *Sh'ma*, *Mi Chamocha, Shalom Aleichem*, it is easy to assume that the melody you grew up singing is the right one. But when you visit a synagogue in a different community or a different country, you may be surprised, and even uncomfortable, to find a different melody.

Wisdom

There's wisdom in that process. You know those words, and you scramble to adapt to this new melody. It gives you pause to make sense of the text, what it means, why we are singing it. You begin to see that Judaism lives in many styles and it works just as well. You are uncovering the intention of the prayer with fresh ears and perhaps a fresh mind and heart.

As a singer, composer and worship leader, this is the terrain in which I dwell and more importantly, how I deepen my faith and sense of humanity. That may sound over the top, but this is what I have known from my core, for my entire conscious life. My earliest memory, sitting at the piano lost in the notes, shows me that music is something both within and outside and has a power like nothing else. It changes our physiology. It's in our brain, not our ears. Dr. Oliver Sacks describes this in his engaging way, in his book *Musicophilia* (Vintage, 2008). Music somehow reaches us in ways that nothing else can. When we combine music with lyrics we can express ourselves with energy, nuance, and clarity all at once.

There is a difference between the experiences of listening (receiving) and playing or singing (expressing, giving) music. When I am singing or presenting a particular song or prayer setting, I know that I am giving a message. I may also be articulating a thought on behalf of the listener. *Kol Nidre* is, of course, a perfect example of this. On *Yom Kippur*, as I begin to sing this, congregants sing along with the familiar first notes. Then, probably because of the melodic complexity, people become active listeners, and my unique intention commences. I sing this extraordinary prayer for myself and for those around me. We take this moment - and it is a holy moment, for sure - to be completely honest about who and what we have been during the year.

Community Expression

When we sing together as a community, everyone is expressing and giving, and the intention is quite different. We are creating a common experience, by sharing a melody, clapping together when the rhythm allows, harmonizing, and even hearing that odd off note from someone who may be out of tune, but enjoying the experience nonetheless. As time goes on, our *minhag* or local custom develops and now the intention of the music has transcended from being a song to being part of what binds our community. We have created a common memory.

It is with these ideas that I choose which songs I will compose or select for my professional and personal needs. I am grateful that our services incorporate a variety of opportunities for prayers of gratitude, praise and petition. We take time to acknowledge the mundane and core human aspects, and those things that elevate our awareness of the world around us. We have prayers to remind us to behave in ways that keep us righteous and safe (for example, *Eilu Devarim*), to remind us to notice a rainbow or a passing ambulance. Chanting or singing our prayers is more than rote. When music is involved, more of our brains and bodies are involved. Ultimately, our souls engage. What a powerful combination to deepen our experiences and personal growth.

A New Day

We all are familiar with the story of Noah. Charged with a confounding task, Noah built an ark; filled it with animals and his family; endured 40 days and nights of rain, and finally came to dry land and a world cleansed and renewed. This story is in some ways problematic, but I was drawn to the poetic lines of Genesis 8:22:

So long as the earth endures,

seedtime and harvest,
cold and heat,
summer and winter,
say and night shall not cease.

What a comfort to know that regardless of all that had been and all that might be, the fundamental stability of life will continue and give us renewed opportunities to be better, to do better. When I was a child, frustrated or self-deflating over mistakes, my mother would say, "Tomorrow is another day." Yes, there are consequences to our decisions and actions, and sometimes we make poor choices, but judging without a solution is not the answer. So, learn and move forward.

Years hence, as a mother I also found myself offering this encouragement, by saying "Every day is a new day." I meant for my children to see that they had choices. It wasn't up to me to make those decisions for them especially as they became older. Interestingly, by saying this to them, I also took comfort when I too made missteps. It was, and continues to be, an effective phrase for finding and giving forgiveness.

My friend and lyricist, Robin Paglia-Dennis and I wrote the song *Every Day Is A New Day*. Robin eloquently used images of the natural world (rain, sun, planting) along with human emotions of fear, anger, and determination. Originally written as a lullaby of sorts, the song's chorus easily moves to be a chant. Sometimes when my husband catches himself in a moment of frustration, he will start singing "Every day, every day is a new day." I smile (and truthfully, sometimes I laugh, depending on the seriousness or silliness of the mistake), and I am gratified. Music has again given us the gift of defining and expressing our humanity. The original intention of the song has been perfectly applied. And I'm delighted that many people have told me they, too, sing it with their children.

I am fascinated to hear from people that this song has served other purposes, in ways I hadn't intended. One man wrote to tell me he sings it every day as his *Modeh Ani* (the morning blessing, offering thanks for waking up to a new day). Cantors have used this song on the High Holy Days, and other times during the year in place of *Elohai Neshama*, a prayer of renewal. A woman told me she listened to this song and the whole album repeatedly while working with her elderly parents as they spent many months cleaning and rebuilding their home which was destroyed in a hurricane. So beyond the original intention of this particular song, it has served to be a benchmark for a moment or time, a prayer of gratitude and hope, a promise of faith and better things to come.

Because so much of my music and my involvement in music are framed around Jewish themes and services, it is natural for me to feel that my intention with music has to do with faith and spirituality. However, I also know that there is a great deal of music that couldn't be classified as religious which is inspiring and moving. As a person who believes in God, it's easy to assign holiness to some music. Or perhaps it's the music that woke my awareness of what is holy? And was that the intention of the composer? How can I know? Actually, I don't feel a need to know. I'm content with finding the sparks that inspire me, from all kinds of sources.

In fact, there's a pop song that for many years was important to me, that gave me reassurance during challenging times. I recently learned that the writer intended it to be a song for teens about rebellion and self-expression. If you are curious, it is called *You Get What You Give*, by the New Radicals. For a while that threw me, but I found my way back to the energy, and the fundamental faith in our dreams and our purpose that the song promotes. Such is the magic of music.

I know, because of my experience, that music matters. I am grateful that the Jewish tradition uses music—*nigunim*, prayer settings, chanting, choral music, contemporary, folk, and the list goes on—in numerous ways to draw us in and near to each other. Learning, singing, playing, and listening to music as part of our faith's language gives us ways to be with God and with our community. There is deep wisdom in that process, for us to uncover and celebrate each new day.

Susan Colin

An award-winning songwriter and cantorial soloist, Susan Colin is the owner of oySongs.com, the largest online distributor of Jewish music. One reviewer wrote, "She sings with a clarity that is breathtaking and rare," *Dallas Morning News.* She combines an engaging, personable style with a variety of enticing musical styles and Jewish themes. Susan says, *"This is the Jewish music for everyone."* Focused on adult spirituality, Susan gives presentations on Jewish music in addition to being a worship leader.

Raised in New York, with formative experiences singing choral music, Susan began singing professionally as a studio musician in Boston, MA and Phoenix, AZ. While working as a worship leader and composer in Dallas, TX, she found her musical home. Susan and her husband currently reside in Phoenix and have three grown children.

Susan has released four CDs to critical and popular acclaim. *Be Strong* (2010), *Every Day* (2005), *Shabbat Favorites* (2003), and *Prayer of the Heart* (2003). Susan's collaborations with lyricist Robin Paglia-Dennis and musician Lee Tomboulian created songs fans refer to as "inspiring." Jacob Delott, Susan's son, plays bass and sings on *Be Strong*, and they co-wrote "*Livracha*," as well as "*Call to Me*" which is featured on Susan's new CD scheduled for release in December, 2014.

Susan's music has been broadcast on NPR stations, used around the world for weddings, funerals, healing and worship services, published by URJ/Transcontinental Music, received two Shalshelet Awards, and has been licensed for video productions.

http://SusanColin.CreatingCalmNetworkPublishingGroup.com

Growing Your Spiritual Community

1. What part does music play in the birth rituals in your life and community? What do you consider a birth ritual: a child being born, a new convert, a beginning or something else?

2. Think about a time you were singing along in a community. If you stop and just listen, does it change the experience? For you is singing different from listening?

3. What "common memories" have you created with a community? How does music "bind" members of your community together?

4. In your community do people get physically involved (clapping, dancing, moving, nodding) in the music?

5. How do you feel when you hear the phrase "Every day is a new day"? What kind of attitude do you have towards the future? Listen to *Every Day Is A New Day*. What purpose can you imagine it taking in your life?

6. How do you find forgiveness? How does your community find forgiveness?

7. Thinking about the phrase, "Music has again given us the gift of defining and expressing our humanity"; how does music help you express your humanity? If you had to define the humanity of your community, what would you say?

8. Think about the music that inspires you. Where do these sparks come from? Is it a particular artist, theme, or genre that inspires you to be great?

Mi Chamocha—Who Is Like Us

Words of *Exodus 15*
float on rising waves
on YouTube
as Moses and the children
cross the sea,
the desert,
meet challenges
and find ways
to say
who is like You
yesterday and today

Styles abound
acapella and unplugged
with a crowd
a single voice
for that special someone
in a community
during prayerful meditation
with guitars and drums
at the wall
in Parody of Gangam style
engaging a new generation
in operatic voice soothing
those used to the way things were
in rhythms reminiscent of an Irish ballad
the deeply moving tune of a folk song

Jews and Christians
pairing images and words
a way to learn Hebrew

as favorite places, scenes, colors
become dancing dreams
of where we can go
what we see
All the ways to feel
all the hearts to touch
with words and music
who is like You
who is like us?

—**Kimberly Burnham**

Mi Chamocha

Mi chamocha ba'eilim Adonai
Mi kamocha nedar bakodesh
Nora t'hilot (osei feleh).

—**LyricsFreak.com**

Growing Your Spiritual Community

1. What is your favorite tune or style of *Mi Chamocha*?
2. Do you and your community tend to like traditional settings? Do you often try new tunes and music with the lyrics and poetry of traditional prayers?

Awareness of Immanent Presence

Shekhinah
l'cha dOdi
circLes mystic hearts
welcOming
Mishnah's soul maggid
tree of life's crOwned tiferet
partner to immaNent presence

shAbbat's
Lecha dodi
Kabbalist
Author authority
Bride and partnership
awarenEss
Turning towards
Zohar blessings and hopes

—**Kimberly Burnham**, in honor of Shlomo ha-Levi
Alkabetz or Solomon Alkabetz, author of the lyrics for a
popularly sung version of L'cha Dodi.

Growing Your Spiritual Community

1. What is in your heart when you turn and welcome in
Shabbat?
2. Consider transitions in your life. What are some of the
beginnings and endings that happen each day, each week
or only once in a lifetime?
3. Do you use poetry as part of your spiritual practice?

Gratitude, Our Thanks To ...

Abraham Joshua Heschel wrote about gratitude, ways to live life and the impact of gratitude in our lives.

"Our goal should be to live life in radical amazement ... get up in the morning and look at the world in a way that takes nothing for granted. Everything is phenomenal; everything is incredible; never treat life casually. To be spiritual is to be amazed."

He also said, *"It is gratefulness that makes the soul great."*

Growing Your Spiritual Community

1. For what are you grateful?
2. What is your practice around gratitude?
3. What makes you great?

Universal Responsibility

It is I
my
relationship with
the eternal
ancient
absolute faith
drawing me in
to the spiral
life's providence

I have no fear
in me when
I hold my companion
letting it go
noticing
the running over
my cup is full

A sound, a look
imbalanced
till gratitude wells up
replacing blame
questions keep coming
a few answers
appear as I see
who am I
in relationship
in an ancient universe
Adon Olam

— Kimberly Burnham

Adon Olam

Adon olam, asher malach,
b'terem kol y'tzir nivra.
L'et na'asah v'cheftzo kol,
azai melech sh'mo nikra.

The Lord of the Universe who reigned
before anything was created.
When all was made by his will
He was acknowledged as King.

—HebrewSongs.com

Growing Your Spiritual Community

1. Does your service typically end with *Adon Olam*?
2. Are you most comfortable with the *Adon Olam* translation of *Master of the Universe, Eternal God,* or something else?

Our Thank You To God
Judy Caplan Ginsburgh

When my young son broke his arm at school, we picked him up and rushed him to the emergency room. They determined he needed surgery. A bundle of nerves, we went out into the waiting room - to wait.

While there, a school bus load of preschoolers was brought in. Their bus had been in an accident and, although no one was seriously hurt, each scared child needed to be examined. Their teachers did not quite know what to do. Being an early childhood music specialist, I gathered the children to sit with me on the floor and I sang with them. Their fear disappeared. The music helped to pass the time as each child was examined and released. And, incidentally, it kept my mind occupied while my own child was in surgery.

Music plus intention can cause wonderful things to happen. Our mission as transmitters of song is to move people, stimulate emotions and add to the beauty of our world with our gifts.

For the past thirty years, I have successfully made my living as a professional singer. I have shared folk music in clubs and at festivals, performed in musical theatre and opera productions, and used music as a vehicle to teach children. Singing at many weddings and funerals, I have shared the music of my Jewish heritage in hundreds of synagogues throughout North America as a cantorial soloist. I have always known that my voice was something very special....a gift from God.

Tikkun Olam

My philosophy has always been that each of us is born with certain gifts. Part of life is figuring out what our gifts are and then learning how to use them. Sharing our gifts is the ultimate goal and our "thank you" to God for blessing us. When we have the ability to discover our gifts, refine them, and share them, then we are making a difference in the world—we are contributing to *Tikkun Olam*, healing the world. Music is my gift and one of the most meaningful ways I can share it is transmitting the music of my Jewish heritage.

But whether singing in a synagogue or performing on a theatre stage, all music should be offered and shared with definite intention. When you look up the word "intention" in a dictionary, you find the following definitions: "something that someone plans to do" and "to have a purpose or plan, to direct the mind or to aim." In order to have intention with music, we – the presenters of the music - must fully understand several things:

What are we singing about?

What sort of mood or feeling do we want to transmit?

What is the relationship between the music and lyrics of what we are singing? How can they complement one another?

Is instrumentation necessary? And if so, what instruments will enhance each other and the intention of the music without distracting?

As singers, what are we singing about? What is the message that the composer wants conveyed with this song? If the song is in another language, attention must be given to translating and interpreting the meaning of the words so that we understand what we are transmitting. If we do not fully understand what we are singing about, how can we sing with intention? When we share a piece of music, we convey intention when we understand the goals of the composer in writing the piece. I personally spend a great deal of time selecting the appropriate music for the event where I will be singing. The music must be appropriate for the venue, appropriate for the space in time in which it is shared, and appropriate for the audience who is listening.

When composing a piece of music, a mood is created. The composer, as well as the transmitter of the music, should have a mood and a goal in mind when sharing their music. This is intention. This is *kavanah*. How do you want to feel while sharing this piece of music? How do you want those listening to feel while hearing this piece of music? What will your listeners take away from your performance or their participation in singing with you? We must present music with *kavanah* in order for it to have meaning to us and to those listening.

There are numerous melodies that have been composed for one piece of text. Often I find that unseasoned composers write from their hearts with all the best "intentions." However, they may spend very little time in thinking about how the melody and the lyrics work together and whether the tone or mood of the composition they have created fits with where it is likely to be shared.

Max Janowski was a genius at composing melodies that enriched text. His melodies are not only glorious to sing, but the music and the lyrics enhance one another – almost as if one could not exist without the other. Instead of fighting each other, they intertwine to create a beautiful blend of music and word. In his *Avinu Malkeynu*, the music conveys exactly what the words are pleading for—"Our Father, Our King, hear our voices..."

This composition is so perfect that if presented with proper intention by the singer, listeners weep when they hear it. The music of *Avinu Malkeynu* becomes the centerpiece of the High Holy Day liturgy, the culmination of the mood and the reason for the High Holy Days.

Y'hiyu L'ratzon

There is true perfection in creating a mood, and marriage between melody and text in one of my favorite pieces of music, *Y'hiyu L'ratzon* by Max Janowski. In this one short and simple composition, I, as the transmitter of this song, sing with the intention I feel was meant by Max Janowski when he composed it, and the intention I feel is meant by the text and where it comes within the worship service. The translation of the Hebrew words is: "May the words of my mouth and the meditations of my heart be acceptable to You, O God, my Rock and my Redeemer. Amen." Max Janowski begins the piece with a melody consisting of a limited range of notes – almost chant-like as we sing softly and introspectively "May the words of my mouth and the meditations of my heart." The melody opens up a bit and repeats almost as if it is pleading with the words "be acceptable to You". Then the melody soars and climaxes with God's name and references to God as our "rock" and "redeemer". The words here are more concrete and the melody reflects this in both pitch and the dynamics used by the singer. This line is also repeated, but again, more introspectively the second time. And the piece ends with "Amen" - as if to say "this is all I ask".

This piece of liturgical music usually follows the silent prayer in our worship service. The silent prayer offers us a special moment with *Adonai* within our community service. It is a time when we can pull within ourselves to be alone with God. And all we can hope for is that God hears our prayers and accepts them. *Y'hiyu L'ratzon* captures this brief, special time with *Adonai*.

Often singing without instruments, I consider my voice the ultimate instrument and sometimes it needs nothing else to accompany it. However, there are times when instruments (or even other voices) are needed to create a mood, to enrich the sound, or to make a larger impact on an audience. Always keep the mood and intention of the composition in the forefront and make tasteful choices to enrich the overall experience of listening.

When I sing in a synagogue, I am a vessel. I am, as cantors were in the days of the ancient synagogue, a "sweet transmitter of song." I have studied a great deal of acting methods in my career and, as with singing; there is always intention when acting. When we are acting, we are not ourselves. We must understand the character's intention in order to determine how that character would speak or move or react.

One of the main reasons I love singing Jewish music is that when I sing, I am also not myself. There are many times when I feel that *Adonai* sings through me. Sometimes I am even transported to another place when I sing and I have no recollection of having sung when the song is over. I feel strongly the imperative to transmit a mood, a feeling through honest intention (*kavanah*). The song sings through me.

As a singer, the emotions I stimulate and ignite may be happy or sad or funny or pensive. This is what music does, especially liturgical music. It triggers something – a feeling, a mood, a need to do something. But it can only trigger something in the listener if the listener is open to listening and listens with focus and intention. This is why Shabbat is so special.

When Shabbat begins, I encourage the congregation to literally step away from the hustle and bustle of the week just past. I ask them to take a deep breath, to let worry, stress and problems go, if only for a brief time. I ask them to use Shabbat as a way to recharge and renew themselves so that they will have more energy to face the week ahead. And then, we begin with a *nigun*—a song without words. The melody lifts and carries us into Shabbat. Coming to Shabbat with the right intention, we come away refreshed and renewed.

As a vibrational or sound healer, I use the vibrations made by various tuning fork frequencies to release negative energy from our energy centers (chakras) and put the body in optimum balance. Sound healing may also reduce pain and stress and put a person in a deep state of relaxation. As healers, we are taught the importance of "intention" in maintaining focus and a positive intention when conducting our healing work. It also helps, if the recipient of the healing has a positive and open mind to accept the intention of the healer. True miracles occur when intention exists along with skill and acceptance.

Miracles in my life teach me the power of music and intention. After my grandmother suffered a stroke, I would sometimes take her to outpatient physical therapy at a local hospital. The therapist would stand in the middle with patients in chairs or wheelchairs surrounding her in a circle. She would call out commands such as, "take your right hand and move it up, now bring it down....move your head to the left....move your head to the right, etc." Some of the participants participated to the best of their ability. Others would sit lethargically in their chairs.

One day, I asked the therapist if I could sing her commands and I proceeded to make up little tunes with her directions as lyrics. Immediately, some patients, who had not moved much before, started moving. Smiles more abundant, I continued to work with the therapist in this way and the staff saw a huge increase in participation, range of motion and morale among the patients. My intention was to create a more pleasant mood and to make exercise or therapy more fun and less like a chore. It worked.

Each of us has special gifts given to us by our Creator. Once we have found these gifts, it is incumbent upon us to share them. In this way, we are taking care of our own individual intentions as well as God's intentions for us. This is our "thank you" to God.

Judy Caplan Ginsburgh

A professional singer, multi award-winning recording artist, and educator, Judy Caplan Ginsburgh has shared her musical gifts on pulpits across North America since 1981. She has a degree in Vocal

Performance from the Indiana University Jacobs School of Music. Perhaps best known for her award-winning recordings for Jewish families, her *Shalom Yeladim* has become a classic and one of the best-selling Jewish children's recordings in the world. Judy is the creator of the popular—*My Jewish World* music curriculum produced by the Union for Reform Judaism (URJ). She has also developed a way to teach prayer book Hebrew through sign language and music enabling learners to really understand what they are praying.

Judy is a certified sound healer and uses tuning forks, crystal bowls, vocal toning and aromatherapy in her healing practice. She is the founder and Executive Director of Central Louisiana Arts & Healthcare, a not-for-profit organization whose mission is to bring innovative arts experiences into healthcare settings to assist with the healing process. In January, 2014, Judy received rabbinic ordination from the Jewish Spiritual Leaders Institute.

http://JudyGinsburgh.CreatingCalmNetworkPublishingGroup.com

Growing Your Spiritual Community

1. Do you feel *Adonai* sings through you?
2. Have you ever been in a situation where music was used to calm a group? What is your experience with music in a therapeutic setting?
3. What projects do you know of or are involved in that exemplify *Tikkun Olam* or healing the world?
4. Think of a favorite song. Imagine yourself in the place of the composer. Can you imagine what she or he was

thinking? Do you know anything about their state of mind or surroundings at the time they composed the piece?

5. Close your eyes. Imagine hearing or singing *Avinu Malkeynu*. What is the effect on your mood?

6. Does your community use musical instruments other than voice? How do you feel about that?

7. In your practice, how do you begin to step away from the bustle of everyday life into Shabbat?

8. What does this statement mean to you, "True miracles occur, when intention exists along with skill and acceptance?"

A Shield, Modim Anachnu Lach
Joy Katzen-Guthrie

Ever feel as if you're daily dodging bullets of bad news blasted at you in every form of conversation and from every direction? Navigating the news, social media and comments of neighbors, friends, and congregants caught within the frenzy of the current political moment, I envision myself at times heading into battle, comfortably wearing a magical suit of negative-resistant armor. My shield is *modim*—gratitude—and without it, I would have been laid low by the slinging bullets of negativity long ago. *Modim anachnu lach*, our prayer of thanksgiving, has given me solace and courage, has put my heart at rest in difficult moments, and has stopped me in my tracks when I have been prepared to overlook the limitless blessings of my life.

*We acknowledge our thanks
to You, our God and
God of our ancestors forever,
Rock of our lives,
Shield of our salvation
in all generations.*

Eyes on Gratitude

Our scriptures overflow with utterances of our gratitude. Our hundred or more daily *brachot* praise acts of human kindness, visions of beauty, experiences of discovery as well as praising our bodies, heritage, and destiny. The first prayer we utter as we open our eyes from sleep is one of thanks for our Creator's creation—

light, goodness, and the opportunity to glorify God. It is no random choice that the first words we are directed to pray as we rise in morning are words of gratitude. The act of acknowledging what is good and expressing it aloud makes an enormous difference in one's perception of living. It orders the mind to notice what is fulfilling rather than what appears to be missing. It directs the subconscious to seek out good. It draws to us, as a magnet, like-minded people and experiences that validate our beliefs—in this case, expansive thoughts of abundance and an increase of the blessings for which we may be continually thankful.

As we immerse ourselves within the *Amidah*, we sense that the *Hoda'ah*—this gratitude blessing—is crucial. Acknowledging appreciation for the kindness of a Divine Presence as well as the good that others bring to our lives inspires the simple awareness that we are not alone. Giving thanks involves both admitting that one is incomplete on one's own, and acknowledging that the abundance of miracles in one's life is never to be taken for granted. From my perspective, it's no coincidence that the *modim* is the eighteenth blessing of the *Tefilah*. It is without question a *chai* prayer, life-giving and life-fulfilling. In this world, we are repeatedly tugged toward an attitude of more lack than blessing, or the drone of a busy routine or the suffering of constant turmoil. Awareness replenishes us with a sense of awe and the value of our everyday lives and the continual stream of life's gifts.

Let us thank and praise You,
for our lives which
are within Your hands,

for our souls entrusted
to You, and for Your miracles
we experience every day.

Indeed, for the miracle not only of sustenance, but of purpose and potential—the wondrous cells, tissues, and organs of our body, the ability of our hearts and minds to discern truth, beauty, and joy, and all parts of ourselves physically, emotionally, and spiritually that facilitate our lives, we are limitlessly blessed.

We acknowledge the miracle of our souls—the source of unlimited greatness within us, the breath of energy, vision, and creation. We are grateful for each and every moment we take the power and inspiration to freely express. For our hope, which when entrusted faithfully in God, allows an experience of the awesome faith of our ancestors as they left behind one life and entered another in endless possibility and promise, singing joyously at the shore of the sea, we give thanks.

Your wonders and favors
are with us every moment,
evening, morning, and afternoon.
You are goodness,
Your compassion never ending,
Your kindness ceaseless.
In You, we place our hope.

No matter the moment, thanks are due. No matter the experience, let me utter gratitude. I cannot deny the stress, anger, or grief that sometimes enshrouds me, from which it can feel impossible to escape. At moments, I am so wrapped in a cloak of confusion, I am unable to see my way out. Nevertheless, every instant regardless of the emotions, allows me to see in a more positive way.

In every experience, let me recognize an element of good. Within my awareness of God's support, let there be the knowing that this turmoil too shall pass. In appreciation of the protection and love I have been afforded throughout my life, let me take refuge and solace in the knowledge that God's presence is ever-constant.

Vitality, Optimism and Joy

At the risk of sounding trite, I would note that there is an opportunity to be more creative, insightful, and, in truth, greater, with every breath. This is a universal understanding. Within every significant faith is the awareness that mindfulness of the good in our lives increases our well being. Within scientific and psychological studies too numerous to mention is the proof that those who feel gratefulness experience increased vitality, optimism, and joy.

When I am faced with an experience in which it is challenging to find anything positive to say about a person or an incident, I dig down and seek a seed of something good, even if small. When I am challenged to find even the smallest fragment of goodness, I acknowledge the goodness that is *possible*. From any negative, I can find a positive, even if it is possibility. The realization that anything is possible reconnects me to God, for God is limitless possibillity.

The awareness that within God's space, possibility is limitless in turn allows me to realize this moment of pain is temporary. The knowledge that pain is temporary, in turn, strengthens me, allowing the pain—physical or emotional—to pass more quickly. Emotions are a spring, feeding upon themselves, cascading into a powerful stream of consciousness. As I express thanks, I mindfully and physically experience the good—for there is no other way to experience gratitude. As that physical and emotional stream of consciousness shifts into positivity, it pulls other beneficial thoughts into itself like a flash flood.

Oh yes, I have had the joy of experiencing this awe-inspiring shift, both from my own turn of attention as well as the powerful energy of another human being inspiring me to turn my attention toward possibility. This remarkable sensation has made me realize the potent effect we have on one another and all life, the profound nature of our choices. What I do, say, and think touches other lives, which touch other lives that also touch mine. The influence of appreciation is never-ending, like the blessings of God.

Modim Anachnu Lach

For all these things,
we will bless Your name
constantly and forever,
as all living things acknowledge
and thank You and praise You.

Kabbalist teaching tells us that we are the story God is telling, the song God is singing. If we, then, are the story or the song on God's lips, what story will we tell? What song will we sing? One of angst, bitterness, blame, and fury? Or one of peace of mind, creativity, support and joy?

As I remind myself of what is good in my life, I increasingly appreciate everyone in my world, from family to friends, colleagues, and strangers. If I am God's song, let me sing of what truly is important. It is not the bills. It is not the limitations. It is those who have contributed to my well being. It is an inexhaustible web of history and humanity that has laid the foundations of a world of immense possibility for me.

I live in a time in which it is possible to be anyone, participate in any effort, travel to any area of the planet, connect with loved ones in an instant anywhere across the globe and beyond, to converse and create with anyone anywhere with no borders or boundaries. A vast web of human beings envisioned and built those physical and technological networks with the sweat of their hands and the dedication of their hearts. Brilliant minds imagined and developed the machinery and technology which I use endlessly. Societies and communities collaborated to create the infrastructure and services capable of uplifting every life on the planet. Let me never fail to express my awareness of these miracles.

Our televisions, newspapers, radios, internet and films continually blast images that would lead us to believe we are capable only of destruction and death. Yet, our connectedness to all humanity results in all we create, hear, and speak. We eat, wear clothing and build dwelling places. these are the activities that engross us and the dreams that fill our human minds. Each activity is a story. Which song or story will you choose to be?

Thank you, Divine Source. Thank you for this blessed moment. Thank you for this amazing vessel in which I live, its magnificent design, and its complex perfection. I have no idea how it all works, but I don't need to know. Through it I walk this earth, as I create, dream, design, and feel deepest grief and splendid joy. Through it I touch, taste, see vibrantly, hear insightfully, cleanse myself with the renewing breath of Your presence.

For the insightful road on which I have walked and the splendid journey I have known, for the continuous pulsing of love, belief, passion, and desire of which I am capable—the pulsing that is part of the heartbeat of God—let me say "Thank You."

For humanity of every color, thought, and capability that expands my own awareness and potential, for relationships—loving parents, caregivers, supporters, family, friends, teachers, coaches and mentors who have devoted themselves wholeheartedly to my growth and well being, I express profound thanks. For those who have served all humanity, making it possible for me and others to thrive healthfully, creatively, and powerfully, for the experiences of my past that I have defined as mistakes or the traits of myself I have called faults, I am thankful for the distinction of what I desire and what I do not—and for the answers and resolutions that have made me wiser and stronger.

Each of us has been given the magnificent right of free will to perceive what he or she desires and to create from that perception. I am aware that in my lifetime, I have seen humanity create what generations before me never could have imagined. Future lives will create far more than I am capable of envisioning. For what I do not know now, I am so thankful for the opportunity to learn and comprehend. For the moments when I believe I experience setbacks, I am thankful for the discovery of that which brings me fulfillment and contentment. Amidst the suffering I see in the world, I thank God for the strength of my own hands and heart to affect a ripple of positive well-being. For infinite wonder and insight that is human life in partnership with the Creator, I sing God's praises.

Modim Anachnu Lach

Joy Katzen-Guthrie

In the last three decades, Joy Katzen-Guthrie has served as a recording/concert artist, composer/lyricist, cantorial leader and writer/speaker/educator. She has devoted herself to uplifting through the arts with Jewish and popular music of all genres. A Memphis, Tennessee native living in the Tampa Bay, FL area since 1981, Joy melds a performance repertoire of some 4,000 songs with a vast knowledge of music and history in congregation, classroom, and concert hall. Joy has 14 published recordings. With a Bachelors of Arts (magna cum laude) and BFA (cum laude) in Broadcast Communications and Music from Stephens College in Columbia, Missouri, Joy served as Executive Producer and Operations Manager in news/talk radio before shifting to a second career in music.

Additionally, Joy has created and led Jewish heritage tours to China and Turkey, and has developed heritage tours to Argentina, Australia/New Zealand, Alaska and Cuba. She serves Congregation Beth Am, Tampa, as Cantorial Leader and is a long-time concert artist and instructor for Eckerd College and University of

South Florida Osher Lifelong Learning Institutes, and Road Scholar programs. With her husband Mark, she operates Tune-of-the-Century Music® recording studios and sound design services for broadcast facilities, artists, and congregations. She is a guest speaker, concert artist, and workshop facilitator, has been a contributing writer to the *Encylopedia Judaica*, and her photographs have been published worldwide. Joy has received appointments to the Florida Artist Residency Directory and has been awarded two arts resource grants. Her official website is her own design and creation, Joyfulnoise.net.

http://JoyKatzenGuthrie.CreatingCalmNetworkPublishingGroup.com

Growing Your Spiritual Community

1. What are your first thoughts or prayers when you open your eyes?
2. When you are stressed or upset, what replenishes you?
3. How do you discern truth in your life?
4. What does the following quote mean in your life, "In every experience, let me recognize an element of good?"
5. In the context of your last year or so, what does the next quote mean? What has passed for you? "Within my awareness of God's support, let there be the knowing that this turmoil too shall pass."
6. What do you want to change in your life and practices in light of this statement: "Within scientific and psychological studies too numerous to mention is the proof that those who feel gratefulness experience increased vitality, optimism, and joy?"

We Give Thanks To You
Rosalie Boxt

I have a hard time being in the moment. "Now" is more distant to me than "to come". I am easily frustrated when things don't go according to plan and when I can't find something and have to replace it, especially when I know "it's somewhere!" I worry about things coming up, that I can't control—in part so that I may prepare in a positive way, but also because I stew and speculate over the many possible outcomes. It is my most significant emotional struggle.

And upon further reflection, I then find it ironic that my favorite text is *Modim Anachnu Lach* (*we give our thanks to you*) from the *Tefilah* (*main prayer section of the worship*). Perhaps, in fact, it speaks to me because it forces me to remember—to pause, to breathe, to stop worrying.

One of the most provocative *iyunei tefilah* (*meditation on prayer*) for *Modim* is excerpted here (author unknown):

I Am Thankful:

For the wife who says it's hot dogs tonight, because she is home with me, and not out with someone else.

For the husband who is on the sofa being a couch potato, because he is home with me and not out at the bars.

For the teenager who is complaining about doing dishes because it means she is at home, not on the streets.

For the taxes I pay because it means I am employed.

For the mess to clean after a party because it means I have been surrounded by friends.

For the pile of laundry and ironing because it means I have clothes to wear.

For the alarm that goes off in the early morning hours because it means I am alive.

Every Moment

Julie Silver and I wrote a melody to *Modim* a few years ago. After studying the entire text, we agreed the piece would need to contain only the first line, "*modim anachnu lach*" and one line found later in the prayer, "*erev, vavoker, v'tzohorayim*", evening, morning, and afternoon. For us that encompassed all we hoped to remember from the text: that every minute of the day, not just in extraordinary times, or in times of worship – or when someone is relieved from suffering, or friends are gathered close for a great occasion – every little moment is full of grace and thanksgiving. This is something I use as my personal intention every week in worship. I try to let the noise and worry, anxiety and sense of imperfection fade into the quiet background, and create opportunities for my congregation to feel their own real acknowledgements of gratitude rise up in that moment. That may happen through multiple opportunities, and not always in song or through these words of *Modim*. Instead, I try to set out a path that leads each of us through the stages in which we might find those ideals visualized.

The beauty of *Modim anachnu lach* in the *tefilah* is that it's plural; it's about our collective gratitude. I'm not as moved by *Modah ani l'fanecha* in our morning liturgy, *I offer You thanks,"* as I am by *Modim anachnu lach.* I do love that moment of morning gratitude, before the trials and dramas that loom ahead can take over; I appreciate the opportunity to begin my day with the words "thank you." And yet *Modim*—We. All of us. We all have so much for which to be thankful. I, as *shali'ach tzibur* (prayer leader), may have no idea what is in people's heart in thanksgiving unless I invite sharing or *chevrutot* (partner sharing), but I know gratitude is there—for every single person. I know they are envisioning the moments of rescue, of serenity, of peace, of family. And to me this is immensely powerful. It makes my intention of quietude and thanks that much more effective, that much more rooted as I lead my congregation through the prayer experience.

Intention is a tricky ideal. I prefer to think of my *kavanah*, my intention, through the lens of focus, of goal, and of centeredness. I don't have intention simply when I prepare to "sing" when leading services, as I use multiple vehicles to engage a community in worship. My guitar, my spoken word, story, movement, congregational voice, harmony and song all come together as tools in my kit to move me and a community toward a common goal. I think we sometimes fall into the trap, as perhaps it's easier, to reflect upon our OWN intention, and what we hope to do as individual prayer leaders, at the expense of considering what our community's intentions are.

We should be asking: What do the people with whom we share the prayer experiences intend to happen in their prayer? Where can the worship lead us all?

My musical intention is important to successful leadership to be sure. I believe the prayer leader, *shali'ach tzibur*, should have a clear vision. This vision of who I think I am in that moment may change for each assent of the *bimah* (raised platform). I consider what kind of leader I want to be. My teacher Cantor Ellen Dreskin suggests that I develop a metaphor for my leadership. Am I a train conductor, museum docent, or team captain? The first step to leading worship is to consider what I see as my role, and how that merges with the congregations' expectations. I think as a *shaliach* I run into trouble if my musical intention is to bring people closer to G-d, but the community has come into worship expecting to grow closer to one another. This does not mean both can't occur, but our success together in worship is reliant upon having similar goals and expectations of what we're doing and where we're going. I think the intention and focus of a leader is important, but runs the risk of being in isolation – in "preparation" or in mentally getting in the "zone" to lead. My concern with this outlook is that it potentially overlooks the fact that each congregation, each moment, each gathering is different and therefore my intention is only a small piece of what is at work.

I think that if everyone in a worship setting, whether six people in a song circle, or 400 people in a large community service, knows that path they have embarked on together, and have a shared expectation for that particular worship moment, there is a greater opportunity for transformation. This is all about transparency–the *shaliach* communicating in multiple forms, what our expectations are of each other, of our spoken and sung word, of our texts and of our silence.

My experience is that while individual intention and focus may help one's own experience, it may not necessarily add to the whole even if the music itself may be familiar or link us all emotionally. This is not to say that everyone must want the same thing or have the same response to music or text in worship. But if we have a sense as a community of some overarching goals our experience will be made more powerful.

When I am leading worship I find myself leaning toward connectivity and energy. This is about the path — the environment, the road travelled, not the destination. I am able to bring more of my own personal *kavanah*, my own vulnerability to prayer and to "what it all means anyway" when I sense that others are open to similar possibilities. When we open a door to each other and agree to travel through it, I am less afraid and I believe the community is more willing to be open to meaningful experiences. When I think I know where I am going, when I think I know who I am in that worship moment, I am more equipped to lead. But that knowing comes from preparation. It comes from considering who the congregation is, how they sit, what *siddur* they use, their facility with language, whether they are in worship to reach for the Divine or lean in toward one another (or both). It comes from articulating where I (and my partner if I'm blessed to have a partner in leadership) would like us to go, how we will get there, and what we might do and see on the way. Simply knowing how I, Rosalie, have intention and focus for my own work may allow me to feel connected to the prayer and to feel confident in my leadership, but I worry about leaving the congregation behind. I can recount (as can you perhaps), being in a prayer setting, observing that a leader indeed believed in something, was confident, had a vision of going somewhere–but it had nothing to do with me, or I didn't know what the vision was, or where it was I was supposed to be going.

I believe that the purpose of prayer is to create openness, curiosity, and exploration. Rachel Cowen suggests that our congregations do not need things to be so bright, that deer can't come out of the woods without being blinded by bright headlights. I try to be aware of the intention I have, the calm and focus I need to feel to do this sacred work, and avoid the work becoming a barrier between my community and me.

Rabbi Joseph B. Meszler teaches that: "the goal of prayer in Judaism is humility. Life is never what we expect it will be, and it is usually when our egos have been damaged and we are forced to look deeply into ourselves that we discover meaning. Even in lofty moments of celebration, we should remember to be humble. A man named Rabbi Yosi understood this:

Rabbi Yosi the son of Rabbi Chanina taught in the name of Rabbi Eliezer ben Ya'akov: One should not stand on a high place when one prays but should rather stand in a lowly place, as it is written, "Out of the low places I called to You, Eternal God."—Babylonian Talmud, *Berachot* 10a on Psalm 130:1"

Rosalie Boxt

The Cantor of Temple Emanuel in Kensington, Maryland, a Reform Congregation just north of Washington D.C., Rosalie Boxt was invested from the Debbie Friedman School of Sacred Music of the Hebrew Union College in 2001. Before that she worked for the

URJ in NFTY Programs in Israel and as a NFTY and URJ Song leader. Originally from St. Louis, Missouri she attended the University of Pennsylvania as a Jewish Studies Major.

Rosalie is the Director of Worship for the URJ Biennial and on the URJ Faculty of Expert Practitioners, as well as on the Faculty of Hava Nashira, a song leading institute of the URJ. She consults with clergy and congregations on issues of worship and music. She is a Synagogue 3000 Fellow and is also a past Vice-President of the American Conference of Cantors (ACC). Through PresenTense, an incubator for young Jewish social entrepreneurs, she has launched a non-profit business called *Kesher Shir* (www.keshershir.org); bringing together Jewish musicians from diverse backgrounds to study and to create meaningful music which will enrich worship and strengthen communities.

Her husband, Jason, is a Managing Director in the Research Division of The Glover Park Group. The two met at the URJ Kutz Camp and have two daughters Tahlia and Arielle.

http://RosalieBoxt.CreatingCalmNetworkPublishingGroup.com

Growing Your Spiritual Community

1. What do you think of the quote, "worrying is like praying for what you don't want?"
2. Do you take leadership roles in your community? Are you a train conductor, museum docent or team captain?
3. If you are familiar with these songs, compare and contrast your feeling on singing *Modim* and *Modah ani.*

4. Consider these questions from Rosalie Boxt, "What do the people with whom we share the prayer experiences intend to happen in their prayer? Where can the worship lead us all?"

5. What does this statement mean to you, "When we open a door to each other and agree to travel through it, I am less afraid and I believe the community is more willing to be open to meaningful experiences?"

6. If you think of your community's service, is there anyone getting too far ahead or anyone getting left behind?

7. What do you think of this idea from Rachel Cowen, "Our congregations need things to be not so bright, so deer can come out of the woods without being blinded by bright headlights?"

Lev Tahor: Taking Out the Trash
Beth Hamon

With a foot in each of my worlds, bike-punk and Jewish professional-in-training, I tried very hard to find balance. It was a huge adventure, and the move to Philadelphia ultimately a mistake...

In July 2001, I moved to Philadelphia to begin graduate studies in Jewish music and Jewish education. I lived in a roach-infested Center City apartment building dating from the 1870s, and commuted by train to a small campus in the northeast suburbs. Most of my few pieces of furniture were scored from free piles around Center City. My bicycle hung on hooks in a corner of my combined living room and kitchen. During the week I went to class. Evenings were spent studying and practicing at home. On Friday nights or Saturdays, I attended services at one of the many synagogues in Center City, enjoying the rich variety of Jewish life in the heart of Philadelphia. On Sundays, I taught music classes in the religious school of a large synagogue near the campus. I wasn't making enough money, even with a partial scholarship and loans, so three afternoons a week I worked at a Center City bike shop fixing bicycles for cash under the table.

East Coast Jewish Scene

I was too rough around the edges and not cut out for the East Coast Jewish scene with its wealth and classism. I was also not prepared to live car-free in a city so unfriendly to bicyclists. I was homesick for my family, my friends and Portland. My advisor implored me to "professionalize," which, in the context of our chat, was clearly code for toning down my dykey-ness, for feminizing my look and mannerisms. She also wanted me to buy a car and to live in the suburbs (where most synagogue jobs were) – and where I could not afford to live. Unbeknownst to her, I had to re-pack my clothes and dishes in boxes and vacate my apartment every other week for spraying because the lady who lived downstairs from me refused to clean her apartment, which attracted more roaches. On those nights, I would practice my *nusach* lessons -- and sometimes doze off -- in a chair at the Laundromat; or I'd sit outside on my front stoop and write songs with my guitar, a pencil and paper and a flashlight.

I completed one semester of graduate school with surprisingly decent grades, but when I returned for spring semester, I knew it wouldn't work out. I didn't belong in the rarefied air, and I wasn't going to become a Cantor or a Jewish Professional Anything Else. I quit three weeks into the new semester and went home. When I returned to Portland, I felt like a failure and didn't know where I belonged. Therefore, I moved in with my girlfriend, went back to the bicycle industry and threw myself into my work there, learning new mechanical skills and eventually becoming the lead purchaser for the bicycle co-op where I had worked before leaving for graduate school.

City of Love

A year after I came home, I took some of the songs I'd written and, through a series of fundraising efforts and a couple of concerts, raised the money to record a very cheap, poorly-engineered "live" album. It was all I could afford and the sound quality wasn't great, but I learned a lot while making *City Of Love*. In the process, I also healed some of the shame and anger I'd brought home with me from Philadelphia. And I promised myself that if I ever heard the call to try my hand at Jewish work again, I would do it on my terms, or not at all.

In 2003, I married my girlfriend. We bought a tiny fixer-upper that same summer and settled down to a simple life in Northeast Portland. By 2010, I was successfully re-established in my bicycle industry career. I was a mechanic, lead purchaser and co-owner at a bicycle collective in Portland, and had been in the business long enough to become something of a *grande dame* in the local bike scene. I wasn't rich, but I had job stability in the midst of a brutal recession. I should have been happy and for a while, I mostly was. But a little voice was nagging at the back of my brain. To quiet it, I took a job teaching two nights a week at the large Reform synagogue where I used to be a member, and tutored a couple of *B'nei Mitzvah* students at the small Reconstructionist *shul* that I had "married into," just a few blocks down the street. I also began writing songs again, songs about my history, my family's history and the growing sense of unease and restlessness I was feeling. One of those songs was my setting of "*Lev Tahor*".

Whenever happiness happens, I can't seem to trust it
Like a rug that's waiting to be pulled right out from under me
I want so badly to believe that all the world's made for me
Can't get past the dust and ash to trust in what I see

Multiple Worlds

Once again, I was standing with a foot in multiple worlds, only now I didn't have enough feet for all the worlds I found myself standing in. I felt adrift and uncertain about my place in the bike scene and my place in Jewish community. With the help of a counselor at a local Jewish non-profit, I realized that I wanted to try again to make a living in Jewish education and music. In September 2012, I left the bike shop where I'd worked for almost twenty years.

That fall, I began working at the large Reform temple four days a week. I also began playing in local coffeehouses, writing more songs and planning to make another album of Jewish music. One of my songs was selected for inclusion in a Jewish composers' festival in Florida. I played a show at a local tavern to raise the airfare so I could go. The story of my unlikely transition from bike mechanic to Jewish performing artist made the cover of Portland's Jewish magazine. Strangers stopped me on the street to tell me they saw me in the magazine, which was both exhilarating and weird. For a few months in the early spring I subbed as a cantorial soloist for a synagogue in Salem – THAT required a steep learning curve! By May, I had begun a fund-raising campaign for the next album. I also signed a contract to spend most of June working as a teacher and artist-in-residence for a summer educational program at a large synagogue in the Midwest. Things were happening very, very fast.

I admit now that it went to my head and freaked me out all at the same time. My trajectory was so weird and so rapid that I didn't know how to keep my perspective. I careened wildly between believing all the local hype about myself, and living in abject fear that I'd be found out as an impostor, a chameleon. I was hurtling headlong into something I couldn't get a grip on, mostly without any real mentorship because I was too freaked out to ask anyone for help – or even, really, to know who to ask. In late August 2013, all my crap caught up with me and I had something very much like a public breakdown. I did and said things that hurt people I loved and cared about very much. I was flailing and did not understand right away the ramifications of what I'd done. Once it was made clear to me, I collapsed in fear and shame, knowing that I had damaged relationships with those closest to me and probably ruined any chance of continuing to work in the Jewish community.

My employer urged me to seek help for the multitude of issues (emotional and, as it turned out, physiological) that I was struggling with. I spent most of the High Holidays at home, not eating much and feeling awful and alone. It was a very difficult and exhausting six months as I rode my bike back and forth between home and work, home and counseling, home and the doctor's office, to sort everything out. There were issues with my past (especially with my Mom – that's SO Jewish!); issues with emotional and physiological changes as I entered the weird world of menopause; and issues with the radical professional changes I'd made. Most of all, I had to let go of a lot of unresolved pain and anger so I could move on with the rest of my life. The emotional heavy lifting this process required wore me out, and some days it was incredibly hard to just get out of bed, dress and go to work.

I was reminded in counseling that, although I had struggled, I had also made some significant changes largely in professional isolation -- and had somehow come out the other side with my sense of self intact. That was no small feat.

Clearing — Good Hard Work

My partner and I had long, deep talks and did good, hard work that reminded me how strong a relationship we have. I reconciled with one of my friends whom I'd hurt deeply; and at work I focused, laser-like, on the well-being and education of my students. It took months of difficult, painful work. With professional help, a very supportive partner, and a willingness to face my fears, I was able to find my bearings again, and to gain a new appreciation for the traits of humility and gratitude. Through the cold, long winter, I also played guitar a lot in the back room of our little house. One song I returned to, again and again, was my setting of *"Lev Tahor"*. I didn't know why at the time, but in hindsight I think I needed the message of the lyrics to keep me calm and grounded as I did the difficult work of taking out the emotional trash – the old ways of thinking that weren't serving me, the habits I'd formed without realizing it, and the self-destructive patterns of punishing myself so hard for every little mistake. There had to be a line—hell, a whole football field of space—between slacking off and beating myself up. I can't say exactly how or why, but singing *"Lev Tahor"* nearly every time I went back there to practice helped me to find that more forgiving, more moderate space as I slowly moved out all the trash piled up in "the back room of my heart".

While still in the painful aftermath of my meltdown, I had to go into the studio in November 2013 and record the album *Ten Miles*. Now I had to summon the strength to record songs that had been written from a very vulnerable place, at a time when I still felt so raw. In the end, this turned out to be the best possible way to do it, the only way I could have achieved the authenticity needed to tell these stories. I had to do it from the broken place that was at the root of some of the songs, and bare my soul in the process. It was a grueling three days of recording, and at the end of it I had a sound that felt real, because it was.

Ten Miles

I released *Ten Miles* in February 2014. I decided to donate all of the proceeds from the release party to the Jewish non-profit that had provided me with counseling, as a way of saying thanks. Since then, I remind myself to walk in gratitude, to think of something every day that I am thankful for. And I have gained a new perspective on my musical gifts, one that allows me to learn from others around me; to use what I learn in the service of others, and not base my every move on what others might think of me. I'm not doing this for their opinions. I'm doing it to give something to my community, and to help calm and ground myself a little along the way.

As I write this, I am preparing for the summer of 2014, during which I will return to the Midwest for another session at the large synagogue, and a July and August in which I will work part-time at a bike shop near my house because, well, I need to. My partner continues to bless me with patience; boundless love and a warm, beautiful smile that I get to wake up to every morning. I don't know what comes next, and I'm mostly okay with not knowing. My life is simple and mostly very sweet, a gift I unwrap daily with all the gratitude I can summon. I still need to pay attention and take care not to let things pile up too much. The human heart is a thing that needs regular care and tending.

Beth Hamon

A musician, teacher, artist, and bicycle mechanic Beth Hamon lives car-free in Portland, Oregon. Her album, "Ten Miles", which includes the song "Lev Tahor", is available at Beth-Hamon-Music.com.

The daughter of nightclub musicians, Beth Hamon is a bicycle riding, autodidactic singer-songwriter whose original material and cover choices straddle the fuzzy line between Jewish and secular themes of social justice, hope, renewal and love. Beth serves as a music-leader and cantorial soloist at Havurah Shalom in Portland, Oregon and as a youth and family song leader and religious school instructor at Congregation Beth Israel in Portland. She also travels around the country, serving other Jewish communities as a visiting teacher, artist-in-residence and performs at folk festivals.

With over twenty-five years of teaching experience in the fields of high school instrumental music, Judaic Studies and Hebrew, Beth holds a B.A. in Music Education and Middle East Studies from Portland State University. Prior to making Jewish education and music her primary career, she spent nearly twenty years as a mechanic, purchaser and small business owner in the bicycle industry.

Beth has released the self-produced CD, City of Love; and performs regularly in coffeehouses and pubs in the Portland-Vancouver area. Her second album of original Jewish folk and roots music, *Ten Miles*, was released in February 2014.

Beth lives in northeast Portland with her partner and two cats. She commutes to work by bicycle and has not owned a car since 1990.

http://BethHamon.CreatingCalmNetworkPublishingGroup.com

Growing Your Spiritual Community

1. Do you have a foot in more than one world? What insight does this essay bring on the subject?

2. What can a rabbi, cantor or lay person who understands the isolation brought about by feeling like an outsider or the challenges of financial struggle offer a synagogue or Jewish community that is looking to grow and have a larger impact on their members?

3. When have you found yourself in a situation where you felt like you didn't fit in? Who "fits in" to your synagogue or community? Imagine someone new coming for the first time. Will they feel welcome or like they don't fit?

4. What does your community offer by way of support to authors and musicians infusing Jewish music with a new and unique spirit? Does your community embrace new pieces by local musicians and artists?

5. Were you familiar with *Lev Tahor* before reading this essay? What do you think of it now?

6. Who are your personal mentors? Who in your community offers mentorship to people searching for ways to contribute to a greater degree? What are Jewish non-profits supporting in your community?

7. Considering the statement, "The human heart is a thing that needs regular care and tending." What are you doing every day to care for and tend your heart or the heart of your community? What is the heart of your community?

The Art of Prayer—The Singer Becomes the Song
Shawn Israel Zevit

Prayer can be electric and alive. Prayer can touch the soul, burst forth a creative celebration of the spirit, and open deep wells of gratitude, longing and praise. Prayer can connect us to our Living Source and to each other, enfolding us in love and praise, wonder and gratitude, awe and thankfulness. Jewish prayer in its essence is soul dialogue and calls us into relationship within and beyond. Through the power of ancient and modern words and melodies, we venture into realms of deep emotion and find longing, sorrow, hope, wholeness, connection and peace. When guided by skilled leaders of prayer and ritual, our complacency is challenged, we can break through outworn assumptions about God and ourselves, and emerge refreshed and inspired to meet the challenges our lives offer. —Rabbi Shawn Zevit and Rabbi Marcia Prager, Adapted From the Davennen Leadership Training Institute.

On Life's Journey

On life's journey, I find I speak less of Jewish music and prayer, and more of the prayer and music that comes through or is an expression of the Jewish people, culture, individual and collective Soul. There are so many varied musical expressions coming through our communities today: a continuum of traditional and experimental synagogue worship, Jewish camp merging musical culture, drumming, chanting and kirtan services and concerts; electric and jazz klezmer; Kabbalat Shabbat services done to the score of Joseph and the Technicolor Dream-coat; the Beatles or Jewish hip hop, etc.

I move between traditional *nusach* and original melodies culminating in my grandfather's *zmirot* from Europe. I find that with *kevah* and *kavannah* clearly connected to the liturgical underpinnings (not just random tunes patched together) and being open to the immediacy of the experience taking place in the room, a wide range of "soul" music is not only possible, but transformative.

There is a continuum of options for inviting a creative musical environment, both innovative and deeply rooted in our musical and textual heritage. A *nigun* can begin a text study session or a service learning *tikkun olam* action. An instrument can underscore a reading or meditation. A choral or multi-part piece can serve as a group building exercise at a board meeting or leadership retreat. *Nusach, trope,* and traditional text are the fundamental to getting inside the carrier wave of our people before adding a patchwork of popular melodies or doing surgery on the liturgy. As in any spiritual practice, music unrelated to the meaning of a service, ritual, learning or social justice event can be self-serving, potentially distracting, and even jarring for anyone trying to connect deeply to the meaning of a moment.

Creative Acts

The Hebrew Bible begins with a grand series of creative acts. Out of a soup of divergent energies, competing elements, and lack of distinctions, the Spirit of God washes over creative potential and with a "Let there be" mission, transforms the unformed into the manifest. Out of a no-thing comes a "some-thing." The "soundscape" begins immediately with the crashing of waves on the newly formed shores of land. Birds are soon chirping and the music of life plays on. Long before the Psalmist details the instruments of the Temple band in Psalm 150, there is chorus of creation declaring its very existence. The song of creation and the score of the world's soul has already been launched.

Music and prayer were intimately tied into spiritual practice during both Temple periods. Even after the destruction of the Second Temple in 70 CE when instruments were no longer part of a lost Temple ritual, the very chanting of the Torah, prayers, *nigunim* (wordless melodies), and mantra-like intonation of Talmud study continued the unbroken musical pulse of the Jewish people's yearning to express an individual and collective response to the acts of hallowing life.

Soul Praise

Soul-praise is an entirely different sort of music. It is purely spiritual, unadulterated by any medium, nothing more than an expression of the simple desire of the soul to rise up in its praise, surrendering its existence to be reunited with its source. In other words, instrumental music is music of the body, and song is the music of the soul. In the Holy Temple, the revelation of godly light was extreme enough to contain both the source of souls and of angels—which is why there was both instrumental music as well as song. (Likkutei Torah, Vezot Haberachah 98d)

I approach both the subject of prayer and music from an integrative perspective. By this I mean my background in commercial scripted theater, ensemble work in educational and social theater, improvisation, Playback Theater, and Bibliodrama, often blends with my work as a rabbi, leading prayer services, singing, and composing. Rarely is my creative work in any of these areas devoid of influences or use of the other modalities. Since 2000, when I co-founded the Davenen Leaders Training Institute with my friend and colleague Rabbi Marcia Prager, influenced by the Davenology approach of Rabbi Zalman Schachter Shalomi (z"l), I have been shaped by and helped train a generation of prayer leaders, musicians, cantors, rabbis and spiritual leaders in the high art of public prayer.

Davenology is discussed in, Rabbi Schachter-Shalomi Zalman (z"l), *Paradigm Shift*, Jason Aronson, Inc, New Jersey, 1993. Reb Zalman was one of the most innovative and inspiring rabbis in the Jewish world today, and a founder of the movement for Jewish Renewal. *Paradigm Shift* is a record of his major teachings that includes contemporary thinking about God and even a sound and movement score for the *Amidah* prayer.

While I strive to find the truth in artistic and educational expression, I am by no means a purist in either of these fields. In fact, the more my rabbinic, educational, performance, and consulting work take me into a variety of settings, the more I feel being of service to sacred values is more fully served by finding the modality, or combination of modalities, that suits the message and the group best. Process and outcome, form and content become mutually enhancing and interdependent ways of being *b'tzelem Elohim* — embodying, mirroring, manifesting and opening up to the flow of Life Itself coming to and through us.

A New Song

Somewhere between singing a new song and acknowledging the very limits of our voices to express the infinite wonders of life is a soundtrack to life that all can participate in. As Rabbi Mordecai Kaplan writes in *The Meaning of God in Modern Jewish Religion Wayne State Press, Detroit, 1994, (Originally published in 1937 and 1962)*:

"The liturgy speaks of God as renewing daily the works of creation. By becoming aware of the fact, we might gear our own lives to this creative urge in the universe and discover within ourselves unsuspected powers of the spirit."

Mordecai Kaplan (1881-1983), ideological founder of Reconstructionism, was a towering figure in North American Jewry. His unusual combination of theology and common sense led him not only to construct new approaches to Judaism geared to our time, but to devise practical expressions as well. He was a champion of creating dynamic Jewish art and developing Jewish artists as one of the highest expressions of Godliness in the world.

Giving Expression

Similarly, finding a variety of places to give expression to our voices (in song, chant, poetic reading, humming a note, choral singing, prayer services, etc.) creates a variety of opportunities for both the gifted singer, composer or musician, and the less vocal or more musically challenged individual to find their place in the soundscape of the community. We inter-act and inter-are in the context of communal prayer. This lifts us out of the confines of our own limited life-narrative to join a song that includes and transcends our personal, denominational, stylistic and liturgical constructs. It is also important to remember that the Jewish way of transmitting wisdom and spiritual truth from generation to generation was aided by chant, *trope* (cantillation for the Torah and *Haftarah*), and *nusach* (melody lines for liturgy).

Tehillim, The Psalms

Of all the liturgical options available to us in the Jewish lexicon, outside of original compositions not related to scripture or liturgy, it is the *tehillim*, the Psalms that invite me most deeply into the realm where pray-er become prayer and singer becomes song. The moments I have felt most encompassed by the holy and simultaneously an expression of the Divine pulsing of creation itself are in these psalm-based expeditions.

The ability of the vast array of classic biblical and contemporary psalms does not limit or judge human expression in the realm or prayer and sacred music. Here are some of my own interpretations that gave birth to music that also came through me covering the depths of despair and bliss of existence:

The first one is from Psalm 27, with words and music by Shawn Israel Zevit, 1994, and inspiration from the psalmist.

When pressures and perspective of a cynical life
Threaten to bring me down
I ride the wave of undying faith
And its lies that finally drown
For one thing I ask, for one thing I long

To build Your house with my life
To see the beauty in every soul
And the light in every night
Hear me, Dear One, when I cry aloud
Have mercy and answer me
My heart won't rest it shouts, "Seek My Face"
And then your soul will be free
Though the world as we know it might crumble down
I know You won't forsake me
Lead me on the path of a righteous life
And I know I shall surely see that
You are my Light and my Salvation of whom shall I fear!
You are the Stronghold of my life of whom shall I be afraid
I will look to You be strong in hope
I will look to You, my GOD
I will long for You
Wait for You
Till eternity with You
Oh, my GOD

The second one is from Psalm 22 with words and music by Shawn Israel Zevit, 1996, and inspiration from the psalmist.

I cry by day, but You don't answer
Numbed at night, I hear no laughter

Eli, lamah azavtani (my GOD why have you left me?)

Oh, my soul is poured out like water
My heart's like wax, its melting over

Eli, lamah azavtani

Others have been here- I know they have trusted
Others have hung in and not been disappointed
Others cried out and found a way through the forest
But what of me?- Eli

Don't be so far when trouble's so near
Why does it hurt so, why do You disappear?
Eli- lamah azavtani

You claimed my heart since its very first breath
You've been my GOD, and will be 'til my death
In the silence, I listen for Your help
Save me now from a hardened heart

Why have You left me? Why have You gone so far?
Shut Your ears to my anguished roar
Eli- lamah azavtani

Let the ends of the universe turn around
Open Your souls and soak in the sound
It's a greater love than you have ever found
GOD has acted, look out now,
GOD in action. Eli....

Yearning

We yearn to participate in the perpetual renewal of creation, as we pray in the first blessing before the *Shema*: *"Hamehadesh betuvo bekhol-yom tamid ma'aseh vereysheit"* the One who renews Creation's work each day. May these words and thoughts help inspire and support you to move beyond the page into the play and sound of the Soul of all Creation waiting within in you for expression.

"The people gave the music life, and the music in turn pulsated in the people, passing from parent to child, and from land to land. The joys and triumphs, the tenderness and warmth, the agony and sorrows, the prayer and protest... made them one, were poured into music; and where they are still felt, that process continues today. When we live for a moment with that music, we are touching the pulse itself, and our own is quickened in turn." Judith Kaplan Eisenstein "Heritage of Music", Union of American Hebrew Congregations, New York, 1972. A leading Jewish composer and champion of music in Jewish congregational and cultural life in the 20th century, Judith was the daughter of Rabbi Mordecai Kaplan and married to Rabbi Ira Eisenstein, a founder of the Reconstructionist movement.

Shawn Israel Zevit

The lead rabbi at congregation Mishkan Shalom in Philadelphia, Pennsylvania, Rabbi Zevit worked for the Jewish Reconstructionist Movement for fourteen years as Director of Congregational Services and Social Justice, consulting with and supporting dozens of congregations, organizations, social justice initiatives in the Jewish and larger world. He is co-director with Rabbi Marcia Prager of the award-winning Davennen Leader's Training Institute (Dlti.org) and is a spiritual director and Associate Director for the ALEPH Hashpa'ah Jewish Spiritual Direction program (Aleph.org), working at the nexus of spiritual formation, development and healing on a personal, interpersonal and communal level.

Mishkan Shalom, a progressive Reconstructionist Jewish community located in a restored historic mill building in Roxborough, named Rabbi Shawn Israel Zevit its new rabbi starting August, 2013.

A 1998 graduate of The Reconstructionist Rabbinical College, Rabbi Zevit is a dynamic and widely known liturgist, teacher, singer, author and consultant to Jewish communities. An accomplished singer and guitarist, Rabbi Zevit is a founding member of the popular Jewish musical group, Shabbat Unplugged.

http://ShawnZevit.CreatingCalmNetworkPublishingGroup.com

Growing Your Spiritual Community

1. "Prayer can be electric and alive. Prayer can touch the soul, burst forth a creative celebration of the spirit, and open deep wells of gratitude, longing and praise." How do you feel about this quote from Rabbi Shawn Zevit and Rabbi Marcia Prager? What do you do to experience prayer as electric and alive?

2. What is the distinction Rabbi Shawn Zevit is making with this quote: "I find I speak less of Jewish music and prayer, and more of the prayer and music that comes through or is an expression of the Jewish people, culture, individual and collective Soul." How does the soul of your community come through in the music and prayers?

3. Think about the natural sounds you hear. Do you have a special place where you enjoy the sounds of the earth and the creatures on it?

4. How would you define or describe "soul praise"?

5. What do you know of Mordecai Kaplan (1881-1983), the ideological founder of Reconstructionism?

6. Have you written original interpretive words or music to the psalms? Which psalm would you start with if you were going to write something? Do you have a favorite psalm?

7. What do you "yearn" for in your family, your community, your work or your play?

Ma'ariv Aravim: Stand By Me
Robbi Sherwin

Blessed is the One Who makes the evening fall,
Blessed is the Spirit Who guides us all
Baruch Ata Adonai ha'ma'ariv aravim
Shechinah, Shechinah

"*Ma'ariv Aravim*" by Robbi Sherwin and Katy Jordan, Aish Hakodesh, MiriamShira Productions, 2000.

Presence and participation; connection (*kesher*) and community; reflection and re-creation; fullness of heart and fearlessness of being; God and gratefulness; *Shechinah* and shalom; all of these things – and more – are what I hope to find and share when I come together with a Jewish community to "pray twice" while singing. St. Augustine of Hippo (+430) is often quoted as having said "*He, who sings, prays twice.*" The Latin cited for this is "*Qui bene cantat bis orat*" or "*He, who sings well prays twice*".

Twilight

Betwixt and between—the time of day immediately following sunset, or gloaming, is a time of magic, of transition. Ancient peoples were anxious when the sun disappeared and suffered from the fear that it would not return without prayers and offerings to the gods. Although science and many millennium have convinced us otherwise, and we no longer fear that the sun will not return in the morning, this is time to take stock in the day that has just passed and breathe and prepare for the new day to come. I find that there is no better way to open my heart and soul to the new day than to sing. I believe that to fully prepare myself and my community for this transition, as the spiritual leader, I must be true and committed in my intention to be a guide during this transcendent time. Together, we are creating a holy circle of trust that benefits the *kehillah*, the congregation or the community. As a conduit the listener/participant along with myself help our prayers soar. As the *shlichat tzibor*—the people's representative—I am here to help facilitate the relationship that each individual pray-er must have to connect personally with God, with the community and within themselves. When I am one with One—it helps others, as well. It is my privilege to be a model of this focused intention.

Ma'ariv

The first service of the "day" is the *Ma'ariv*, or the evening service. We are about a make new start, to embrace a new day. From the very beginning of the Torah, in *Bereshit*, Genesis 1:5 says: "It was evening, it was morning, the first day," followed by verses that end each day of six days of creation with "it was evening, it was morning... the (3rd, 4th, etc.) day. We begin our new day at sundown, not at midnight as the secular world does, allowing us to start anew as the sun goes down.

As with all our prayers, the *Ma'ariv Aravim* begins with praising God and defining God's role as Ruler of time and of space. God is defined as the "bringer of dusk." The prayer lists a litany of God's power in this transition into the new day, and we are in awe as God "brings it on."

Ma'ariv aravim: a blessing for evening:

Baruch atah, Adonai, eleoheinu melech ha-olam, asher bidvaro ma'ariv aravim, b'chochma poteach she'arim, u-vitvunah meshaneh itim, u-machalif et ha-zmanim, um'sader et ha-cochavim, b'mishm'roteihem b'rakiya kirtzono. Borei yom valaila, golel or mipnei choshech, v'choshech mipnei or. Uma'avir yom u-mevi laila, u-mavdil bein yom u-vein laila, Adonai tz'vaot shemo. El chai v'kayam, tamid yimloch aleinu l'olam va'ed. Baruch atadh Adonai, ha-ma'avriv aravim.

—A modern translation from *Siddur B'chol L'vav'cha*, Congregation Beth Simchat Torah, p. 81, 2007, New York:

Blessed are you, Holy One, Creator of All:
With wisdom, You open the gates of dawn;
With understanding, You make time and seasons change.
You arrange the stars in the sky, according to Your plan.
You created day and night, rolling light into darkness,
darkness into light.
You cause the day to fade away and bring on night.
You separate day and night.
Adonai Tzva'ot - "Source of all beings" is Your name.
Living and Ever Present One, you rule over us forever and ever. Praised are You, Eternal One, who brings on the evening's dusk.

Another contemporary translation – this one through song, can be found here in Steve Brodsky's version of *Ma'ariv Aravim*, recorded by Sababa on the 2005 release, *"Pray for the Peace"*:

Holy One of Blessing, Your Presence fills creation.
Your word brings on the night.
You make the days pass by
The seasons go in circles
You separate the darkness from the light
Baruch Ata Adonai Eloheinu Melech ha'olam
Asher bidvaro ma'ariv aravim, ma'ariv aravim

Ma'ariv Aravim is my favorite evening prayer – every day God renews creation, meaning that we all have chance for a 'do over,' starting at the most beautiful part of the day. God's paintbrush spreads from the east to the west, painting the sky and the land with vibrant colors of orange, pink and purple. This prayer is full of colorful imagery: I can see the melding of the evening with the day and the day with the evening – and imagine what it would have been like to order the stars. You are only limited by your own internal visualization with this prayer. And we can appreciation the separation, the new beginning. We have the opportunity to be grateful for the past, and to anticipate the future – all in living color.

Magnificent Mountain Jews

The image of God as nature particularly moves me. My congregation, B'nai Butte in Crested Butte, Colorado, is located at 8,900 feet above sea level in the "Wildflower Capital of Colorado." This magnificent place with jutting mountain peaks and colorful valleys, located in the East River Valley, is just 12 miles trailhead-to-trailhead across either the East or West Maroon pass from Aspen, Colorado. It explodes in vibrant color all over the mountains in the summer wilderness. In the winter, the Crested Butte Mountain Resort also boasts the #1 ski area in the country with stark, jutting white peaks. You haven't seen God transform the world until you have witnesses the pink "alpenglow" as the sun touches the very tip of the peaks at sunset.

Thinking Outside The Bimah

Crested Butte is quite remote and Jews who live there – about 10% of the population - are not only looking for organized religion here at the "end of the road." We are blessed when the amazing visual artists, opera singers, spiritual seekers, scientists at the Rocky Mountain Biological Laboratories, students at Western State University in Gunnison, musicians on tour and our very active 2nd homeowner community are present. Their participation swells our ranks with Jews from all over the world that come together to "think outside the *bimah*." With God and nature as our guide, we share events such as Shabbat on Skis at 10,000 feet; "Torah and Java" at a local coffee shop, hiking with Torah and *shofarot* on *Rosh Hashana* morning (the elk often answer the *shofar*!), tossing our crumbs (and shortcomings!) during *tashlich* in a real mountain river; or our annual eight-hour, hike across West Maroon Pass (at 12,000 feet!) to join with the Aspen Jewish Congregation. We do much of this at sunset, and we are awestruck as we are touched by the gold and orange of the quivering aspen trees, and the palette that transforms us day-to-night in the crisp air as the sun sets.

Composing in Sun-Soaked Pine Forests

Musically, the prayer has many beautiful settings. The version of *Ma'ariv Aravim* at the beginning of this chapter appears on my second album, *"Aish HaKodesh"* and was written with my daughter, Katy, then 13, while lying on a picnic bench at the Burning Bear campsite at Guanella Pass in Colorado at 10,000 feet. The day had been filled with rafting, hiking and fishing and everywhere was the delicious smell of sun-soaked pine needles. This heady tonic, along with the crackle of the campfire, "filled up my senses," as John Denver— *zichrono l'bercha*—let his memory be for a blessing—so eloquently put it. There were millions of stars visible, and as there was no light pollution in this remote location, we could even spy the Milky Way. As the evening fell, we could count the shooting stars as they danced above us. Grateful for the opportunity to witness the color and majesty of the heavens at the same time, Katy and I came up with the three lines that became a sacred round. I didn't realize, at the time, I was playing the exact same chord progression from the mega-hit, *"Stand By Me."*

Stand By Me

Much has been said about Jewish influences in contemporary composers, especially those of the "American Songbook" era like George Gershwin. I often wonder if Mike Stoller, Jerry Leiber and Ben E. King, the three composers of *Stand By Me*, knew they had written a love song to God that mirrors the *Ma'ariv Aravim* prayer. Both Stoller and Leiber were Jewish. Although an anthem for teens in the Sixties, the words of *"Stand by*

Me" are truly a prayer in and of themselves. I often "mash up" the Hebrew in the *Ma'ariv Aravim* with this "prayer." Imagine that the "you" in this song, is God.

The chords: *C Am Dm G* play over and over again. *"Blessed is the One Who makes the evening fall,"* I intoned on that picnic bench at Burning Bear. *"Blessed is the Spirit Who guides us all,"* my daughter, Katy, answered.

"Stand by Me" speaks of the night coming and the darkness of the land. The theme of not being afraid as long as (God) stands in support is prevalent throughout the song. Even though mountains may crumble and the sky may fall, God is with us. You can find a complete set of lyrics to *"Stand by Me"* at AZlyrics.com/lyrics/beneking/standbyme.html

Thank you, God.
Over and over again.
For the chance to renew ourselves day by day.
For the opportunity to share sacred moments of transcendence with our communities.
For not fearing the darkness.

Thank you, God.
For delighting us with stars.
For the seasons that go 'round'.
For bringing on the evening.
And may we all transition into the next day without fear.

Robbi Sherwin

Austin's "Rockin" Rabbi-Cantor Robbi Sherwin travels the world as a Rabbi/Cantor and Artist-in-Residence specializing in Jewish retreats and congregational songwriting. Raised as an Air Force 'brat' in small towns all over the U.S., she brings an infectious love of Judaism to all who encounter her – babies to Bubbies!

An award-winning, multi-published composer of 100 Jewish songs, Robbi tours extensively with her popular folk-rock band, Sababa! and with Steve Brodsky and Scott Leader. She has recorded five CDs of original Jewish folk/rock music. A multi-instrumentalist and exceptional harmony singer, her "spirited Jewish songcrafting" has been published, sung, recorded and performed from Tulsa, Oklahoma to Tel Aviv, Israel. Robbi's music can be found in Voices for Israel II; Shalshelet: The Foundation for New Jewish Music; URJ/Transcontinental Music's Ruach series, Tot Shabbat Curriculum and Shabbat Anthology; Women of Reform Judaism's 100th Anniversary CD; and many others.

Robbi is also a Storahtelling Maven, Vice-President of the Women Cantors' Network and one of the few female artists featured on Jewish Rock Radio. As the spiritual leader of Congregation B'nai in Crested Butte, Colorado, she enjoys the Rocky Mountain "chai" of a shul at 9,000+ feet, with Ski Shabbats, Alpine hikes and an attitude of high-altitude gratitude. Listen to Robbi at SababaMusic.com

http://RobbiSherwin.CreatingCalmNetworkPublishingGroup.com

Growing Your Spiritual Community

1. Consider the idea of "betwixt and between". Where in your life, in your community, or in your work are you betwixt and between?
2. What does this quote mean to you, "*Ma'ariv Aravim* is my favorite evening prayer—every day God renews creation, meaning that we all have chance for a 'do over', starting at the most beautiful part of the day?"
3. How do you do with transitions from one place to another or from one perception to another or from one activity to another? We sometimes talk about how children transition. There are those who are good at transitions and those for whom transitioning is more challenging. How are you at transitions? Have you ever used songs to ease the transitions?
4. Have you participated in services outdoors? What kinds of settings have you enjoyed?

Family

In Finkelstein's translation of *L'dor Vador*, we see a connection between the generations, families and our individual connection to God.

"From generation to generation,
we will make known Your greatness,
and to all eternity proclaim
Your holiness.
Your praise shall never depart from our lips.
Blessed is Adonai, the holy one."

—*Jewish Liturgical Music for Treble Choirs* Prepared by Miriam Altman, July, 2014

The prayer expresses an essential tenet of Judaism and other faith traditions—the importance of carrying on good works and faithful beliefs to your children and your children's children.

Growing Your Spiritual Community

1. What are you teaching your children or the children in your community about music, songs, and prayers?
2. Imagine how your children's children's generation will be different from you in their use of liturgical music.

My Yiddishe Grandma and other Healing Tales
Jeff Gold

My relationship with Judaism has changed over the years, but my connection to Jewish culture and its music has always been there for me. These beautiful songs and melodies have moved me and helped me grow and develop as a musician. My earliest musical memories are of my grandmother singing and humming her favorite eastern European lullabies and folk songs. She always had a song in her heart and she hummed while cooking, sewing, cleaning or just passing the time, but when it was time for bed, for those of us lucky enough to be a grandchild, niece or nephew, she was magic.

The Music of Ashkenazi Eastern Europe

The music which originated in Eastern Europe (the Balkans, Romania, Bulgaria, Poland, among others) and moved westward and northward throughout Europe and later into North America and Israel, belongs to the Ashkenazi tradition. These were the songs of Grandma's youth, born of the rich oral tradition of Jewish story-telling and melody, depicting life in the vanished world of the *shtetl* or village, evolving into the popular songs in the late 19th and early 20th century as arranged and composed by people like Sholom Aleichem, Mark Warshavsky and Joel Engel. It wasn't until I was much older that I began to understand the re-connection with her own youth that Grandma must have been experiencing as she comforted me to sleep.

Grandma Judith was all about kids. Each of her 10 grandchildren was her "favorite" and that's what made her so special. She had a way of figuring out what made each child unique, and then exploring their individuality. This deep and very special connection began very early on, in her comforting arms, hearing her soothing voice singing those beautiful lullabies, *"Shlof mein kind...sleep my child..."*

Out like a light, it worked every time.

She didn't possess a powerful voice; that wouldn't be her style. Her singing was a warm and comforting instrument of reassurance as I drifted off to blissful sleep. When I woke, the air was sweeter, my dreams were more colorful, and I woke up relaxed and refreshed. Weekends with Grandma and Grandpa were special. As the years passed, I was lucky enough to hear her sing to my own children, always a pleasant reminder of my youth: it never lost its effect on me.

Grandma's Influence

People often tell me that many of the songs I've composed sound like they may have been influenced by Yiddish music and I really hope that's true. As Grandma sang me to sleep she was making a magical connection with me that contained a message of love and comfort. My own intention is to make the same sort of spiritual connection with others through my music.

The appeal my songs have had to children has truly surprised me, especially when I play at fairs and events. Children always stop to listen and watch me play. When they can make their parents stop and listen, they become my best salesmen! Something about my music connects with children, I'm guessing in the same way Grandma Judith's music connected with me.

Grandma is no longer with us, but I think she'd be especially proud of the connection my songs have made with the Special Education community. My very special nephew Russell was Grandma's last great-grandchild and he only knew her for a short time, but it seems to have been long enough to have established his magical musical connection with her. Russell was one of my earliest fans and would listen to my CDs over and over again as the music became attached to the routine of getting him to relax, go to bed and actually fall asleep.

Uncle Jeff's Healing

One night, Russell announced to his Mom (my sister) that "Uncle Jeff's Music makes me feel better!" He then began to share the songs with his classmates at his school, many of whom also experienced a positive effect and I'm proud to say that my music has become an integral part of many families' bedtime routines throughout the world.

The healing effect is by no means limited to kids. I am especially moved when my songs reach out and touch people of all ages in unexpected ways. Once while I was taking a break from playing at a public event, a homeless man walked up to me and wanted to tell me his story. He was a Desert Storm Vet, former helicopter pilot who evacuated the wounded. He had seen and experienced many awful things but has been unable to get any meaningful help since returning home. Now here he was homeless in Southern California. He told me he was very stressed out, unable to sleep and was hoping that listening to my "relaxation" music might help. So he sat down on a park bench and listened quietly while I played.

After I'd played for an hour or so, as I put down my guitar for another little break, he walked back up to me, thanked me and said he felt much better. Then he reached into his pocket and pulled out a dollar and put it in my tip jar. I pleaded with him to keep it, but he refused, said he wished he could give me more and then disappeared into the crowd.

It happened again last week. A homeless man dropped a couple of bills and some change into my tip jar, but this time I did not chase after him, as I now know better. Instead, I acknowledged him with a wink and thanked him for listening as he pushed his shopping cart down the parkway. He had sat under the shade of a palm tree for over an hour listening to me play, occasionally flashing a thumb up and making sure to be the last person to finish applauding after the conclusion of each song. As he walked away I was thinking that if I'd been born in the past, I just might have made a pretty decent Fiddler in the *shtetl*.

From the dawn of civilization, music has been used successfully to induce states of physical, mental, and emotional relaxation as well as promote healing. King Saul was soothed by David's harp music. In ancient Greece, Apollo was both the god of medicine *and* music. In ancient Egypt, the professions of priesthood, musician and physician were combined as one. Priests from ancient Egypt, Greece and Rome chanted incantations as they administered medicine to the sick. Yiddish lullabies deeply rooted in Hasidic *nigun* still exist to this day.

These are just a few examples of how the belief in the power and intent of music to affect change within ourselves was passed down through the generations in so many cultures throughout the world. It was not until the late 1700's, as music became separated from its role in science and medicine, that music's ability to entertain became more important than its possible therapeutic benefits. Possibly more so than any other type of music, Jewish music in general has been able to find a balance between the two philosophies.

Human Emotions

The ability of music to influence human emotion is very well known. You probably experience it daily while watching the television or at the movies. A variety of musical moods may be used to create feelings of calm, tension, excitement, or romance. Music also evokes memories of times gone by, and triggers all sorts of emotional reactions like joy, warmth, fear and sadness. When you hear Tevye sing "*Sunrise, Sunset*" in *Fiddler on the Roof*, and you gaze out over your own family, my guess is at the very least, a lump forms in your throat and your eyes well up.

According to the American Music Therapy Association, the 20th century discipline of Music Therapy began after World War I and World War II when community musicians of all types, went to Veterans hospitals around the country to play for the thousands of veterans suffering both physical and emotional trauma from the wars. The patients' notable physical and emotional responses to music led the doctors and nurses to request the hiring of musicians by the hospitals. This then lead to formal studies of music as a healing practice.

A number of famous Jewish musicians including violinist Yehudi Menuhin, singer Emma Schaver, and conductor Leonard Bernstein travelled to the "Displaced Persons" camps though out the American and British occupation zones after WWII. I read an account of a nurse who was present at one of Menuhin and Benjamin Britten's concerts at Bergan-Belson who noted, "It was inspiring to see these two compassionate men, clad simply in shirt and shorts, creating glorious melody and moving amongst the people in the crowded hut who were difficult to rouse from a deadly mental lethargy as a result of the horrors and privations they had suffered. They were successful in some cases in wooing them back to life and hope and commence the healing of the mind and body."

Songs from the holocaust have played a crucial role, both as historical sources that would enable future researchers to reconstruct what had happened, and as artifacts that could perhaps preserve the voices and the memory of the victims. Precious few documents survived WWII and the "Jewish Blues" that Jews sang in the ghettos and death camps might be the best picture that will ever emerge of our struggles during WWII and before.

Where Shall I Go?

One of Grandma's favorites was *"Where Shall I Go"* (later recorded by Steve Lawrence and also Ray Charles, among others), that begins with a haunting and melancholic first verse....

> *Tell me, where can I go?*
> *There's no place I can see.*
> *Where to go, where to go?*
> *Every door is closed for me.*

The folk music created in Eastern Europe and Israel in the past century has taken on significance for Jews across the world that looks to Israel for cultural and religious inspiration. The intention of Israeli folk music old and new, true to its original creativity, is to facilitate the unification and common identification among Jews throughout the world.

The second verse of "Where Shall I Go?" answers with soulful jubilation...

Now I know where to go,
Where my folk proudly stand.
Let me go, let me go
To that precious promised land.

Lullabies

When I try now to remember Grandma's voice, I think the first song I hear is *Dona Dona*, which was originally written by Aaron Zeitlin (lyrics) and Sholom Secunda (music) for the Yiddish musical Esterke" in the early 1940s and became popular again a generation later when it was recorded by Joan Baez in 1960, Donovan in 1965 and Patty Duke in 1968. Sadly, the world of Yiddish language and music is disappearing as it is assimilated into other cultures. It's important to try and preserve what we can. For my part, I'm going to start recording a few arrangements of Yiddish lullabies. There are so many beautiful healing melodies to choose from.

Recently, I asked my father to share his memories of his mother and the Yiddish music of his youth. I asked him if he still listens to any of the songs Grandma used to sing and I wanted to know what some of his favorites are. We were alone in the car at the time and we were very late. He's a great driver, but he was doing quite a bit of bobbing and weaving to try to make up time. His answer surprised me. He said, "Yeah, there were a whole bunch them, in fact I have a CD right here." And he popped it in the CD player and Abraham Goldfaden's "*Rozhinkes min Mandlen*" started playing...and he started singing along. Just like that we were driving with the flow of traffic, slowing for yellow lights and having a grand old time...and for a few wonderful moments, it seemed Grandma was riding in the back with us.

I've always been in tune with the healing effect music has on me. Grandma got me started on something, and while I probably didn't realize exactly what was happening at the time, I learned that playing the guitar lowered my blood pressure by transporting me to a place within me, where I can feel both relaxed and exhilarated at the same time. This love continued to grow while participating in sing-alongs at the Jewish summer camps I attended and also listening to the musical hymns and prayers in temple. As I sat listening, I would focus on the melodies, the cantor's majestic tenor, the choir's harmonies, and especially the organ. It was so beautiful I could have listened all day.

Lullabies like *Durme Durme* and *Zing Faygeleh Zing* were my first experience with music and our Jewish culture, and while I don't actually speak Yiddish, these songs have left an indelible mark on me and my music. These melodies are forever swirling within my heart and in my mind, sometimes inspiring new songs and emotions I enjoy expressing through my guitar and piano. This journey began for me as an infant in my grandmother's arms as she sang beautiful Yiddish lullabies in her warm, inviting voice as my love for music germinated. This love grew to encompass a place within me where I find warmth and comfort, energy and recharging; and where I can clear my mind and get creativity flowing. It is my proudest achievement that I am able to share this gift of beauty, peace and comfort through my musical compositions.

Jeff Gold

California native Jeff Gold composes soulful and spiritual instrumentals for relaxation, meditation and healing. His music has also become popular within the special education community, especially for children with autism, many of whom have found that his soothing music helps them focus and relax.

Jeff has released three CDs, *"Simple Treasures, "Escapes"* and *"Soul of a Mountain"* —each one is a soothing and relaxing collection of melodies featuring beautifully arranged acoustic guitars, piano, strings and flutes. While he composes and arranges his own music, he also plays guitars and piano. He does his own mixing, editing and mastering, skills he perfected as a television editor for shows like *"Baywatch,"* and *"The Office."*

Jeff's earliest musical memories are of his grandmother who loved to sing Yiddish, Romanian and Russian Lullabies to her grandchildren as they fell asleep. She had a rich, warm, beautiful voice and was always singing or humming. These Eastern European influences are evident in many of Jeff's compositions. He is also inspired by his wife, Diane Gold, who he describes as an invaluable resource.

He composed the soundtracks and also produced nine guided imagery CDs for *"The Live Well Series"*, with hypnotherapist, Janet Montgomery. Programs include stress management, coping with cancer treatment, and their latest, *"Sleep Well for Kids."*

You can listen in at JeffGold.com and Music as Therapy.

http://JeffGold.CreatingCalmNetworkPublishingGroup.com

Growing Your Spiritual Community

1. Do you have memories of older relatives singing or reading to you? Do you ever sing to or sing with children?
2. Do you feel connected to an Ashkenazi tradition?
3. Do you have a favorite Yiddish song?
4. Do you experience physical and emotional healing through music?
5. What is your earliest memory of music?
6. Is music or prayers part of your going to sleep ritual?

My Father's Tunes
Hannah Seidel

It was Friday night in Indianapolis. We were a small group of bicyclists crossing the country with Hazon, a Jewish environmental organization, and we were joined for the weekend, as the culture of the road makes common, by a friendly cyclist met on the way. He was genial and curious, and watched politely as we celebrated the holiday together. When we parted ways Sunday morning, someone asked him what he had thought of his first experience with the Jewish Sabbath. He paused for a moment. "Well, you sure do a lot of singing."

Why does music seem to go hand-in-hand with Jewish prayer? Why do Jewish services never consist solely of sober and silent reflection? What is it about the addition of music that allows reciting a poem, prayer, or psalm to become a truly religious experience?

Music is beautiful. It can allow us to focus our attention away from our everyday world and towards the divine. It can make us happy, and it can make us sad. It can make us feel the support of our community, and it can bolster us in our individuality. But I believe there is another reason that music is so prevalent in Jewish services and celebrations.

A Childhood Full of Jewish Music

My childhood was filled with Jewish music. My father is a rabbi who writes alluring new tunes as easily as I wrote bad poetry in elementary school. These melodies permeated my childhood. Even now I find

115

myself humming them in the shower or on the bus. Throughout my childhood I sang these tunes like second nature, and doing so felt, well, natural; I didn't think much of it.

Chanukah

In third grade at my Jewish Day School, we were assigned to write about our favorite Jewish holiday. I chose *Chanukah*. I will spare you the poetry I composed (I could not think of anything to rhyme with *"Chanukah"* except *"Chanukah"*), but I was so overcome with the warm memories of that holiday that I ended my paragraph saying: "If we never actually make it to heaven, *Chanukah* will be the next best thing." At the time, it seemed the most obvious assertion in the world. My mother, a teacher, who was helping me, delicately asked if this was really what I meant to say, or if it wasn't a little too… strong. My face scalding, I hastily crossed out what I had written and replaced it with something calm and inane that I no longer remember. I was embarrassed, but I was also upset, because that *was* what I had meant to say.

If I had had the words, I might have described the warmth of the *Chanukah* candles in the window, or the warmth of my older brothers' arms, normally scorned, around my shoulders, or the sound of our small family chorus singing *Maoz Tzur* and *HaNerot HaLalu* to my father's tune. Our reflection sang back at us from the window, and the candle waxed dripped in a hundred colors, and I felt loved. I didn't have the words to translate that feeling into a homework assignment, but I did have the music, and my father's tunes. These tunes accompanied me as I grew up, and every time I sang them, I remembered that feeling of being loved.

Ki Eshmerah Shabbat

The first time I realized that my father's tunes were not all that they seemed came a few weeks before my *Bat Mitzvah*. We were singing *z'mirot*, Shabbat songs, at synagogue after lunch, and I requested one of my favorites, *Ki Eshmerah Shabbat*. The group cheerfully launched into a strange and grating tune, which I had never heard before. Confused and mortified, I didn't even try to keep up; I couldn't. I sat in my seat and stared at the words in the *benscher*, the mealtime prayer book, not understanding them.

It didn't take me long to figure it out, at the same time as my mother whispered the truth in my ear: "I don't think they know Dad's tune, sweetie."

Not know Dad's tune? Impossible. There only *was* one tune to *Ki Eshmerah Shabbat*—we've been singing it for years! How can anyone not know my father's tune?

Easily, it turned out.

From that moment onwards, I was always a little wary of large groups singing *z'mirot*. I collected tunes relentlessly, determined never to be caught off guard again. And I searched out which of my childhood favorites were, in fact, my father's tunes, and I kept them to myself (the list is long: *Yom Shabbaton, Yikum Purkan, Adon Olam, Lecha Dodi*, even part of the grace after meals). It was safer that way.

Music of the Israel Trail

When I was fifteen, I went to Israel for the first time on a program called *Derech HaTeva*, in which Israeli and North American teenagers backpack a portion of *Shvil Yisrael*, the Israel Trail, together. It was a meaningful and transformative experience for me in many ways, not the least of which being that I learned dozens of handsome, unfamiliar tunes from all over the world. I acquired new favorites and found the confidence to teach my old favorites to the group. Everyone was learning together, whether how to find a trailhead, cook for Shabbat on a single camping stove, or sing *Modeh Ani*. As I learned to lead our way through the wilderness, I was also learning to lead a group in song.

When the program ended, instead of returning home I remained an extra week in Israel, joining with my synagogue's tour, which my father was leading, and which conveniently coincided with my own. One afternoon as we were waiting for the tour bus, someone suggested we sing a song, so I taught the group the new *Modeh Ani* tune I had just learned. It wasn't one of my new favorites, but it was easy to learn and to teach, and (it soon became apparent) that it was as new to the synagogue group as it had been to me.

As we gathered our things to board the bus, my father remarked to his congregants, "That's how you know you've done a good job, when they grow up and start teaching you new tunes."

He made it a joke, and I laughed along, even while I was thinking (though old enough to know better)—But Dad knows all the tunes. I was embarrassed, but also proud of myself. Maybe Dad was right. Maybe this meant I was growing up.

A New Attitude

My father's tunes, friendly and familiar, had comforted me for most of my childhood. As I grew older, I came to hear just how vast and varied the world of Jewish music is, and my father's tunes became landmarks as I explored. They were places I knew I could always come back to and feel welcome. And finally my father's tunes became presents, ambassadorial gifts I carry with me always, to share and to receive equal gifts in return from whomever I meet.

Because of my father's tunes, I came to love teaching tunes to others. Teaching his melodies was a chance for me to share with other people a little piece of what was, for my grade-school self at least, the next best thing to heaven. And the act of sharing always made the words of the prayer or song ring a little more soundly.

What good is a song sung by only one person? What value is there to a tune a child is too embarrassed to sing, for fear that no one else will know the melody and she will be left to sing alone?

The song that started it all for me, *Ki Eshmerah Shabbat*, impacted me so powerfully not because of its words (which I did not learn to translate until much later) or even my father's tune (which, though I liked, I did not realize was unusual in any way), but because of the context in which it was sung: Friday night, with friends and family around me, and tea and dessert still on the table. It made me happy because I associated it with happy circumstances.

However, the song itself has its own thoughts on the matter of Jewish music and *kavanah*, or prayerful intention. *Ki Eshmerah Shabbat* is a poem of promises. Written by Abraham Ibn Ezra, a 12th-century Spanish rabbi, it is a vow the singer makes to God: I will keep Shabbat so that You will keep me; or alternatively, it is a declaration of faith: look everyone, I keep Shabbat, and so I know that God will keep me. The poem goes on to list the rules and practices of Shabbat and the singer's dedication to each one of them. In the vision of this poem, Shabbat is a contract or at least an important clause in a larger agreement, not a lighthearted party.

Why, however, is such a notion immortalized in a casual song, and not in a prayer or some other weighty medium?

Ki Eshmerah Shabbat presents the idea of obedience as delight, a covenant made of love as much as duty. It evokes a compact obeyed not out of dull obligation or fear, but out of wonder, gratitude, and joy: "It is an honored day, a day of pleasures...Those who mourn on [Shabbat] are set back, for it is a day to rejoice, and it shall make me happy. Because I keep Shabbat, God will keep me; it is a sign between us, forever."

Which is more revealing about the nature of Judaism: God's actions in the world, or how we, as Jews, react? We do not fear, but approach; we do not ignore, but wonder; we do not solemnly obey, but celebrate in song. We do not cloister ourselves, but share in the delight of the community.

Inner Beauty

Kavanah, intention, is often thought of as spiritual focus towards God. We strive to have good *kavanah* in our prayers, to remove distractions and really feel the meaning of our words, not just mouth along to them.

Attaining *kavanah* is serious business. But *Ki Eshmerah Shabbat* encourages the idea that true *kavanah*, true attention and connection to God, is as inextricably tied to joy, appreciation, and song as it is to resoluteness and solemnity.

When I teach a song, it is true; I do not always have good *kavanah*. I do not always think about the meaning of the prayer. Instead I am listening—should we try that section again?—and guiding—One more time from the top! When I teach a song; it is true, my thoughts are not on God. My thoughts are on the people around me. But perhaps that is just as it should be.

The 11th-century Muslim mystic and philosopher Abu Hamid Al-Ghazali once wrote, "The beautiful work of an author, the beautiful poem of a poet, the beautiful painting of a painter or the building of an architect reveal also the inner beauty of these men." Music, too, is a natural expression of this inner beauty; it reveals the soul. And as we are all made in God's image, is not the inner beauty of all mankind divine? So what better way is there to commune with God, and to appreciate the inner beauty of our fellow man, than through song? Music in this light, then, is a naturally religious experience.

In my own changing relationship with Jewish music, the joy contained in song bridged the gap between embarrassment and confidence, between fear and

121

delight, between complacency and bravery, and between childhood and adulthood. It is, perhaps, the only thing that could have done so. It allowed me to stop worrying about the sounds I was making and embrace the beauty within each song, within myself, and within the community. As the singer of *Ki Eshmerah Shabbat* accepts God's covenant of Shabbat and reciprocates the gift joyously, so was I able to take my father's tunes and find joy, for myself and others, in passing them forward.

Ot hi l'olmei ad, beino u'veini.
May it be a sign forever between us

Hannah Seidel

A writer, Hannah Seidel is a native of Washington, DC. As the daughter of a rabbi with a tendency to compose new tunes when dissatisfied with the traditional ones, she has been surrounded by Jewish music all of her life.

Hannah recently graduated from Oberlin College, where she studied Religion and English. Her time at Oberlin exposed her to new tunes, prayers, and opportunities for Jewish leadership. At Oberlin, Hannah led High Holiday services, regular Shabbat services, and taught many of her peers to *leyn* Torah and *Megillat Esther*. She was also a member of Oberlin's Kosher-Halal Co-op, which piqued her interest in interfaith cooperation and friendship.

Hannah's senior thesis explored modern Jewish prayers for healing, delving into questions of theology, history, tradition, and the ultimate value of prayer. In the process of research, Hannah discovered dozens of new and rare Jewish prayers, and was inspired to begin writing her own.

After graduating, Hannah became the Jewish Student Life Coordinator at Oberlin Hillel, continuing to serve the community to which she has become so attached. She is currently working on her first novel.

http://HannahSeidel.CreatingCalmNetworkPublishingGroup.com

Growing Your Spiritual Community

1. Have you ever unexpectedly joined in a religious or spiritual service that is different from your own? What did you learn or take away from it?
2. Have you ever been caught by surprise when a community you are visiting sings a familiar song in an unfamiliar tune?
3. If you think about a favorite song, is it the words, the tune, or something else that moves you, engages you, and draws you in?
4. What is your Shabbat practice? Are there different times during Shabbat when your observance feels like a burden, as opposed to a joy? What do you think distinguishes these times from each other? Is it possible for Shabbat to be both challenging and joyful simultaneously?
5. Do you agree with Al-Ghazali that art can reveal its creator's inner beauty? Is inner beauty a necessary precursor to creating art? How else might a person's inner beauty be expressed?

The Song of Solomon, A Personal History
Marci Vitkus

Why do certain songs strike a chord with individuals? A) Is it the piece of music itself? B) Did the composer find a perfect combination of notes and beats? C) Did a moment happen while we listened to the song that forever fused together the melody, meaning and moment? D) It may be that years later, we hear it again in a whole new light, in a way in which we weren't prepared for the first time it's set upon our ears?

In my case I think it may be E) All of the above.

Early in my cantorial career, I was preparing for a wedding I was to officiate between two congregants; Leah, who was 72 and Al, who was 80. At the time, I had only officiated at six ceremonies so I didn't have a deep repertoire to pull from. I called on the professional, my Dad. As a retired cantor he has done his fair share of weddings.

"Do you have a nice traditional piece of music I could sing for Leah and Al's wedding?"

The Song Grandpa Wrote

"You could always sing 'Set Me as a Seal Upon Thy Heart' written by Grandpa." And so my journey down memory lane began...

My grandfather, Hyman Reznick, comes from a long line of cantors. Technically they weren't "official' cantors, as we know them today. Back in the early 1900's and before, the town had one person who served in a unique capacity. They were the town *shochet*, (ritual slaughterer), as well as *mohel* (performs the circumcision) and the *baal t'fillah* (keeper of special prayers) and *tzaddik* (wise man). My great grandfather, Morris, was the last in the family who served in this capacity. His four sons were raised on Jewish music and the art of butchering. According to my Great Uncle Nate, Hyman's younger brother, they were well known in town for their voices and incredible harmony, which they honed while, plucking chickens and singing *chazzanut*, simultaneously. From my grandfather on down, the family tradition began to look more like the cantorial role we see today, predominantly serving in a synagogue as the co-spiritual leader and conductor of music. The role of *cantor / shochet / baal t'fillah* goes back 15 generations from Hy, thus making me a 17th generation cantor, as well as the first woman in the line.

The fascinating thing to me is I learned all this after I had been serving a congregation for several years. It feels like *B'shert* that I ended up becoming a cantor, because it was not at all in my life plan. I have a bachelor's degree in Early Childhood Education from Indiana University. I was the director of a cooperative preschool for 5 years and co-owned a preschool with my husband for seven and a half years. In my college days, I went home for *Passover* and *Hanukkah*, and went to whatever local *shul* I was near for High Holidays, but that was the extent of my religious involvement. I always felt pride in my Judaism but never felt a direction for it. However, one statement my Dad made always stuck with me. He would explain to people "My religion is Jewish music."

Unconsciously I adopted this philosophy as my own although I remember feeling uncertain about that answer. Turns out it is a very Jewish belief. Music as a way of commuting Torah in ceremonial moments and in times of great joy is commonplace in our history and in our modern synagogues. And in my case it has been the connecting thread throughout my life.

Song of Solomon

This song my grandfather wrote includes the lyrics from the *Songs of Solomon,* a series of lyrical poems organized as a lengthy dialogue between a young woman and her lover. The introduction calls it "the song of songs", a superlative commonly used in the Scripture to show it as the greatest and most beautiful of all songs.

Chosen Words

The words my Grandfather chose for his piece are:

"Set me as a seal upon thy heart,
for love is strong as death so strong is love.
A flame of God is love.
The flashes of love are flashes of fire,
a very flame of the Lord.
Many waters cannot quench love,
neither can the floods drown it"

The Confidence to Sing

So it was surprising for me to hear Great Uncle Nate say my grandfather doubted himself. This man, revered by my father, so well loved by the Jewish community, and co-founder of the Halevi Choir lacked serious confidence. It affected him so much that he never had his *Bar Mitzvah* because he felt he couldn't learn all the material and he froze up. Yet he composed a song filled with vivid imagery and passion for his wife.

Instantly, I connected with this because I too was a very reserved youth. I loved to sing but was never confident in my voice. Yet once I started to take voice lessons and learn to maximize what I had, I started liking how I sounded. I sang in choirs for years and had cameos in numerous youth theater productions. As a preschool teacher, I loved singing with the kids. But, it wasn't until I auditioned for a women's club performance at age 22 that I really believed I had a nice voice. I distinctly remember the response and the looks on the people's faces when I tried out. At first I thought "What happened? Did I miss something?" Then the accolades began and it felt truly genuine and really good. It changed the course of my life.

I had another moment when I shared this song with my colleagues at a Women Cantors' Network conference. This is a group of approximately 300 women who come together each year to learn, support one another, chant together, pray together, but most of all sing together. One of the highlights is called the *Kumsitz*, wherein we sit around and share new songs with the group. I learned much of my repertoire this way in the first few conferences. After attending for five years I decided I could get up the nerve to present this special song. It was well received with lovely compliments, but more importantly for me it marked another step on my journey. Music, especially this song, was transporting me through my life.

I am still conscious today of how deeply one's voice can move people. I view my role as Cantor through these eyes. I try to remain ever grateful for the gift of song and what it does for people. I try to sing with intention, not as a performer and not as a song leader even, but as someone commuting the sound of music intended to enhance the spiritual experience. But more than ever, when I sing this piece of music, *Set Me As A Seal Upon Thy Heart*, I carry all that intention—imbued deeply with my family history. There is powerful forward movement in my voice, in my heart and in the music as I sing the song of my family going back hundreds of years.

Marci Vitkus

Cantor Marci Vitkus has served the Jewish Congregation of Venice, Florida since October 2001. She has proudly officiated at over 100 weddings, mostly Jewish-interfaith marriages, as well as baby namings and funerals. Marci feels blessed to be part of an amazingly warm and accepting congregation. She doesn't have lots of fancy awards but thinks her husband, Andy, and two kids, Max and Sadie are rewarding enough. She serves on the Board of the Women Cantors' Network.

http://MarciVitkus.CreatingCalmNetworkPublishingGroup.com

Growing Your Spiritual Community

1. How would you answer this question, "Why do certain songs strike a chord with individuals?"

2. Share some moments or experiences that taught you something about your voice or ability to communicate something significant.

3. Are you familiar with *Shir Ha-Shirim*, the Song of Solomon? What do you like about it?

4. What have your ancestors or one particular ancestor contributed musically to your life or the world at large?

Avot v'Imahot Through The Generations
Rebekah Giangreco

"Blessed are You, *Adonai* our God,
God of our fathers and mothers,
God of Abraham, God of Isaac, and God of Jacob,
God of Sarah, God of Rebecca, God of Rachel,
and God of Leah,
the great, mighty and awesome God, transcendent God
who bestows loving kindness,
creates everything out of love,
remembers the love of our fathers and mothers,
and brings redemption to their children's children
for the sake of the Divine Name.

Sovereign, Deliverer, Helper and Shield,
Blessed are You, *Adonai*,
Sarah's Helper, Abraham's Shield."

— Frishman, Elyse D., ed. *Mishkan T'filah: a Reform Siddur*. New York: Central Conference of American Rabbis, 2009. page 244

Satisfied

We were famished,
Bleary eyed blind.
Morphine took her last breath.
Her hand was cold in mine.
Blood oozed into the catheter bag, thick and cool.

When *Bubbie* died, I asked
my mother what she remembered
of her mother.

She replied, "I remember
sitting in front of her,
begging her to eat."

Bubbie was bipolar.
Or a misunderstood mystic
depending who diagnosed her.
Mother witnessed *Bubbie*'s flurries
of baking and cooking,
songs, and praise, or
floods of tears,
starvation, dirges and sorrow.

Stuffed or starved
she was never satisfied.
Mother took care of siblings and home.

Bubbie was often away in mind,
medicated, or institutionalized and
mellowed with electro shock therapy.

Mother barricaded her heart to keep it sound.
She stunned the whole family.
When she met a man from another faith
and a far away home.

She left behind the familiar drama
and entered the unknown.
Six years after their wedding,
I was due to arrive.

Mother delivered me at the end
of a work day.

She began labor
in the grocery store line.

Hungry and bleary eyed.
Shaved and numb:
The doctor handed her
a clump of my hair he cut
as he sliced her perineum.
Blood dribbled onto the table, thin and warm.
I was wrenched out and whisked away.

Other than that she remembers little
of my childhood and neither do I.

Shrouds of armor shielded our memories.
We were starved or stuffed, never satisfied.
I married a man.
Within months, we were expecting.

As I labored with my first child,
my husband and mother were by my side.
It was dark, the warm bath soothed
and rushes carried us closer to birth.
My mother was there, uninvited,
but there.

The swells rolled in stronger,
the imminence of motherhood
crashed toward me,

I reached out
and held my mother's
dry cracked hand.

An illumination coursed
through me: My mother
did the best she could.
Shields surrendered;
distress dissolved.
Not stuffed,
not starved,
somewhat satisfied.

I sang,
roared, and pushed my baby out:
Marveling at the soft head
emerging from my core.
The burning I will never forget.

I stroked her fuzzy hair, ears, and little nose
as she looked around half out half in.

My womb emptied,
and my heart filled.
One last hand-clenching song,
wail and push delivered her into the tub.
We floated in the bloody water,
warm and welcoming.
Many hands brought her to my chest.

She took her first breath.
Clear eyes swallowed each other whole.
We were full.

Baruch atah, Adonai, magein Avraham v'ezrat Sarah.

Rebekah Giangreco

A Spokane, Washington resident, Rebekah Giangreco is an active member of Temple Beth Shalom.

She is an acupuncturist, East Asian Medicine Provider and Acutonics® Sound Healer at New Moon Family Acupuncture. Valuing each client, Rebekah loves her work. The blending of acupuncture and moxibustion, Acutonics® Sound Healing and clinical nutrition with redox signaling supplementation is a powerful trilogy in helping those ready to heal, ready to take control of his or her health and achieve true wellness

Enjoying life with her husband and four children, she believes in the power of *teshuvah* (healing and transformation) across the generations.

http://RebekahGiangreco.CreatingCalmNetworkPublishingGroup.com

Growing Your Spiritual Community

1. Where do you come from? What is the legacy your ancestors have given you?
2. If you have children, think about the ways having children has changed your relationship to and appreciation of your own parents.
3. What did you learn about God and life from your parents?

Communities of Chant

"Our history and our people and cultures have influenced Jewish music. The music is a reflection of the times in which it was written and the communities from which it emerged reflecting diversity. Current interpretations of our liturgy and texts had, in the past created discussion and may not have appealed to everyone, but I think the consensus is that most composers are to be acknowledged and respected in their attempt to bringing a new perspective to text. The new music cannot stand alone. Our history must have a voice and represent. One of those ways is by using traditional modes. Without blending the two worlds of music we are left with a singular experience that offers us no spiritual challenge; teaching us to hear in a new way. "

"May the source of strength
who blessed the ones before us,
Help us find the courage to make our lives a blessing."

—Debbie Friedman (z"l), *Mi Shebeirach*

Debbie used both English and Hebrew lyrics, and wrote for all ages. Some of her better-known songs include the *Mi Sheberakh, Miriam's Song, Birchot Havdalah, Not By Might, I Am a Latke, 613 Commandments, Sing Unto God, Sh'ma and V'ahavta (Thou Shalt Love), L'chi Lach, T'filat HaDerech, The Angel's Blessing, Kaddish D'rabanan, Devorah's Song,* and hundreds of other compositions.

Where Might I Go To Find You
Lisa Doob

Music is an art that has always fascinated me. To be experienced, it must be heard. Once it has been heard, it disappears into the ether, and is gone. How can a medium that is so ephemeral have such an impact? What are the subtleties inherent in music that make it so powerful—so essential to who we are?

Although I play the acoustic guitar, I most closely identify with vocal music. Indeed, I cannot remember a time when I did not sing. I only became aware of how often I comforted and entertained myself with song when I lost my voice for the first time, at the age of six. Over and over, I would start to hum a melody to myself, only to find, once again, that I could not. It was as if I were instinctively reaching out to grip something with a hand wrapped in bandages, not remembering that I would not be able to use it. And though my childhood bout of laryngitis lasted for only a few days, it stands out in my memory as a time of intense frustration, of disconnectedness, of unhappiness. Communication through singing is an inextricable part of who I am.

It is clear to me that music is more than a few notes in the air, or even notes on a page. What are the layers of meaning intrinsic to even the simplest of vocal melodies, and especially to the music of prayer? For even music without words is rich with emotion, with communication, and with memory.

A Sung Prayer That Speaks

It is challenging to unpack why certain prayers and melodies affect us so powerfully—the underlying reasons can be deeply personal. I invite you, therefore, to choose a sung prayer that speaks to you, and to ask yourself some or all of the following questions about it. Perhaps, through your answers, you will be able to determine why a given prayer has an impact on you, and, by extension, understand why certain sung prayers have such broad appeal.

First, one might reflect on the melody itself. Is it slow, matching the heartbeat at rest? Does it have a defined pulse, possibly inspiring you to dance? Does the tune repeat, making it easier for others to join in? Does the melody swoop and leap with joy, or does it have a smaller, perhaps more accessible range? Can voices join together in harmony, creating a sense of wellbeing, consonance and community? All of these physical characteristics of the melody will have an impact upon how it is received and used within a prayer setting.

Equally important to the melody is the cultural context of those who are hearing it. Does this melody sound like others that you have heard before? Is the structure of this melody familiar - for example, for those versed in Western European classical, folk, or pop idioms, that of multiple verses and a refrain? Is the tune perhaps unfamiliar or exotic, awakening the senses through its otherness? Or does it blend the exotic into the familiar? These factors may determine, in part, how immediately connected a listener may feel to a given melody.

Often, the melody is wrapped around text. What are the words, and do they speak to you? Are they in sync with the music? Or - like many settings of the *Kol Nidre* prayer, for example - does the tune become so central to the experience of the prayer that the text becomes almost incidental? Are the words in a language that you speak with fluency? If not, is the text a familiar one, perhaps borrowed from another prayer? Is it translated in such a way that you can understand it easily, or will it be understood primarily through its melody? For those who do not speak the language in which a text is written, the importance of the music becomes all-the-more pronounced.

An important component of a prayer is the emotion that it inspires in the listener or participant through memory. Have you sung this prayer during a time of happiness, of crisis, or of connection to others? Is it a text that you may remember from your childhood? Do you associate this prayer with being in a certain place, either regularly, or on a single occasion? Does this prayer remind you of the people with whom you sang it? What emotions do these memories inspire? Your link to a given prayer, through memory, adds a significant degree of nuance to your experience of it.

Once you have begun to answer some of these questions for yourself, it is possible to look at a given community's experience of prayer.

What is the relationship of the individuals praying as a group to one another? If they are connected to one another, will this affect how they relate to the prayer they are singing, or to which they are listening? What are the emotional needs of the community at the moment of their prayer? Are individuals tired as they enter morning services, and in need of a gentle wake-up? Do they need to tap into the rejuvenating joy or restfulness of Shabbat? Are they in search of comfort during troubling times? Most importantly, having identified the community's emotional needs, what are the texts and melodies that will enable the congregation to connect with one another? What are the prayer settings that allow those assembled to feel their needs have been heard and addressed?

Challenges of a Prayer Leader

My challenge as prayer leader is to connect with those who pray with me. Within a service, I plan for moments of active singing and moments of participatory listening. All of those moments, however, are bounded by an emotionally-based intention set for that service - one which is intended to meet the needs of the congregants at that moment, whether expressed or unexpressed. Sometimes, prayer settings are changed during the service itself, depending upon the emotion in the room at that moment. My challenge as prayer leader is to be attuned to those shifts in emotion, and to respond to them. There is a conversation going on during the service, not only between the congregation and the Divine, but amongst ourselves. Through the subtleties of prayer, we are able to reach out and support one another.

Ya Ana Emtsa'acha

When I write music, my intention is to allow others to enter into the experience of the prayer with me. Most often, I write an accessible melody paired with guitar, and written with sensitivity to the text. One recent example of this is a setting of a fragment of a Yehuda Halevi poem, printed in the publication of the Central Conference of American Rabbis' most recent prayerbook, *Mishkan T'filah*. One short section of Ya Ana Emtsa'acha is translated by Rabbi Dr. Lawrence Hoffman and Dr. Joel Hoffman as follows:

Where might I go to find You,
Exalted, Hidden One?
Yet where would I not go to find You,
Ever present, Eternal One?

My heart cries out to You:
Please draw near to me.
The moment I reach out for You,
I find you reaching in for me.

—Frishman, Elyse D., ed. *Mishkan T'filah: a Reform Siddur*. New York: Central Conference of American Rabbis, 2009. pg 53.

When I first encountered this text, it reminded me of an experience I once had as a university student. I was standing by myself outside on a clear, winter night, during a break between classes. The air was crisp and cold, the sky inky black. The stars, bright and faint, seemed to go on forever. And suddenly, looking up into that endless night, it was as if I were being drawn up into the firmament, pulled toward that sense of eternity. My feet were on the ground, but my soul was flying.

The melody to which I set this fragment of Ya Ana, floats somewhat but it is also firmly grounded. It is a quiet song which reflects an intensely personal experience. And yet, it is a singable melody, inviting others to taste a bit of that experience of reaching out towards something greater than oneself. It is an attempt to connect with the community through emotion, melody, memory, and text. The listener of this setting may not know the back story that informs it. However, if I sing it with this memory in mind—with the intention to share this personal experience, in some fashion—the story, on a basic emotional level, is transmitted.

In many ways, the experience of music is fleeting. We hear it, and it disappears. Yet, once linked to memory, emotion, and community, the experience of music is a durative one—powerful and long-lasting.

Lisa Doob

Born and raised in Winnipeg, Manitoba, Canada, Cantor Lisa Doob has written songs in English, French and Hebrew since the age of eight. Her love of music as a communicative art has been expressed in performances – both planned and extemporaneous – while living in England, France, Israel, Canada, and around the United States.

Lisa earned her cantorial ordination from Hebrew Union College-Jewish Institute of Religion in 2001. She has served congregations in the Baltimore, Brooklyn, and the Chicago area. Lisa writes songs for all ages and teaching songs for children that combines a love of Judaism with childlike, engaging enthusiasm. Her reflective music—in Hebrew and in English—gives people a meditative entry point to experiencing the rest of Shabbat. Some of Lisa's music can be found in *The Complete Jewish Songbook for Children, Volume II; Tzedek*

Tirdof: The Social Action Songbook (URJ Books and Music; and *R'fuah Sh'leimah: Songs of Jewish Healing* (Synagogue 3000).

Lisa is the Cantor at Temple Isaiah in Lexington, Massachusetts, and lives nearby with her husband and three children. She is a *Kesher Shir* fellow, and is currently working on her first recording project.

http://LisaDoob.CreatingCalmNetworkPublishingGroup.com

Growing Your Spiritual Community

1. Have you ever lost your voice? What was that experience like for you?
2. Do as Lisa Doob suggests and pick a favorite liturgical song and explore the ideas she brings forward. For example, explore the melody and the cultural context in which the song was created. Notice how the words and music fit together, are in sync or maybe they are not in some way.
3. Do you write poetry?
4. What poems set to music are you familiar with? Do you enjoy them?

Benching

Blessings, Yiddish bentshn,
Birkat hamazon
benching after meals
bread shared
meals forming communal ties

Blessing *Adonai*
a *mitzvah* of satisfaction
good land
a homeland where
three or more gather
as a *Zimmun*
back-and-forth goes
the invitation

First praising God
for sustaining life
providing
food for all creatures
then gratitude
for the compassion
nourishing the Jewish people
food and Torah, then and now
you and me on into the future

—Kimberly Burnham

Growing Your Spiritual Community

1. How does it feel to share bread, food and songs with
your community?

Jewish Selves in Song
Shira Wolosky

In memory of my mother.

Perhaps uniquely in the period of mourning, song becomes another dimension of relationship. Song binds communities not only in space but in time. Both the words and melodies of Jewish song can go back very far. The Psalms we share with Jews in the ages of kingdoms and Temples. Other "*piutim*," hymns and acrostic poems, date from antiquity and medieval into modern time. Words and tunes can carry a myriad of years; but melodies also bring innovation and renewal. The music sung to verses can be taken from the most wide-flung places and experiences, from all musical genres and origins, from many times including totally contemporary ones. In song we carry forward a living tradition, connecting us not only to each other but to a past that we share among the dead and the living.

We have received it from the past, we have shared it with those no longer here; but feel an ongoing relationship with them drawing us from deep within ourselves upwards. During the mourning period for my mother, the songs of Friday night services unlocked the gates to emotional depths that suddenly pressed upwards. Especially the song *Yedid Nefesh*, "Companion of my Soul," felt like entering a strange but intimate connection with her life and my life and the life I help carry forwards. *Yedid Nefesh* is sung in many tunes. It was sung by my own children at the wedding of our eldest as she walked down the aisle. It marks the border-moment between ordinary time and the unique moment of change into Sabbath. That twilight transformation is one braided between mothers and daughters, when they light candles together, as I did with my mother. That transport of light turns into song, in the welcoming of the Sabbath in synagogue.

There is no pure tradition, but only many mixtures. Melodies are realized and interwoven. Communities borrow and combine, recast and select, admit and omit. This mixing is not an assault on community but enrichment of it, and of the individuals who are its members. Today there are new senses of the world through globalized communication, economics, art, music. How to define these while retaining a sense of the particular—of one's own culture as distinct but not detached, unique but not suspicious, combining a variety of sources but not thereby dissolving into sheer cosmopolitan, post-national, borderless non-identity— that is a pressing challenge of our day.

But Jewish communities were never self-enclosed and self-defining. Jews were always members of their own community and of others as well: of the country in which the Jewish community was situated, whether in strife or in harmony; connected to other Jewish communities in other countries, by language, commerce, tradition, religion; and finally connected to Israel, which always had ongoing Jewish communities in some contact with communities in other places, sending emissaries throughout the Jewish worlds. These different memberships might be more or less in tension, more or less in competition, more or less mutually supportive of each other, both as communities and for members participating in them, changing in changing times and circumstances. All of these memberships have left their mark on Jewish song. Song weaves bonds among the variety of memberships that Jews have always had, and have today more than ever, in the form of worldwide translateral communities ranging from North to South America, through Europe and Russia, and into Israel as the Jewish community exercising sovereignty, in a renewed, struggling and miraculous attempt at self-determination.

Certainly from today's perspective, this multiple membership as participation in diverse communities is normal. In some ways it challenges the sense of who we are together as well as the sense of who each of us is separately. And yet this multiple participation makes possible a greater creativity in enacting and shaping the lives each community and self makes from that multiple membership; as well as a greater contribution in shaping what and how the shared worlds of community mark each other. What emerges is a more realized uniqueness: not as unitary but as directions and conjunctions that each self and each community undertakes and expresses.

Voices Joining Voices

Unless participating in a formal choir, there are in general few occasions in which people sing together: except, that is, in religious services. Singing is a weekly practice in the Jewish home as well, around the Sabbath table to welcome the angels of rest into the pressing schedules we keep. The Sabbath is an opening that lets us breathe. The walls it builds, which from one point of view seem to be restrictive tyrannies, in fact, stone by stone, come to enclose a garden, where we can break away and extend ourselves in directions hemmed in by the driven courses of the week. There, breath turns into song.

Singing together is an experience that is spiritual, in a deep calling of breath out of the self into the open, at once wide and high. But it opens the self exactly in being deeply communal. In synagogue, song voice joins to voice, breath to breath and in the process something more than the merely individual is gathered. What do we precisely gain from joining together, and specifically joining together the power of our breath and the reach of our voices? Interchange produces additional effects. All knowledge is partial; all vision, all experience, all selfhood is partial. Through meeting in common space, act, commitment, each person gains from the other: in knowledge and vision, as one member knows and sees and feels what others don't; in strength, in support that each can supply the other. Daring and venture; security and protection, are all more possible, more realized when offered to each other. This common space of shared histories and memories, words and chants, melodies and rhythms, hopes and purposes, is the substance of cultural identity—although identity, a Latin word meaning fixed sameness, is truly not a good term for the participation in culture that people experience and enact. I believe that what we are speaking of is less identity in this fixed and seductively self-referential way than membership. Each person is a member, some more active, some more passive, in a community of shared experiences. In community, each member brings his and her own world into contact with those of others, offering, combining, enjoying, also contending and conflicting; although in a community, rather than in a collective, this does not demand that each person cease his or her separate

147

selfhood so as to be absorbed into a greater unit that commands the individual members. Members remain both separate and committed to each other. They share, gain from and sustain common experiences; but each in individual ways, bringing individual senses to the common.

Creativity and Contribution

Community in this sense of membership among committed but separate individuals can be seen in age-long traditions of Torah study. In learning, each intelligence is called on to contribute his, and now also her, *hidush*, new insight, into texts ancient and modern, sometimes learning in a *shiur*, a lecture; sometimes together in *hevrutah* or with study partners. Jewish learning offers a provocative educational model in which each person's voice intensely challenges and engages the other's voice. This learning model realizes the two core values of membership: creativity and contribution. The individual person calls on his or her own creativity, but in ways that contribute to common cultural life.

In study this is mainly, although not only intellectual. But song brings in many more facets of the self than intellect alone. The sense of hearing in song is primary, in a way not only received but produced, not only external but internal, as vibration that is tactile, and also rhythmic in bodily senses, like dance. Of course intellect is also engaged if the song has words; but words in song mean more than intellectual understanding. Words become themselves sounds and rhythms, repeated and interlocking. And language is directed to everyone at once, addressed to each other by all those singing in a widening of exchange that is immediate and active. Perhaps above all, song unbars emotional deeps that stream into body, soul and intellect, with full range from mourning to joy.

Faces of Torah

Unity in a static and total sense has ever been a more Greek than Hebrew ideal. Even the core declaration, that "God is one" has been interpreted to mean not unity but uniqueness. Each person as unique is one sense of creation in the divine image, as in the *midrashic* parable of the coins in which only God as minter creates coins, each of which has a different face.

Torah, we are taught, has seventy faces for each of its words. So song has seventy faces and seventy voices, experienced as interweaving, yet also felt in each one's own soul, heart, and breath. We gather together to sing, appearing to each other in a public space of visibility, very old and very young, in the synagogue or home – no longer merely a private sphere but itself a core community, in turn interlocking with others.

Individuality is not absorbed or erased in a group, nor is it self-defining in separation. This balance is directly felt in song. Traditionally in synagogues there have been no formal choirs, trained and authorized. Instead, in more traditional synagogues leadership of the service rotates among members – until now only men, but at last also, more and more, including women. It is an irony that in the history of the modern synagogue, introducing a choir or official cantor has tended to lead to a decline in participation by members, not their enlistment. The less formal, more distributed leadership of tradition has also meant greater, if less organized, participation. Different tunes are introduced from service to service, drawn from the many communities of Jews in time and space, in creative combinations as the service (or Sabbath meal at home) unfolds. The song is thus woven and bound together through multiple histories, cultures, customs, of music as of texts; each self emerging from their own unique combinations in interlocking memberships that crisscross among communities.

In "*The Sayings of the Fathers*," the Rabbis praise those who speak words of Torah to each other, who thus have the *Shekhinah* among them, "for it is said, Then they that feared the Lord spake often one to another" *Pirkei Avot* 3:3. Even three who speak words of Torah together "are as if they have eaten of the table of the Lord" *Pirkei Avot* 3:6. Even one "that sits and studies [is] as if he fulfilled the whole Torah, for it is said, He sitteth alone and keepeth silence, because he hath borne it upon him."

The *Shekhinah*, as the presence of the divine that dwells in the world, is felt among those who converse and resonate together, addressing and inviting all the voices of the past, the dead with the living, in exchanges with each other across time and unto today. Words when sung, or a song without words, awaken breath and body, gather inner world with the outer senses, bringing the whole person into ongoing, echoing interspace, each addressing each other, with the divine dwelling among them.

Shira Wolosky

With a PhD from Princeton, Shira Wolosky was Assistant and then Associate Professor of English at Yale before moving to the Department of English and American Literature at Hebrew University. Her books include *Emily Dickinson: A Voice of War*; *The Art of Poetry*; *Language Mysticism*; *Defending Identity* with Natan Sharansky; *Poetry and Public Discourse*; *Feminist Theory across Disciplines*, and she has written on literary theory and poetics; American poetry, history, and religion; and on Jewish topics. Her awards include Fulbright and Guggenheim Fellowships, a Fellowship at the Princeton Institute of Advanced Studies, and a Tikvah/NYU Law School Fellowship. She has twice been Drue Heinz Visiting Professor at Oxford.

http://ShiraWolosky.CreatingCalmNetworkPublishingGroup.com

Growing Your Spiritual Community

1. How would you answer the question, "What do we precisely gain from joining together, and specifically joining together the breath and reach of voices?"
2. Consider some individuals in your community, what do they bring to the group? What changes because you and they are part of the community?
3. Think of the different communities to which you belong. What other communities intersect with them?
4. How does the presence of the divine show up in your community?
5. How do you feel about this quote from Shira Wolosky, "Song weaves bonds among the variety of memberships that Jews have always had." How many different communities do you feel connected to?

The Intangible and Tangible Effects of Music
Sheldon Low

"Nature is saturated with melody; heaven and earth are full of song."
—Nachman of Bratslav

Several years ago I found myself on an airplane next to a particularly friendly (read talkative) older man. He had very little reddish hair left on the top of his head, spoke with an eastern European accent, and consistently failed to notice me closing my eyes to rest. He informed me that he worked in a machine shop manufacturing metal parts for various uses. Afterward he asked me what kind of work I did, and I told him that I was a musician. Before I could realize my mistake, I received a full half-hour lecture on how I, and by extension, my generation, were dooming humanity because we didn't spend our time creating real tangible things. My second mistake was letting him know that I used to work as a mechanical engineer and that in that role I had in fact worked with our in-house machine shop to build several real, tangible, practical, and horribly uninteresting things before embarking on my joyful music career. For the rest of the flight he implored me to quit music as a career and go back to engineering. I'm not entirely sure what his motivation was, but as we disembarked from the plane we shook hands and he promised me that I would never forget him. About that, he was right.

*"If I were not a physicist, I would probably be a musician.
I often think in music. I live my daydreams in music.*

I see my life in terms of music."
  —Albert Einstein

But on his other point, I must wholeheartedly disagree. The longer I "work" as a professional musician, the more I'm convinced that music is one of the most critical ingredients for life. Even before the scientific revolution, humankind has understood the power of music—to tap into the spiritual realm. Some believed, and some still do believe, that it is precisely this mystical, intangible, and perhaps elusive quality to music, that relegates it strictly to and for the spiritual world. They believe that music should only be sung for G-d and that certain types of music are akin to devil worship. I don't ascribe to those beliefs, but I have witnessed firsthand the power of music to heal, transform, and unite. I've seen otherwise disinterested and disengaged teens, break out in dance and join together with youth from around the world singing Jewish songs of peace. I've watched adult hospital patients howl with laughter or burst into tears at the first few notes of an old Beatles song. Most poignant of all, I've seen music consistently inspire the most important and most powerful human force—hope.

I'm reminded of the story of Rabbi Hugo Gryn, who survived the horrors of Auschwitz. He tells of the freezing winter of 1944, when his father, a fellow prisoner at the camp, attempted to celebrate *Hannukah* by lighting a wick dipped in his margarine ration. When Rabbi Hugo Gryn objected to his father using the precious food in this manner, his father responded by declaring "You and I have seen that it is possible to live up to three weeks without food. We once lived almost three days without water: but you cannot live properly for three minutes without hope!"

"The inner history of a people is contained in its songs."
—Rabbi Adolph Jellinek

Back in college, I took a course in MIDI, the electronic music computer language. As part of the course, I was assigned to design and build a system to measure the precise movements of a percussionist playing a Lunga (Ghanaian talking drum). If you are unfamiliar with the Lunga, it is a drum made from wood carved into a hollow hourglass shape and open on each end. Each end of the hourglass is then covered in a goatskin drumhead, and the drumheads are connected to each other and held to the wooden drum body by many animal skin cords strung around the entire body of the drum. By squeezing and releasing the drum underneath your arm, the chords tighten or loosen the drumheads and thereby raise or lower the pitch of the drum. Through precise movements, the Ghanaian drummers create a handful of sounds and intonations, through which they are able to tell the history of their people. Each of these drums is considered sacrosanct and so upon assigning us this project, our professor warned my team that the idea of wiring up one of these drums is a sensitive issue at best, and borderline blasphemous.

He then informed us that his friend, Alhaji Dolsi-Naa Abubakari Lunna, a well-respected Lunga player from Ghana who had actually built the very Lunga we would be "roboticizing", would be traveling to the U.S., and would visit our class to perform on our "Robolunga". When it came time for his arrival, a tall broad man dressed in traditional Ghanaian clothes stepped into our lab and wrapped his massive hand around mine in a handshake, before picking up the drum and beginning to play. The symphony of sounds and rhythms he created far exceeded our expectations of the drum's versatility, which were based of course, on our pathetic and unfamiliar attempts at the drum. It was actually hard to not stand up and dance while Alhaji Dolsi-Naa played. When he finished, we rushed to look at the data created by our Robolunga's sensors, eager to understand exactly how Alhaji Dolsi-Naa had managed to create such an amazing array of sounds. To our dismay, almost all of our Robolunga's sensors had failed. We were left with the mystery unsolved, along with questions and the sounds of the Lunga echoing in our heads.

"Music can name the unnameable and communicate the unknowable."
    —Leonard Bernstein

For me, it is precisely that intangible nature of music, coupled with its very palpable and measureable effects, which makes it so magical. Just as certain scents and smells are capable of thrusting our consciousnesses to a specific distant memory, music has a way of transporting us emotionally and spiritually. We all have songs that confirm this. When I hear Steven Sher's *Bless This House* or even just think about the melody in my own head, I can literally feel the sadness of the last day of camp in the back of my throat, and practically smell the trees under which we would hold our final friendship circle. I'm happy and contented hearing anything from

John Mayer's *Continuum* which reminds me of my excitement at moving to New York City to embark on my Jewish music career.

Every song occupies its own sonic, chronological, contextual, and historical space in my mind and conjures a unique emotional color and feeling. If none of this makes sense, I would argue it's because I'm trying desperately to describe something I believe we all feel and know, but I'm constrained to words printed black on a white background. If I could provide you with a musical soundtrack to this paragraph, I'm willing to bet that you could feel it too.

"In the high spheres there are temples which may be opened only with song"
—Shneor Zalman

It's not important to me how it works, or why it happens; only that it does. Music has the ability to resonate with us in such a way, that it can instantly tap directly into our souls, our hearts, and our emotions. If you have ever created a slideshow, then you know you can add just about any piece of music and your project goes from being a simple collection of pictures into a rich and emotional experience. If you've ever driven down an open highway on a warm sunny day with the windows down, and turned the radio way up, you know what I'm talking about. It expresses all of the ideas between the words, which words themselves somehow fail to communicate. It can serve as a bridge to our ancestors, a common gathering place for our present, and a link to our future. It is with this belief that I approach my songwriting, and my song and worship leading.

"Song is obligatory in the ritual of the sanctuary."
  —Talmud, Arakin

To me, there is no greater example of the comprehensive nature of music than in the *Mi Chamocha* prayer. When we sing, *daven*, or say these words, we are instantly reminded of one of the most central stories of our people's existence, the Exodus from Egypt. When I say these words as part of a *minyan* or congregation, I can't help but imagine being surrounded by these very same people, only thousands of years ago in the Sinai desert. I think about all of the freedoms which I enjoy daily, and of all those people in the world still in the literal and figurative shackles of oppression. I think about my Grandfather Hans, who in 1937 at the age of 16 left his home, family, and everything he knew in Vienna, eventually crossing the Atlantic Ocean in his own march to freedom. I give thanks to my great Aunt Ada, who's involvement with the American Jewish Congress inspired me by demonstrating that the collective power of a group of ordinary devoted citizens can accomplish anything, including bringing to fruition the 2000 year old dream of the creation of a Jewish state.

I give thanks to those who marched this earth before me, on whose shoulders I stand, and I commit myself to leaving this world a little bit better than I came to it. In fact, I sometimes like to suggest to my fellow worshippers that we can accomplish loving G-d "with all your heart, with all your soul, and with all your might" which we recited from *Sh'ma* only moments earlier, by standing and marching in place. In doing so, I propose that we are honoring the memory of our ancestors by symbolically walking in their footsteps, and dedicating ourselves to the cause of freedom and the future of the Jewish people by singing the exact same words of freedom sung millennia beforehand. I feel connected to my ancestors, both distant and near, and to my community surrounding me. I feel centered, present, focused, and hopeful as I am reminded of all the blessings in my life. Most importantly, I feel committed to *tikkun olam*. Through this literal song and dance, we are transformed from a group of individuals, into a holy community.

"Music is a universal language, and needs not be translated. With its soul speaks to soul."
 – Berthold Auerbach

I believe that Judaism has a tremendous amount to offer. One of my favorite *midrashim* revolves around the story of Exodus. The *midrash* begins as the Red Sea crashes down on the Egyptians, guaranteeing the Israelites' freedom from slavery. In the *midrash* G-d silences the Israelites saying, "My creatures are perishing, and yet you rejoice?"

I love this and the many other lessons found in our tradition. I find meaning and purpose as part of a people. I find timeless and universal wisdom in the biblical and historical stories of our people. And most of all, I find joy.

"Everywhere in the world, music enhances a hall, with one exception: Carnegie Hall enhances the music."
 —Isaac Stern

This is perhaps the heart of my purpose as a Jewish musician. Many of my fondest memories are centered around a Jewish holiday, with my closest friends and family gathered around a holiday meal— often times singing. I want to write and lead Jewish music to help others find that same joy that I've found.

Life is precious and fleeting, so we must take care to live each moment with intention and joy. Judaism gives us a beautiful framework to add meaning to each moment in our life. The values and lessons contained in our history and traditions give us the tools to continue the work of creation and do *tikkun olam*.

If I can use music to spread joy, educate, build community, inspire hope, add meaning, and help make the world a little better, then I will know that I have indeed created something real and tangible.

Sheldon Low

One of the brightest young stars in Jewish rock music today performing rock concerts, Sheldon Low, 'Light Up Shabbat' services, seminars, and leading Artist-in-Residency weekends in Jewish communities, camps, youth groups, and festivals throughout North America. Sheldon has released four albums to date and his recordings have been featured in numerous compilations including *NFTY Ruach 5767*. His two children's albums have been widely distributed by PJ Library.

Born and raised in St. Louis, Missouri, Sheldon is a third generation song leader who from an early age developed a strong Jewish identity attending Hyman Brand Hebrew Academy, Solomon Schechter Day School, Camp Ben Frankel, and USY. In high school, Sheldon was fortunate to meet and be mentored by national touring Jewish musician, Rick Recht. In 2005, Sheldon graduated Magna Cum Laude with a BS in Mechanical Engineering from Tufts University and spent nine months working as an engineer before embarking on his music career. In 2013, Sheldon started Hallelu Records, an independent Jewish record label based in New York City.

Sheldon resides in New York City with his beautiful partner, Hadar Orshalimy. Learn more about Sheldon and listen to his music at SheldonLow.com.

http://SheldonLow.CreatingCalmNetworkPublishingGroup.com

Growing Your Spiritual Community

1. Do you often have the opportunity to talk with people about how you choose to live your life? Does anyone ever try to convince you to do something different?
2. Do you think of singing music as creating something tangible?
3. Ponder Sheldon Low's statement, "I have witnessed firsthand the power of music to heal, transform, and unite." What have you witnessed in the power of music?
4. Do you play an instrument? How do you think about your skill, your contribution to the world as you play?
5. What songs affect you in this way: "Just as certain scents and smells, ... music has a way of transporting us emotionally and spiritually"?
6. Do you have memories that pull on you as you sing or hear the *Mi Chamocha* prayer?
7. Where do you find your joy and hope?

Building and Inhabiting the Mishkan Through Chant
Shefa Gold

Ozi v'zimrat Yah vay'hi li lishuah
My strength (balanced) with the song of God will be my salvation (Psalm 118:14; Exodus 15:2)

In this practice I find and express my strength, my will, my effort, and my desire when I chant "ozi." When I chant "*V'zimrat Yah,*" I open and surrender to the God-song and let it be sung through me. Then in the last phrase, "*vay'hi li lishuah,*" I balance those two aspects of my practice.

My love and longing led me to study philosophy. As the thoughts of each philosopher were revealed to me, I wanted to understand what engendered these ideas. From what state of consciousness did they emerge? How might I step into that same place that I could know and perceive the world like this? I wanted to be each philosopher, to see from their perspective and tune into the same source of wisdom that had inspired them.

Now, as I develop a spiritual practice from a sacred phrase, I bring those same questions. How do I step into the state of consciousness from which these words emerged? When I embody the truth of the sacred phrase, how is my world transformed?

My philosophical studies led me to an exploration of consciousness. I practice astral travel and shamanic journeying. And I cultivated a deep respect for my dreams and the power of imagination. I was drawn to the mystical traditions of Christianity, Islam and Judaism. I went through a rigorous training to lead sweat lodge from a Native American Lakota teacher. In the sweat lodge I learned how to pray as if my life depended on it.

Bhakti Judaism

My exploration of consciousness led me to meditation. I practiced the art of letting go of the content of thoughts so that I might rest in God. My inspirations as I developed my own practice of meditation were Buddhism, centering prayer and the Hasidic ideal of *d'veikut* (cleaving to God).

One night I had a dream in which I was told explicitly by a booming authoritative voice, "You will create *bhakti Judaism!*" I woke up startled and asked, "What is *bhakti?*" I didn't even know the work but soon found out that it refers to the devotional path within Hinduism, the path of love and complete surrender to the mystery of the Divine.

Chanting

When I first began chanting, I was in love with sound. I experimented with melody, rhythm, harmony, tone, and pitch. But after a while I began to notice that the silence that followed the chant was simply extraordinary. I just couldn't wait for the chant to end because I knew that I would get to dive into that beautiful silence. It was as if the chant opened a door, and in the silence I could enter and received the true blessing of my efforts. I fell in love with the silence.

This movement from sound to silence to sound to silence eventually began to reveal the secrets of the silence at the very heart of sound, and the sound at the very heart of silence. And these secrets sent me on a path toward listening every more deeply.

A song may entertain, but a chant is meant to transform. It is as if we are building a *Mishkan*, a holy sanctuary with the sound, intention, meaning, and fine attention to detail. Then in the silence afterward we must learn to enter the *Mishkan* and experience God's presence that we have invited in with the chant.

Three Phases

There are three phases that transform chant from simple singing into a contemplative, ecstatic meditation practice:

1. Establish the ground of a chant.
2. As the chant is happening, cultivating an awareness of the components of the chant - variables that affect consciousness.
3. Learning to enter the silence that follows. This is when the transformative power of the chant does its work.

The Ground of a Chant

The ground of a chant begins with an understanding of why you are chanting. What is the need of the group? Or, if you are chanting alone, what is your own need? What is the spiritual challenge that we are facing at this moment? When that challenge is clearly perceived and articulated, then we can find the power and inspiration to rise to the challenge. The leader of a chant must learn to perceive the potential of the group that she's working with, creating a strong and safe container for practice, and communicate an enthusiastic expectation of what's possible. All participants must surrender themselves in service of the group and to the sacred purpose of the chant. Before you open your mouth to chant, it's important to formulate a clear intention and direct your heart toward that purpose.

1. Perceiving the spiritual need or challenge
2. Rising to meet that challenge
3. Perceiving the potential
4. Inviting co-creation of group energy
5. Creating expectancy and the sacred container.

Under The Wings

Va'ani matzati m'nuchah mitachat kanfei HaShechinah.
Under the wings of Shechinah I have found my rest.

I wrote this chant in honor of *Sukkot*. I imagine sitting in my *sukkah* under a delicate roof of branches that gives me a glimpse of the vast deep blue sky. The Divine Presence also protects me, yet allows me to see through Her wings and connect with the beyond.

Components of a Chant

The chant begins with a piece of text. The sacred phrase, drawn from liturgy or scripture, becomes a doorway. We enter through that doorway by using each of the components of the chant as variables that have an effect on our state of consciousness. by becoming aware of those effects, we can use these components with more and more awareness and skill.

1. Meaning of the sacred phrase
2. Breath
3. Intention
4. Sound-- vowel and consonant
5. Melodic story and harmonic intervals
6. Tone and rhythm
7. Visualization-imposed or discovered
8. Context from which the sacred phrase is drawn
9. Balance of will and surrender
10. Vertical and horizontal axis
11. Stereoscopic consciousness

By bringing attention to the rhythm of breath, to the sounds of the words, to the many layers of intention that evolve with the chant, we transform a simple melody into an opportunity for transformation and healing.

Kabbalah's Four Worlds

When we chant, we are building a *Mishkan* at four distinct, yet interconnecting levels. The *Mishkan* exists at the level of the group, in relationship, in the body and in the heart. During a chant for the purpose of healing, we call on the fullness of our passion and generosity to build and strengthen the *Mishkan* at all four levels.

In *Kabbalah* there are four worlds, which correspond to the following realms:

1. The physical world of action
2. The emotional world of expression, feeling and creativity
3. The world of knowing
4. The spiritual world of being and interconnection

The chant becomes a healing force when all four worlds within the chanter are engaged. The chant vibrates through the body opening up and enlivening the physical world. The emotions are engaged through the building of intention. The world of knowing is engaged through learning about the context and content of the sacred phrase. And the spiritual world is activated in us as our sense of separateness dissolves and we open up to the One through expanded states of consciousness. Through the practice of chant, we can activate all our disparate parts at once and become the vehicle for God's healing power.

Guardian's of Truth

Notzeir t'einah yochal piryah.
Those who guard the truth will be nourished by her fruit.
(Proverbs 27:18)

The literal meaning of this verse is, "Those who guard a fig tree will eat its fruit." But since this is from the book of Proverbs, I receive its meaning figuratively rather than literally. When I can bring my attention to the fullness of this moment, in all its complexity, beauty, poignancy, and meaning, then I will be nourished by its fruit. When I become fully present, attentive, reverent, and receptive to the holiness and truth of each moment, I receive the bounty of my experience.

Shefa Gold

Rabbi Shefa Gold is a leader in Aleph: Alliance for Jewish Renewal and received her ordination both from the Reconstructionist Rabbinical College and from Rabbi Zalman Schachter-Shalomi (z"l). She is the director of C-DEEP: The Center for Devotional, Energy and Ecstatic Practice in Jemez Springs, New Mexico and around the world.

Shefa composes and performs spiritual music, has produced ten albums, and her liturgies have been published in several new prayer books. She teaches workshops and retreats on the theory and art of Chanting, Devotional Healing, Spiritual Community Building, Meditation, and trains Chant Leaders in Kol Zimra, a two year program for rabbis, cantors and lay leaders.

She is also on the faculty of the Institute for Jewish Spirituality. Shefa combines her grounding in Judaism with a background in Buddhist, Christian, Islamic, and Native American spiritual traditions to make her uniquely qualified as a spiritual bridge celebrating the shared path of devotion. She is the author of *Torah Journeys: The Inner Path to the Promised Land*, released in 2006 and *In The Fever of Love: An Illumination of the Song of Songs* released in 2008.

http://ShefaGold.CreatingCalmNetworkPublishingGroup.com

Growing Your Spiritual Community

1. What other spiritual traditions have spoken to you?
2. Think about what this quote means: "This movement from sound to silence to sound to silence eventually began to reveal the secrets of the silence at the very heart of sound, and the sound at the very heart of silence."
2. Does your community or do you in your individual spiritual practice pay attention to the silence after or within the music, song or chant?
4. What is a phrase you would enjoy chanting?
5. Look at the list of ways to ground a chant. What does each one mean to you? How might you use these suggestions to create deeper engagement in your community?
6. How do you imagine this directive, "The leader of a chant must learn to perceive the potential of the group?" How would you perceive the potential of your group?
7. Do you chant? What is your intention as you chant? Is it different depending on whether you are chanting alone or with a specific group? Does your intention change depending on the setting in which you are chanting or praying?

Elohai Neshama
P. Faith Hayflich

Elohai Neshama Shena Tata Bi, T'Hora Hi
My God, the soul you have created in me is pure.
You breathed it into me.

Before dinner, I chant, hearing my breath in the 'H' in *eloHai* and *t'Hora* ... My breath, my soul. Are they different? In a Shefa Gold melody I connect to this prayer. The words, while meaningful, have little resonance. The melody carries them inward. Singing makes an impact. It fills me with vibration. I am full of prayer.

Many years ago while living in California, I learned to chant. A series of events propelled me to go to Canada and meet the guru of Yasodhara Ashram, Swami Sivananda Radha. Going there changed my life. I began chanting Sanskrit mantras and doing a standing meditation practice that taught me to receive and accept Light and offer it to others. I learned how to change my thoughts, give new content to my mind, question my internal critic, and look askance at the guilt that seemed to guide me.

I'd grown up a Reform Jew and attended National Federation of Temple Youth (NFTY) camps as a teenager. I lived in a house of people who wanted to explore Judaism when I was in graduate school. But after going to the Ashram, the next time I went to High Holy Day services and began the *Viddui* prayers, I thought, "I've had enough guilt to last a lifetime." I didn't see how Jewish prayers could uplift. They just made me feel bad. I left the services and didn't go back for almost 25 years.

I chanted Sanskrit prayers and sang Indian songs. The idea of singing things I didn't really understand came naturally to me after growing up with Hebrew songs in synagogue. But I could never really sustain a chanting practice. I tried often, sometimes succeeded in chanting every day for a week, a month, and once, a year. I often listened to Swami Radha chant as I slept. But somehow, it never completely took hold. Some part of me held back.

When Swami Radha was alive, she told me about a rabbi who had lived at her ashram for two years, who came to explore the heart of Judaism. She told me to explore Judaism and its mystical aspects. She said that yoga is basically a science for transformation and that its practices (including meditation, the yoga of work, the yoga of dreams, etc.) could be applied to any religion.

I listened to her, but remembered the guilt I felt. I am part of a different community now, I thought.

Then, seven years ago, I was invited to a community *seder* or Passover meal with Congregation Emanu-El, a reform congregation in Spokane, Washington, where I now live. People were friendly. We ate. We sang. I recognized how much I missed Jewish community—the warmth, the passion, and the ritual I grew up with.

I began exploring. Our small congregation had a student rabbi. She introduced this chant. I read the words. The tune sank into my soul. She wasn't sure where it came from, so I searched online, found it on YouTube.

Now, it has taken hold. I chant it almost every day, and though I know it's a morning prayer, in my non-*halachic* way I chant it at any time—during the day, under my breath, and in my mind. I listen to it sometimes on my iPhone.

I wake up on occasion in a dark or emotional mood, and the chant reminds me, I am pure. There is something essential to me, as close as breath, which defines me. I become like Teflon. My mood rolls off me. I know I am essentially pure since G-d has implanted that within me. I become grateful.

I wonder now where all the guilt came from. Why do we Jews feel so guilty?

We are pure.

When I remember this, I see things differently. As a human being who is pure, I have the potential to express that, to be authentic, without the overlay of competition or desire to please others or to act on a myriad of internal expectations. We all have that potential, I know, to let go of whatever we do that gets in our own way. We can become a little closer to who we are.

Visiting the Ashram for the first time in a year, I take a workshop, where we are asked to go away for an hour and do a spiritual practice. I chant a Sanskrit mantra, *Hari om*, the healing mantra. The chant has a mystery about it. It's ethereal and less than tangible. It inhabits my body and lifts the vibrations of my mind. I feel inspired and elevated.

Then I chant *Elohai Neshama*. This Hebrew chant feels like me. This is who I am. There is no difference, no separation. I am wholly this experience.

This all seems ironic to me because yoga means *unity*—no separation. I find unity not in the Sanskrit mantra I was given, but in the Judaism that is in my bones.

Recently, my husband and I bought a vacation home. Although it's mostly furnished, we still need things—paper goods and garden tools, towels and linens, tables and a bed. I have been shopping madly. I feel not like a human being, or even a human doing, but a human shopping. My mind is full of want.

Then I am in morning services and we chant *Elohai Neshama*. While I may appear focused and concentrated, I am in fact composing a list for Costco in my mind. Then, I remember, my soul is pure. Who am I? I wonder underneath this desire? Miraculously, to me, the spinning thoughts and lists subside. I become present and enter into the chant.

Two weeks later, I am at *Ruach Ha'Aretz*, a Jewish Renewal retreat, taking a workshop with Shefa Gold and *davening* with her in the morning. We chant *Elohai Neshama*. It's a different tune than the one I've been chanting, but the effect on me seems to be the same—a sense of presence, congruence, lack of separation between myself and the world. I completely inhabit my world. I hear the voices of those around me. We sing and sway, joined by the fine vibration that floats through the air.

On the day of leaving, we sing it again, with still a different tune. I am not completely present, my mind on leaving. Reb Shefa brings a different interpretation to it this time, asking us to consider how not only our own, but everyone's souls are pure. She adds a line "Oh, pure soul, in you I see endless possibility" and asks us to think of encountering this, rather than the flawed manifestations we often experience. At one point we sing to each other *Elohai Neshama Shena Tata Bi, T'Hora Hi*. Our eyes are open. I gaze at the person next to me for two or three lines, singing to her, looking into her eyes. It is incredibly intimate, difficult to sustain beyond a few rounds with someone I don't know well. I challenge myself to keep open, vulnerable as long as I can. Then I turn to look at another. We smile while singing. Our eyes light up. In my singing I become present, opening myself to another's gaze.

P. Faith Hayflich

President of Congregation Emanu-El, a small Reform congregation in Spokane, P. Faith Hayflich spent many years as a small business owner in Silicon Valley. She visited Yasodhara Ashram in British Columbia, where she explored the mind-body-spirit connection, reflected deeply on her life, and learned how to meditate on light and chant. She eventually moved to Spokane, Washington in order to teach yoga and meditation and spend additional time at the ashram. In 2008, wanting to learn more about the tradition she grew up with, Faith began exploring Judaism. She is currently studying for her adult *Bat Mitzvah* and combines Jewish and yogic meditation practices. Faith sings, laughs, and tries to meditate daily.

http://FaithHayflich.CreatingCalmNetworkPublishingGroup.com

Growing Your Spiritual Community

1. What is your experience with meditation, yoga, and chanting?

2. What is your experience with singing in a language you are not so familiar with? Is Hebrew comfortable for you? Does it feel familiar?

3. Do you have a sense of your purity? Do you have a sense of the purity of those around you?

4. Do this exercise from Shefa Gold: Chant "*Elohai Neshama Shena Tata Bi, T'Hora Hi Oh, pure soul, in you I see endless possibility.*" Do the chant in Hebrew then in English. Do it alone the do it with someone else. Look into their eyes. Notice how you feels.

7. Try this exercise with another song or chant, looking into someone else's eyes as you sing.

Musical Connections Through Time and Space
Victoria Carmona

For 400 years, there were Jewish communities scattered throughout the vast Ottoman Empire, mostly established by refugees fleeing from the Spanish Inquisition and the expulsion of Jews from Spain in 1492. The Ottoman sultan, recognizing the folly of Spanish Monarchs Ferdinand and Isabella expelling a huge part of their educated, professional, artisan and merchant classes, invited the Sephardim (the Jews of Spain) to settle in his lands.

My grandparents came to the United States just before WWI, from what is now Turkey. My mother's parents had lived in the large Jewish community in Smyrna (now Izmir). At its height, 55,000 Jews lived there, and it was an important center of Jewish learning. The Ottoman Empire lasted for 470 years, but by the dawn of the 20th century, it was weak and failing. Events leading up to WWI destabilized what had been autonomous Jewish enclaves within the larger Turkish society. Revolution was in the air. The relative safety and security that the Jews had enjoyed in Ottoman lands was ending and Jewish young men, including both my grandfathers, fled the country.

My mother's father, Nissim Saul, a well-educated and religious man, found his way to New York City in 1910. There he joined Shearith Israel, the Spanish and Portuguese synagogue, the oldest Jewish congregation in the United States. Unofficially he was a part-time cantor there for many years and very active in that community until moving to Los Angeles in 1935. My grandmother's father was also a cantor in Smyrna, so singing was a strong part of my heritage, but one from which I was disconnected.

I grew up in a small desert town with few Jews, and no others of Sephardic heritage. It was a two-hour drive across the desert and over small, winding mountains roads to visit my grandparents in Los Angeles, where there was a sizable Sephardic community. Isolated in Lancaster, I was part of an invisible minority within a tiny minority, within a post-Holocaust Jewish world that was in shock, depression and deep mourning.

I only understood this much later, in hindsight. But the lived experience was not a source of comfort or spiritual connection. Nor did I feel that I had any place in Jewish life as a girl. In the small conservative synagogue to which my family belonged, I, as a female, literally did not count.

Connection to Singing

Singing was always an important part of my life. I sang all the time, but because of the Jewish disconnect, the singing in my soul came through in secular ways: primarily show tunes, folk songs, and camp songs. Every summer found me at Girl Scout camp in the Greenhorn Mountains of the southern Sierra Nevada for two weeks. Singing was a really big part of camp life at the very rustic Camp Mountain Meadows. Each year our big competition was a singing contest, called Singing Rocks. For the first week of camp each of the four to five units practiced four songs—fast, slow, round and ballad. Each unit practiced and practiced, hoping to win the Singing Rocks pennant. In addition, when all the units came together each day for breakfast and dinner, we sang a great variety of songs all together both before and after meals. And, of course, there were guitars and singing around campfires in the evenings. We learned rhythm, harmony, how to listen, and blend our voices together, and we sang our hearts out. On the evening of the contest, just before dusk, each unit would hike up the hills surrounding the camp and hide behind the large rocks. The campers were invisible from below, where the camp director and staff were the judges. "Let the singing rocks begin," called out the camp director, and sweet harmonies floated down from our hiding places among the trees and boulders. The winning unit was announced at the last campfire. Those are fond memories of learning to sing, listen and be in that common, cooperative space of vocal music. Singing with others requires unique skills that are transferable to other parts of life.

Sacred Harp

The circuitous path of my life wove through northern California before unexpectedly taking a sharp turn to the east coast. On my path to Jewish chant, I made an early stop in the world of Sacred Harp, a tradition of four part polyphonic a cappella sacred music that originated in the Protestant Churches of the American South. That form of chanting creates a sacred space in sound and in silence, as everyone breathes together and sings with great gusto. In the silence following that full-throated plunge into vocalization is an indescribable feeling of movement and stillness at the same time.

A few years later, I spent a year living in a Hindu ashram where chanting was a big part of every day and Sanskrit chants were used as prayers in worship. I was finding the heart connection to sacred space that was missing from my early experiences of Judaism. During this period of time, I was deeply involved in the study of religion and spirituality. Of particular interest to me were Hinduism, Buddhism, Christianity, Sufism and Shamanism. Missing from this list was Judaism, which seemed to me to be dry and lifeless and utterly lacking a spiritual dimension.

Fast Forward to Resonant Chanting

Fast forward to the early 21st century! Life brought me to West Hartford, Connecticut. For the first time in my life, I am living in a Jewish community. The Jewish resources in this town are fantastic, amazing and mind blowing to someone who has never had this experience before! It feels like water to a parched landscape. I am reading, learning, and studying both Hebrew and Judaism. I am learning about Shabbat. Attending services at different kinds of synagogues, immersed in the richness of this thriving community, I find Jewish Renewal, where chant is integral to the worship service. All the things I had been looking for and finding in other places I was surprised and delighted to find in my own tradition! This included a rich and profound connection with spirit, which I had never suspected was there.

For the first time I am chanting with others in Hebrew rather than Sanskrit. I am beginning to connect the dots. I am singing and chanting those same songs and words that my grandfather chanted so long ago in New York, in Smyrna and back through the generations. I finally have a place of belonging within my own heritage and tradition. And it is tied in with that physical, vibratory practice of chanting.

There is a resonance in the chanting—not just the physical resonance of the vibration in your own body, but through time and space. There is a connection with everyone else that ever chanted these words and contemplated their meaning, reaching for greater connection with others, with the divine, through the deep immersion in that sound, both words and music.

Giving voice.
Giving heart.
Opening and receiving.
Listening.

Being enveloped in the sound
as it rises and flows and fills the space.
Feeling the vibration very personally,
deep inside my own body.

Being surrounded by it
as it fills the space I'm in for that moment.
It creates a timeless quality as it connects
me with those who have come before and
those who will come after.

Connects me with my grandfather
who sang and chanted many
of these same words and prayers.
Connects me with the heritage

that I both so strongly feel
and, paradoxically, only vaguely got to know.

Healing Sounds

I soon discovered the healing dimension of chant. I have been a massage therapist for many years. Over time I have studied all kinds of healing modalities. In Connecticut, I took courses in Integrative Manual Therapy (IMT). An essential piece of IMT is a simple process called NeuroFascial Process (NFP). It involves the laying on of hands, connecting together the different organs and systems of the body. It can be done with your own hands or by someone else's, or by a group of people, laying hands on the body and making those connections all at once. Out of the desire to improve our health, a group of eight women came together to do NFP one night a week for several years. Each week, four participants would have 30 minutes of treatment time lying on the massage table, while the other seven members placed hands on various parts of her body. For two hours each week, we gave and received these treatments.

At first, there was idle conversation while we passed the time. But for the receiver, that was not conducive to the healing state the NFP was creating. Then one of us had the inspiration to chant as we lay on our hands, and a truly amazing healing process was born.

Most often we chanted Hebrew songs and prayers. The effect was profound. Rather than being dissipated in gossip or idle talk, the energy became focused and beautiful. The person on the table received not only the gift of healing hands but also the gift of healing voices--soothing, inspiring, uplifting, relaxing, and at times angelic. That coming together in focus and intent, with voices raised in praise, created a deeply healing experience for both givers and receivers. The blending of voices in song created an effortless focus that would have been impossible to generate in any other way.

Focus is an odd word here because in using it I mean two almost opposite things. It created a unified field in which all participated. Not a sharp, narrow focus, but rather a broad, wide, spacious focus—a very relaxed state of participation and belonging to a greater whole, a greater harmony. Both creating and being affected by it. Giving and receiving at the same time, becoming part of a larger whole while also retaining your own particularity and identity, and contributing from that place within yourself. Contributing to the big picture we created from the smaller picture of our own self. In essence it created a doorway for us to enter a sacred space.

For the person on the table, the beauty of the chanting and the focus it provided supercharged the healing environment and experience.

Chant is like a vehicle that transports. In the case of the NeuroFascial Process it moved us as a group to a higher, clearer, more connected place. It provided the receiver with a container for the healing experience and made the energy provided by the givers into a coherent whole. Just as a laser is coherent light, the chant created coherency of energy and consciousness that increased the power of our intention for healing for ourselves and our friends. Inherent also in chant is the silence that follows the singing. That silence is integral to the chant—it allows you to experience whence the chant has transported you — where that coherent wave of the chant has carried you.

Entanglement in the Present Moment

For me in particular, chant is about coming into the present moment: letting go of the pain of the past or anxiety of the future, wherever my mind might take me – in a sense the idle chatter and gossip of my own mind. In a group, it is a joining together in a great unity in the moment. The sound and vibration are happening in the now. They are present-time sensory experiences, not conceptual ideas or thoughts. This is a real and shared experience.

In modern physics, there is the concept of entanglement, i.e., that every particle that was ever in contact with any other particle in the universe is forever linked to and in communication with that other particle. I believe the power of singing and chanting creates that same kind of connection through time and space. It links me with my grandfather and ancestors before him. It links me with King David, singing and chanting songs and Psalms. It links me with all the Jewish people — in a sense reiterating the idea that we all were standing at Sinai, and that we all are — or have the potential to be if we choose to be — forever deeply and intimately connected.

There is a *sh'ma* moment of unity, where all who are present are one, and that unity or oneness expands beyond the present to all who have sung and shared in that. By bringing us into the present, the chant experience liberates us from our particularity and connects us with that broad, wide altogether, the eternal now, where vibration and stillness are one. That moment is, to quote William Blake, to "Hold Infinity in the palm of your hand and Eternity in an hour."

Victoria Carmona

The granddaughter of four Sephardic Jews from what is now Turkey; Victoria Carmona grew up in the high desert of Southern California, where there was only a very small Jewish community.

She has grown to love the refreshingly lush and green state of Connecticut, where she participates in *P'nai Or*, a Jewish Renewal congregation and *Shir Hamakom*, a monthly musical Kabbalat Shabbat service, lead by Arnie Davidson and Shelly Aronson.

Victoria has been a massage therapist for 36 years (double *chai*!). Using the many different modalities she has studied over the years, she helps clients to relax, heal and reconnect with their bodies in West Hartford, Connecticut.

She recently added Nutritional Therapy and Biodynamic Craniosacral Therapy to her practice. Visit ACaringTouchMassage.net for more information.

http://VictoriaCarmona.CreatingCalmNetworkPublishingGroup.com

Growing Your Spiritual Community

1. What is your heritage? What part has music played in the stories you have heard from or about your ancestors?

2. Do you know any Sephardic songs or tunes? Are they sung in your community?

3. Have you ever visited a Sephardic synagogue or some other synagogue? How was it similar or different from your community?

4. Think about your community and spiritual practice, what is the larger setting? Are there many or few like-minded individuals in your city or country? How do you find like-minded individuals?

5. Have you ever done a treatment or healing session in conjunction with music? How would you feel if your health-care provider incorporated sound, chanting or singing into the treatment session?

6. What do these words from Blake mean to you, "Hold Infinity in the palm of your hand and Eternity in an hour?"

Ayn Od: Non-Dual Perception
Brian Yosef Schachter-Brooks

Music has been inextricably connected to spirituality for me ever since my grandmother played me the sound track to Jesus Christ Superstar when I was four. The impression made by Deep Purple's Ian Gillan, crooning and screaming as the musical Jesus character, hardwired music and spirituality as inseparable in my nervous system. No wonder I eventually became a musical prayer leader for today's *neo-hassidic* Jewish community- the Jewish Renewal movement.

Passover Seder

However, I never wanted to be a musical prayer leader. I wasn't even brought up with Judaism. For that, I had to visit my Uncle Howard and family in New Brunswick, New Jersey. There I would have my annual dip into the ocean of Torah at the *Passover Seder*. During those *seders*, I could feel the drama of the ritual, of its reverent remembrance, of a past liberation, and its hope for future redemption. Through all of it, however, I had the sense that something was being missed. The past and the future had to be hints, I thought, of a reality accessible in the *present*. Those early childhood experiences seeded my yearning for real spiritual liberation- a liberation that could be found by piercing the traditional "shell" of drama, rituals and words into a totally different reality space.

In my teen years I experimented with all kinds of meditation and mystical practices. When, at the age of eighteen, I finally received a temporary taste of what I was yearning for in an experience I will not attempt to describe here, I became even more of a seeker. I wanted to get back to the absolute freedom and simplicity of that experience. When I went away to college at the Eastman School of Music, I studied the mysticism of Kabbalah and Hassidism both on my own and with *Chabad*. It was there, with the local *Chabad* rabbi, that I was introduced to the power of *nigunim*—wordless Hassidic melodies that function as portals into prayerful *devakut*, or "cleaving to the Divine".

Chochmat HaLev

After college I moved to the San Francisco Bay Area where, over the next six years, I tried to connect with different Jewish communities. None of them seemed to work for me; I was always turned off by this or that. Then, in 1998, everything changed. I felt like I had come to the end of my spiritual seeking. Something shifted in me, and I realized that the liberation I sought was being kept away by *the seeking itself*. I imagined that liberation was something I could "get" or "achieve", and it was that imagining that prevented me from seeing what was already present. I realized that the answer must lie in a radical commitment to the truth of this moment, to Reality as it is. When I made this commitment, all excess thinking dropped away, and my whole perception of everything underwent a total transformation. The "oneness" or "non-duality" of everything became apparent. In the wake of that shift, everything began to change for me externally as well. I met a man named Dr. Avram Davis who had founded a Jewish meditation center called *Chochmat HaLev* in Berkeley. He invited me to create a musical service with him. Although I initially declined, he was persistent and eventually I caved. When we opened the doors to the first Friday night service in February 2000, it was a huge hit. Hundreds of people showed up. I couldn't believe it. Avram, who has since become a good friend and teacher, had a vision in which music would help resurrect the power of prayer within Judaism. I didn't see it at the time, but that vision changed the course of my life.

During those first years of the early 2000's, musical prayer leading was fun, but I didn't take it all that seriously. Over the years, however, I began to see it as an art. I've been doing it now for fifteen years and have come to take it very seriously, and composing (*Barukh Hashem*) many musical liturgical settings. My intention in composing remains aligned with the original vision: to make Jewish prayer accessible through the power of music. Many American Jews are alienated from Judaism and Jewish prayer. Through music, prayer comes alive in a way that many have never before experienced. I often receive feedback from new folks after a service that this was their first time experiencing prayer in a way that actually meant something.

Torah of Awakening

In recent years, an approach to teaching Jewish spirituality that I call "Torah of Awakening" has begun to emerge. Torah of Awakening is based on the teachings and inner technologies of non-duality in Kabbalah and Hassidism. Its purpose is to help people make an experiential shift in their perception and tap into the non-duality that the tradition points to. One of my favorite musical pieces I've written is a setting of a verse from the *Aleinu* prayer that expresses this non-dual perception.

Aleinu

The *Aleinu* is chanted at the end of all morning, afternoon and evening services. It is an affirmation of one's commitment to the spiritual work, and to its ultimate goal of transforming the world into an expression of holiness and goodness. The line I set to music reads, "... *hashevota el l'vavekha ki Hashem hu ha Elohim bashamayim mima'al ve'al ha'aretz mitakhat, ayn od-* return to your heart that Existence is the only Divinity in the heavens above and the earth below- there is nothing else!" I am translating the divine Name Y-H-V-H as "Existence" because this divine Name is formed from the letters of the verb "to be". Thus, the verse is a wonderful expression of non-duality, in which G-d is not a separate entity, but is rather all that is, and "all that is" is somehow sacred and divine. There is nothing else!

I love this verse and what it expresses, but I didn't come to it on my own. A month or so before High Holidays in 2012, Rabbi SaraLeya Schley of *Chochmat HaLev* asked me, "What does this verse from the *Aleinu* mean to you? I am thinking it could be a great theme for High Holidays." Now, I am not much of a "theme" guy. I was thinking, "Yeah, whatever you want," but then I realized what an amazing verse it is. I couldn't believe I had never noticed it before, even though I had been chanting it three times every day!

I was inspired to write a melody for it. There was a melody I had already been playing with in a slow five meter. One day I was driving somewhere and I started to experiment with the words of that verse and the "five" melody. I soon realized that, miraculously, it seemed to fit perfectly. At some point I got the idea to take the two syllables *"Hu"* and *"Ha"* from the phrase that says *"Hu HaElohim"* and make a chant to outline the slow, five meter. This *"Hu Ha"* chant is a little tricky but is simple enough for a congregation to chant as a constant ostinato (repeated pattern) while singers sing the more complex melody. Thus, the congregation chants, *"Hu, Ha! Hu, Hu, Ha!"* over and over again. This piece was premiered in the High Holiday services a month later. I call it *Ayn Od*.

Sufi Zikr

Another interesting thing that evolved with this piece has to do with body movements inspired by *zikr*. *Zikr* is a Sufi practice of "Divine Remembrance" that utilizes chanting and body movements. The word *"Zikr"* shares a root with the Hebrew word *"zakhor"*, which means "remember". My good friend and teacher, Shaykh Ibrahim Baba Farajaje, leads *zikr* with his son Issa in their Sufi community and had begun to share their *zikr* leadership with us at *Chochmat HaLev*. I thought it would be wonderful to combine the *"Hu Ha"* chant with *zikr*-like body movements. Ibrahim Baba and Issa led the movements in the services at that time and have many times since. The piece has thus taken on an extra quality of embodying Sufi-Jewish connection.

Some people who experience this piece in the congregation are uncomfortable with this connection. There may be discomfort with elements that don't seem "Jewish", and especially with elements connected to Islam. For many, however, the connection with Sufism and Islam is a refreshing and healing balm for the ills of mistrust and separation in our contemporary dominant narratives. But despite these narratives, the truth is that Jews and Muslims have a long and deep history of connection and sharing between the two traditions. And, on a deeper level, this connection serves as an external symbol of the underlying Unity pointed to by non-dual teachings within both Hassidism and Sufism.

Just as I had not set out to be a musical prayer leader, I also hadn't set out to connect Judaism and Islam. In doing so, I am not motivated by anything political, but only by a love of the music, the practices, the people with whom they are shared, and the Oneness at the heart of both traditions. It seems to me that real change will not come about primarily through political means, but through relational means. When Jews and Muslims sit together, make music together, pray, discuss and sip tea together, the old destructive narratives will become less and less relevant. If anyone doubts this is possible, come visit us! I am grateful to help Jews reconnect with their own tradition, as well as help to melt the walls that separate us from our Muslim sisters and brothers.

Brian Yosef Schachter-Brooks

Inspired by Martin Buber's writing while procrastinating from piano practice at High School Jazz camp, Brian Yosef Schachter-Brooks began a quest for finding the inner truths of Judaism, beyond dogma and tradition. Finding that Truth ironically led him back to tradition. Brian Yosef currently serves as a spiritual leader, teacher and music director at Chochmat HaLev in Berkeley, CA. His teaching, "Torah of Awakening", teaches Judaism as a path of awareness and inner liberation. His band, Captain Zohar, plays original Jewish devotional and concert music. He holds a Bachelor in Musical Composition from the Eastman School of Music.

He received *smikha* (ordination) as Minister of Sacred Music from Reb Zalman Schachter-Shalomi, *z"l*. He lives in Oakland, California with wife Lisa and two children, to whom he owes constant gratitude for keeping him far from cheap substitutes for G-d.

Listen to an original musical piece from Brian Yosef Schachter-Brooks, The *Hashkiveinu* prayer at TorahOfAwakening.com

http://BrianYosefSchachterBrooks.CreatingCalmNetworkPublishingGroup.com

Growing Your Spiritual Community

1. Do you feel your spiritual practice started as a child and was continuous or have you weaved in and out of various spiritual traditions?
2. What is your experience of *niguns* or wordless tunes?
3. What do you feel about this quote? "Something shifted in me, and I realized that the liberation I sought was being kept away by the seeking itself. I imagined that liberation was something I could "get" or "achieve", and it was that imagining that prevented me from seeing what was already present. "
4. What do you imagine when you hear the words, Jewish meditation, Sufism or Mystical Islam?
5. How do you incorporate movement into your prayers or songs?

The Art of Nigun as Prayer
Dahlia Topolosky

Song as a form of prayer is rooted deeply in our Jewish heritage. When the Israelites left Egypt, Miriam played the drums alongside her brother, Moses, and the people sang to express their gratitude to G-d for being free. When King Saul was depressed, David played music for him to restore his spirit. Elisha, like many prophets, called for a harpist to play so that he could receive prophecy. When the Temple in Jerusalem stood, the Levites were responsible for adding music to the worship. Still today, the *siddur* prayer book is filled with verses from the Psalms on the use of instruments and singing when praising G-d.

In my own life, song has always been a conduit for me to express myself deeply and genuinely. I was a child who loved to sing songs with my family at the Shabbat table. I enjoyed performing "shows" for my parents and I would sing karaoke for hours with or without an audience. Choir and play performances filled my early years. I sang in an acapella group and learned to play guitar in college.

Yet, despite my love of song and music, I still found myself struggling with my personal connection to religious prayer. In synagogue as a child, I did enjoy the moving and melodious tunes of the chazzan or music leader, but I did not feel comfortable singing along out loud. I also wasn't paying much attention to the words we were chanting. There seemed to be a disconnect between the words on the page and the music in my heart.

In college, we had a strong Jewish community, and I went to religious services often during the week and certainly each Shabbat. On Friday nights we sang in unison the Kabbalat Shabbat tunes that were familiar and beautiful, but I remember still feeling disconnected from the other students around me and disappointed that I was unable to fully immerse myself in the service. Several of my friends shared similar feelings, and we decided to experience a Friday night at the Carlebach *Shul* on the Upper West Side of Manhattan, known for its long, yet powerful singing service. Perhaps there we would find a spiritual home.

Belonging

Rabbi Shlomo Carlebach (z"l) once taught, "Exile is the feeling you get when you know the words, but you can't remember the tune."

While I didn't know this teaching at the time, Reb Shlomo's words now seem to perfectly capture the spiritual frustrations of my younger years. His tunes and teachings would help me rediscover my prayer.

Indeed, my first Shabbat *davening* at the Carlebach Shul was life-changing. I can still picture the incredibly diverse congregation, many of whom appeared to be guests like me. Some women were dressed in special colorful Shabbat dresses, and others arrived in jeans and more casual clothing. There were elderly men and women sitting right next to small children smiling and dancing to the sweet Shabbat melodies. Everyone seemed to equally belong.

At one point in the service, I realized that I was singing in a full voice and that my voice did not stand out; rather, it blended harmoniously with those around me. For much of the davening, I kept my eyes closed, but somehow, I felt more connected to people around me than ever before in a religious service. The chazzan's passionate voice inspired everyone to join him. His voice did not overpower the crowd. Instead, his style seemed to invite the opportunity to pray together.

Prayer is often an offering of thanks or an exercise in requests. But on that Friday night, I discovered that prayer could also be about achieving a Oneness with all of G-d's creations made in G-d's image. It was an awesome experience, for even just a few hours, to leave the judgments beside, take a step out of myself, and hold hands with the other. This type of *davening*, which embraced a communal consciousness, was new to me, and it was deeply fulfilling.

Nigun

There were many factors that contributed to that inspiring evening at the Carlebach Shul, including the smiles of the people we met, their warm greetings, and the energized singing. But perhaps most revealing of all was the transformative power of the *Nigun* in prayer – where songs continued with the melody but without the words. The mere sounds of *Nai Nai Nai*, nonsensical syllables sung together, somehow increased the intensity beyond when we were singing the actual words. In those moments, the Hebrew skills of those seated around, or even their religious backgrounds, took a backseat to the ability of the *Nigun* to create a sense of Oneness in the room. The tune seemed to lift everyone out of their individual spaces and bring them towards a common place.

My first encounter with Kabbalat Shabbat at the Carlebach Shul was not my first introduction to Reb Shlomo's music. When I was younger, my parents had taken me to Reb Shlomo's concerts and they played his records in the house. I even had the blessing of watching Reb Shlomo perform a musical wedding in Jerusalem one summer where the *chuppah* lasted more than two hours and no one seemed to mind. But although his music was not new, the uplifting communal experience of that Friday night *davening* forever changed my personal connection to prayer. I had witnessed the transformative power of the *Nigun* - not only as a means of enhancing the *davening*, but also as a tool to create an incredible sense of unity among the worshippers.

Admittedly, there are occasions where I still appreciate a quiet, reflective *davening*, all alone, but since that fateful Friday night; I tend towards *shul* services where the unifying, communal *Nigun* is the norm.

Nigun as Prayer

Outside of religious services, I also found that the *Nigun* allowed for meaningful moments in many other musical contexts. I would sit for hours with friends, or even alone, and play a Carlebach *Nigun*. I was amazed that after singing the same tune 10 times in a row, I could still sing it differently the 11th time. In my twenties, I led concerts and sit down *kumzitz* gatherings for women of all ages, utilizing the holy power of the *Nigun* to build connections and spiritual bonds. I enjoyed gathering women together to sing and celebrate Rosh Chodesh, the celebration of the new moon. At one point, my roommate and I, together with some friends, hosted a regular Carlebach Friday night service in our apartment. Through all these experiences, I began to appreciate that "prayer" could be achieved outside of the standard *davening* times (*Shacharit*, *Mincha*, and *Maariv*), and that with each time we sang a *Nigun*, we were potentially realizing a deeply, prayerful moment.

The *Nigun* also brought answers to my personal prayers. I met my husband-to-be for the first time while each of us was playing guitar and singing a *Nigun* at the Western Wall in Jerusalem. A few months later, we met again in New York, and that first musical evening in Israel was rekindled. We soon played together at a Melava Malka (a Saturday night festive meal to usher out the Shabbat) and immediately felt a connection. We both knew that together we wanted to bring some music to the world in a way that brought all different types of people together. At our wedding, we incorporated the various *Nigun* melodies from the *Kabbalat Shabbat* service to frame the *chuppah* ceremony. We wanted others to actively participate in the joy of our *chuppah*, and we knew that *Nigun* was a holy tool to invite everyone to help us dance into our new home.

Together with my husband, who is a pulpit rabbi, we engage with music and the power of *Nigun* to build community. When we lived in Riverdale, New York, we opened our home each Saturday night for musical *Melava Malkas*. We organized soulful gatherings at our *shul*, the Hebrew Institute of Riverdale, bringing together our diverse community with the calm of candlelight, heartfelt teachings, and of course, the *Nigun*.

Hurricane Katrina

After Hurricane Katrina, my husband was hired to be the rabbi of the Congregation Beth Israel, a synagogue that had been inundated by over ten feet of floodwater from the breached levees of the failed Federal flood protection system. While we thought we had come to bring direction and strength to a weary congregation, we were inspired to find a city where music unites the people, and in this case, served to invigorate the renewal efforts. For our own part, we brought Carlebach tunes into our services and many programs, hoping it would add to the energy of a rebuilding community.

Wordless Inspiration

We now live in Maryland, and are tasked to help grow a relatively new community in Rockville. Again, I believe that music and the transformative power of the *Nigun* are some of the keys to our success. A friend once said to me that she wished that "daily *davening* was just one very long *Nigun*," because then she "would find *davening* each day meaningful and relevant." I do value the structure of the *siddur*, but her wishful *Nigun* reflects a sentiment that many of us surely share – the desire to personalize our prayer. The repetitive tune, free of set words, gives space to my friend, and to all of us, to offer our own inner thoughts alongside the words on the page.

Another congregant who was studying for conversion told me that she loved the *Nigun* at *shul* because even though her Hebrew is insufficient to keep pace with the service, at least she can hum along to the tunes. Here we uncover another aspect to the art of the

Nigun: it is accessible. In addition to its energizing, unifying, redemptive, and personalizing qualities, the *Nigun* offers an invaluable entry point to help make *shul* a more welcoming environment to those less familiar with its rhythms.

Tears

Finally, I have found the *Nigun* to be a uniquely powerful form of prayer in times of mourning and healing. In one instance, we had friends who were visiting our community in the process of adopting a baby. When the baby was born, however, the birth mother changed her mind and our friends were left bereft with only unfulfilled dreams. The following Shabbat, we invited them to stand amongst the congregation, and we sang a *Nigun* – we hugged them with song to offer our support in their pain. In another example, I led a *kumzitz* with a woman who lost her brother to cancer to mark the end of her mourning period. She felt that by bringing everyone together and singing the songs that were special to her brother, it gave her a voice in her own grieving process. A final example was an evening for women to join together in song and *Nigun* to pray for the safe return of three Israeli teenagers who had been kidnapped. This gathering was not about reciting psalms or standardized prayers, or hearing from politicians and community leaders. It was simply about the power of *Nigun* and the unstructured beauty of a song without words that allowed our tears to flow, each in our own unique way.

Birth and Rebirth

As a married adult with four children, *Nigun* has always played a central role in my family. When pregnant with each of our children, my husband Uri and I carefully chose a unique hope-filled *Nigun* to sing repeatedly to our growing baby. Although they are now older (10, 8, 5, and 3 years old), our children always remind me to sing "their song" before I kiss them goodnight. My hope is that somehow through their *Nigun*, each child will always feel connected to us and remember how much they are each loved.

I bless my children, and all of us, to embrace the redemptive power of *Nigun* – to offer ourselves the gift of awareness that rises above words, and connects us to G-d and all of creation.

Dahlia Topolosky

A psychologist, musician, and mother of Elyon, Itai, Adi, and Liat, Dahlia Topolosky, Psy.D. plays guitar and dumbek drum, and uses song to create meaningful experiences for those from all types of Jewish backgrounds. She believes in the spiritual power of female energy and continues to lead concerts and *kumzitzes* for women for any occasion (at Jewish conferences, memorials, *rosh chodesh* celebrations, etc.). Dahlia was greatly influenced by the music of Rabbi Shlomo Carlebach, and through her sharing and understanding of mystical teachings and songs. She has a unique gift of being able to make a whole room of people feel connected. Dahlia and her husband Rabbi Uri Topolosky helped rebuild Congregation Beth Israel in

New Orleans after Hurricane Katrina. They were inspired by a city whose music brought everyone together.

Dahlia and her family now live in Maryland and continue to use music to inspire others in their efforts to grow a new, affordable, and warm community in Aspen Hill. BethJoshua.org.

When she lived in New York, Dahlia co-led a Jewish "Parent and Me" Jewish music and movement group and in 2007, produced her first album called Kol Nearim—Voice of Children. Her album is used in many schools and synagogues, and continues to be sold in Jewish bookstores in America and Israel.

http://DahliaTopolosky.CreatingCalmNetworkPublishingGroup.com

Growing Your Spiritual Community

1. How does your community embrace *Nigun*—when music goes beyond the words?
2. What types of personal experiences have you had singing a *Nigun*?
3. How does your community deal with grief, loss and tragedy?
4. Rabbi Shlomo Carlebach, "Exile is the feeling you get when you know the words, but you can't remember the tune." How do you appreciate this quote?
5. Do you have a *nigun* or a song that you think of as "your song"?

Torah Cantilation—Meaning and Mantra

Torah Trope on Mobile Apps

"Two new mobile apps are poised to revolutionize bar/bat mitzvah preparation, and possibly the whole practice of learning to chant Torah. Rabbi Charlie Schwartz and Russel Neiss—Jewish educators, techies and friends—released PocketTorah, which enables users to read and hear every Torah and Haftarah portion from virtually any Android or Apple device.

In addition to containing the entire Hebrew text (viewed with or without vowels), plus English translation and links to a range of commentaries, the app has "on-demand" audio, with a karaoke-like feature highlighting each word of text as the recorded voice chants it."

PocketTorah and PocketTorah Trope are available for free and funded with a $36,750 grant from the Jewish New Media Innovation Fund.

"But will they put bar/bat mitzvah tutors out of business? No, said Neiss. Instead, they will "liberate *b'nai mitzvah* educators to focus more on the content and meaning," rather than on teaching the more mechanical aspects."

—Julie Wiener, TheJewishWeek.com

A Taste of Ancient Melodies
Mindy Sandler

"Why do you do it?" As a lay reader of Torah and *Haftarah*, I often get asked why I read Torah on a regular basis. "What's your story?" People are curious.

It was never something I dreamed of doing but here I am. At the age of thirteen, I was encouraged, like most girls at our conservative Philadelphia area synagogue, to have a Friday night bat mitzvah and read *Haftarah*. In my extremely introverted girlhood, I was relieved to be getting out of reading Torah and only required to chant *Haftarah*.

Thirty Years Changes You

Thirty years later, with five children of my own, a Saturday morning "regular" at services in Spokane, Washington, and several years experience on the synagogue Ritual Observance Committee, I became more and more fascinated with Torah reading and was even thinking maybe I should actually try it out. When a local need arose in our small northwestern city for someone to teach *Torah trope* to *b'nai mitzvah* students that was all the incentive I needed to finally plunge in at the age of forty seven and learn *trope*. The Rabbi who hired me for this opportunity lent me her textbooks and CDs, and a year later I proudly watched as my first bar mitzvah student chanted *maftir* and a lengthy festival *Haftarah*. I also managed to talk him into reading ten verses from the Torah for our community at a regular Shabbat service about halfway through our year of study together.

He never believed it, but all year long I was swimming as fast as I could just to stay a few inches ahead of him. It didn't hurt that the summer immediately preceding his bar mitzvah, our other local congregation was also in desperate need of Torah readers to fill the vacuum left by our Rabbi, who was on an extended sick leave. Our community's misfortune led some of us to explore radically new waters and, as the Temple president kept exhorting us to do, "step out of our comfort zones, and step up to the plate." I became a weekly Torah reader that summer.

A Taste of Ancient Melodies

Three years into my Torah reading journey, I am still fascinated by the ancient melodies associated with our sacred texts and what they must have meant to our ancestors. No doubt they served a purpose in preserving the oral history of the Jewish people and transmitting our ethical teachings from generation to generation. Moreover, melody not only helps us remember but also interpret our ancient stories. This is why I believe *trope* offers clues to understanding our sacred texts as well as insights into understanding what our medieval rabbis and ancient predecessors may have been thinking.

The Hebrew phrase for *trope*, or sacred musical cantillation, is *ta'amei ha'mikra*, which literally translates as taste or sense of the reading. It is a form of musical punctuation or interpretation, which thereby influences the listeners' understanding or helps make meaning of the text. Thus, *trope* is a very powerful art form and as much subjective and personal as it is objective and communal. Just like the Torah itself, *trope* is lovingly and meticulously handed down through the generations but inevitably sounds different coming out of different mouths and entering different ears. The chanter, or *baal kriyah* (literally master of the reading), has a tremendous responsibility to sing true to the Hebrew words on the parchment, as well as follow the prescribed musical notation as handed down in his or her community. Different communities have developed different melodic traditions with slight variations in how the *trope* are chanted and recorded. While we have a responsibility to convey the sacred script of our Torah along with our ancient music, the rules of the reader's cantillation system still has room for individual differences in interpretation and expression within the fixed boundaries of the codified and regulated language of *trope*.

My favorite example comes from a rare *trope* found in the Torah. The existence of these rare *tropes* is a phenomenon I find even further thought-provoking. When Joseph refuses Potiphar's wife's offer of sexual indiscretion (Gen 39:8), his answer comes in the form of a *shalshelet*, a *trope* that occurs only four times in the Torah and isn't found in any other scroll or prophetic reading. Do we sing the four trills intrinsic to the essence of this visually as well as audibly undulating *trope* with a sense of uncertainty, as if Joseph's decision is a personally difficult and challenging one for him; or do we sing the *shalshelet* with four-fold purpose, conviction and emphasis, as if Joseph's answer reflects a solid and sure sense of justice and morality? Is Joseph wavering in his response, or is he adamant? Needless to say, the chanter has a lot of influence over the reading here and how the listeners hear it.

Seasons of the Trope

Another area in which the art of chanting *trope* is so important is the way in which our sacred melodies change over the Jewish year. We use different melodies at different times of the year, including the High Holy Days, the end of *Sukkot, Purim, Passover, Shavuot* and *Tisha b'Av*. At each of these special times of the year, the appropriate readings from Torah or other scrolls (and at least once for *Haftarah*) designated for the season are traditionally sung in *trope* reserved for the occasion. So, just the way we associate different holidays with different foods, songs and rituals, so, too, should we appreciate the seasonal and festival changes in the sacred music we hear at these times used to tell our stories.

Just as important as smelling and tasting the different holiday foods over the course of our annual Jewish journey is hearing and experiencing the different *trope* melodies:

Unique and ancient melodies that belong to Torah read on high holy days;

The scroll of Ecclesiastes read at the end of the harvest season as we face approaching winter; the crazy and exciting scroll of Esther read on Purim;

The strange and eerie shifts in *trope* used only when we hear and relive our people's experience of liberation at the crossing of the Reed Sea during the chanting of the Song of the Sea; and

The dirge-like *trope* we use to relate our people's tragedies in the scroll of Lamentations on *Tisha b'Av*.

I believe it is essential for our communities to hear and experience these musical changes over the Jewish year just as we do with our foods, customs, rituals and holiday service liturgy. In this way, the "keeper of the *trope*" has a significant role in the observances of the congregation. Our annual musical journey should be preserved.

Time on the Bimah

On a much more personal level, I find the experience of reading from the Torah to be one of my strongest and most spiritual connections to Judaism. The time I spend on the *bimah* or altar practicing from the Torah scroll, when the sanctuary seats are empty, is about as peaceful and whole, in the sense of the Hebrew word *shalem*, as it gets for me. It is very satisfying (also connoted by the Hebrew word for peace and wholeness) to introduce others to this and other rewards of reading from the Torah.

Every time I read from the Torah, it is a "religious experience" for me. I feel a special connection to the unknown and unknowable. I bring what I can in human knowledge and preparation to each reading, but still I don't know how it will turn out, or how it will be heard. There is something otherworldly about the sounds and experience of Torah *trope* that I don't hear in the more pedantic, human-to-human transmissions from our prophets in *Haftarah*. I feel honored and blessed to be part of the long oral tradition of preserving our ancient words and melodies and practicing the art of sacred cantillation.

Mindy Sandler

A Hebrew School teacher, Mindy Sandler also teaches *b'nai mitzvah* students in Spokane, Washington, where she lives with her silviculturalist husband and five busy children between the ages of seven and seventeen. Before starting a family, she worked as a wilderness ranger and interpretive naturalist in the national forests of the Pacific Northwest. Later, she taught English to international students, including fifteen months abroad in Slovenia. She still likes to take long walks, though now primarily in the city, often accomplishing errands or appointments on foot. Locals recognize her as "the lady who walks everywhere." Her formal studies include a Bachelor of Arts degree in Biology from Amherst College, a Master of Science degree in Zoology from Oregon State University and a Master of Arts degree in English from the University of Idaho. Her current passion is reading Torah and *Haftarah*, teaching, and inspiring others to do chant Torah at Temple Beth Shalom.

http://MindySandler.CreatingCalmNetworkPublishingGroup.com

Growing Your Spiritual Community

1. When have you been asked to "step up to the plate" in your community?

2. Did you do a formal bar mitzvah or bat mitzvah or celebrate in another way? Did you read or have you read from the Torah? What was the process or experience like for you?

3. Does this chapter encourage you to learn to read Torah in your community? Does it change how you feel about Torah reading?

4. How does this tradition of reading Torah influence your connection to the divine?

5. Do you feel or respond differently when you listen to different Torah readers?

Leyning in English: Torah Reading in English Brings New Meaning to the Torah Service
Jack Kessler

A friend who is an active officer in a large New York synagogue, attended a ritual committee discussion about the quality of services at the *shul*, and proposed that the Torah service be dropped. The shocked worthies wanted to know how he could suggest such a thing. He replied that Shabbat morning services in this *shul* were indeed engaging, emotionally and intellectually satisfying experiences. Everyone sings, discusses, and participates ... that is, until the Torah service. Then, he observed, the energy in the room drops dead.

Yes the columns of Hebrew are nicely chanted and melodically correct, but hadn't everyone present on the ritual committee seen for themselves how during the Torah Service the participation and engagement dropped to near zero, how people zoned out, drifted to the back to chat ... and disengaged. Yes, the *aliyas* are called, and those chosen dutifully or cheerfully march to the front to recite the *braches*, but as a whole, what might in earlier times have been a highlight of Shabbat morning, was now deeply dull. All in all, it was not working. And if that was so, perhaps it should be dropped.

The committee certainly was not about to approve the idea, and thus my friend arrived at his purpose. He challenged them. If they were unwilling to drop the Torah service as he had anticipated, were they not then obligated to discover and implement ways to make the Torah service come alive. If they had succeeded with the other components of the service, why couldn't the Torah service be re-visioned and renewed to match the quality of engagement and participation of the rest of the service?

I relate this episode to address a crucial issue for our communities: we need Torah to be alive for us as a living source of wisdom – brimming with meaning, relevant to the challenges of our lives, informing our choices, inspiring our spiritual journeys. Yes, of course Torah will always have a default iconic status, but for Torah to be alive, it must speak to us in compelling and inspiring ways.

My friend was hardly the first person in our contemporary scene to raise this challenge. Others too have been hot on the trail of making Torah-engagement a participatory experience. Amichai Lau-Lavie crafted 'Storahtelling' which itself grew out of earlier experiments with bringing Torah text dramatically alive. Bibliodrama was championed by Peter Pitzele, his colleague Rivkah Walton and others. The use of "theme-based *aliyot*" in which congregants self-selected and come up to Torah in response to the message of the reading, as explained by the brief *dvar-torah* that is shared before the *aliyah*, is yet another part of the widening effort to renew our engagement with Torah.

For myself, I was already an experienced *Baal Korei* (Torah reader) when, about twenty years ago, I encountered my first experience with a way of chanting Torah that changed my experience of Torah reading forever. This has become not only my personal "new normal," but also how I teach my cantorial students, the rabbinical student with whom I work, the participants in the Davvenen' Leadership Training, and even my Bar and Bat Mitzvah kids.

Leyning in English

Twenty years ago I first heard Rabbi Zalman Schachter-Shalomi (*z"l, zichrono liv'racha*—let his memory be for a blessing) *leyn*—read publicly from the Torah—in a flowing combination of Hebrew and English. He was *leyning* in the traditional *trope*—the Torah melody—moving seamlessly from the Hebrew into English translation and back into Hebrew without breaking the melody, and using the English to not only translate, but in his choice of how he translated—interpretively and dramatically teaching the text on the spot. It was stunning. A tour-de-force! I was riveted! The text practically jumped off the page. I had never heard Torah so passionately alive, so powerful. I've been *leynen* Torah my whole adult life, and I know the Hebrew reasonably well, but others around me, for whom the Hebrew would typically be a blur without meaning, they were riveted too! They heard the ancient Hebrew, its inflections and rhythms, but interspersed with English in a way that brought them inside the experience. The public reading of Torah had come alive! The words leapt from the scroll into their hearts. People who were hearing Torah read from the scroll and understood for the first time, wept.

Reb Zalman (*z"l*), a master, was not using a separate English translation printout; he was translating in the moment, directly from the open scroll! And he was singing the English! He was melding the *trope* with the English, using the traditional Torah chant so we could really hear how the song of Torah becomes the carrier wave for the emotional power of the text.

For me, this was one of those aha! moments. I realized that even for the non-Hebrew-speaking Jewish world, Torah could be immediately alive and vital. I too began *leyning* this way, and have watched the reactions. Because not every synagogue is prepared for such a shift, I began with *Megillat Esther* on Purim, selectively and of course often humorously, translating passages directly from the scroll as I went along. I'd watch as the crowd, typically restlessly waiting for the one word they understand – Haman! – would suddenly wake up and pay attention. Then gradually I began to bring my "direct-from-the-scroll" translations to the Torah service. I'd watch to see the ripple of surprise among those hearing Torah like this for the first time. The energy shifts in the room. There is an elevation of attentiveness. People smile, and lean forward in their seats to hear..., as if to say: "Wait a minute, I *understand* this! It *means* something! Torah is speaking to *me*!"

There are any number of ways to *leyn* in Hebrew and English. Because every translation has a *midrashic* element and is an interpretive rendering of the sense of the original Hebrew, the process opens up the opportunity to share the multiple layers of meaning in the Torah text. And of course, the translation of a given text will not necessarily always be the same, but may vary depending on the reader's understanding of the text at that time, and what she or he wishes to stress on that occasion.

The pattern I have developed is to always begin and end in Hebrew, no matter how much of a blend of Hebrew and English may fall within the section I am chanting. This puts the translation/interpretive reading squarely inside the frame of the original language which has unique power. Inside that frame, there are diverse ways to *leyn*. One can alternate Hebrew and English sentence-by-sentence (less becomes too choppy) or in larger segments. One can make sure all the Hebrew one *leyns* is translated, or only some. Or the reverse: one can switch into *leynen* in English, and add in Hebrew phrases or whole segments as feels appropriate.

Torah Trope

At this point, I wish to share a word about *"trope."* *Trope* is a precise system for the public singing of Torah. It was developed for dramatic expression, to provide punctuation, and as it is structurally linked to Hebrew grammar it is also a means of delivering the text with grammatical nuance. The current system we use was developed in the 8th century, and combines two earlier systems, a Babylonian and a Palestinian tradition. English is of course a very different language; singing English using *trope* means significantly disengaging the *trope* from its link to Hebrew. When you are singing English in *trope* you are using the *trope* to serve both a musical and dramatic purpose. If you are considering undertaking this new musical and spiritual adventure, I suggest that you not try to apply the *trope* from the Hebrew overly rigidly, but rather take the Hebrew *trope* settings as a guideline, and freely create an English version that does the job in that language.

My successful experiences with Hebrew/English Torah *leynen* have led me into other texts. Based on my earlier work with *Megillat Esther* I went on to create and record an original abbreviated version of *Megillat Esther* entirely in English, set of course in *Megillah trope*.

Imagine hearing "…now this was the Ahasuerus, whose empire *extennnded* from India to Ethiopia. In the third year of his reign he threw a *huuuge paaarty,"* and you can hear the *trope* at work!

Next I developed English *Haftarot* using my own English translation of the standard *Haftarah*, also of course set in *Haftarah trope*. Then, going boldly where no *hazzan* had gone before, on a year in which July 4 fell on Shabbat, I set the Declaration of Independence to *Haftarah trope* and offered it in my *shul* as an alternative *Haftarah*. This text, drawn from the American revolutionary experience, came alive as a prophetic text in an extraordinary way. You can hear it on the Shalom Center website. Then using selections of excerpts from several of Reverend Dr. Martin Luther King Jr's speeches, I crafted a *Haftarah* for the Shabbat of MLK weekend. The power of his faith, witness, and call to justice rolled into the room with a challenge to us to live the dream. As you can see, I offer the possibility that, while not officially part of the Jewish canon, from time to time alternative texts like these can be brought into our congregations in ways that honor our American and Jewish spiritual legacies.

An Invitation

I invite you to experiment and join me in this adventure! Torah, our prophetic literature, the other scrolls and texts that we chant at holidays and festivals and the classic musical carrier wave of the *trope* can meet our creativity, and can come alive in many ways. This experiment of blending Hebrew and English *leynen* is one way that I have found to be both powerful and successful

And there is more…Torah can be *leyned* in any language: Hebrew mixed with German, Dutch, French,

Spanish and… yes… Norwegian, all of which—thanks to my students—I have also heard! And it works!

Jack Kessler

Hazzan Jack Kessler has been described as a one-man force of nature in Jewish music. He was ordained as a Cantor at the Jewish Theological Seminary of America, and went on to have a twenty-year career serving Conservative congregations. During that time he received a Master's degree in voice from Boston Conservatory and pursued studies in composition in the graduate department of Brandeis University, where he worked with Arthur Berger and Harold Shapero, and Bethany Beardslee at Harvard. A lyric baritone, he has performed opera, oratorio, and premiered new works, in addition to his ongoing career as a singer of Hazzanut, the sacred cantorial art. Originally trained as an *Ashkenazi Hazzan*, his performance style and original compositions also embrace *Sephardi* and *Mizrachi* styles.

Hazzan Kessler has lectured and taught master classes in Jewish music at New England Conservatory in Boston, the Academy for Jewish Religion in New York, and presented many concerts in an educational format. He is the dean of the Cantorial department of the professional training program of ALEPH: Alliance for Jewish Renewal, and teaches a number of cantorial students.

His current performance projects are directing, composing for, and being the vocal lead of the two touring ensembles Atzilut Concerts for Peace, a duet format of Arab and Jewish musicians performing

215

together, and Klingon Klezmer, which does Jewish music from other planets.

http://JackKessler.CreatingCalmNetworkPublishingGroup.com

Growing Your Spiritual Community

1. Imagine yourself in the ritual committee discussion where it was proposed that the Torah service be dropped. How would you have responded? What would you have said?
2. Have you ever heard someone chanting from the Torah, using the *trope* but not using Hebrew, instead using another language which everyone present understands? How did it feel? What was your response?
3. What has been done and what can be done in your community to increase engagement and bring the Torah service alive?
4. What do you think about this idea, "The use of "theme-based *aliyot*" in which congregants self-selected and come up to Torah in response to the message of the reading, as explained by the brief *dvar-torah* that is shared before the *aliyah*?"
5. Have you ever heard Klingon Klezmer music?

What Are Jewish Blues?

Saul Kaye describes this new form of Jewish music saying, "So where does the African blues tradition come from? The slave experience has been the foundation of so much of the music that has shaped American culture. Jews have been enslaved in many countries over the centuries including Egypt, Babylon, Persia, Rome, Greece, Germany, and Malta. So, like the African Slave experience proved to be a catalyst for blues, so the path of Jewish history fostered its own form of soulful tears, from Jews crying out in Egyptian slavery (Exodus) to the prophet Jeremiah weeping over the destruction of the Temple in *Eicha* (Lamentations). Jews know the pain of spiritual crisis and call to *Hashem* with their own form of blues. You can hear it in the synagogue when the Torah and the books of Prophets are read, chanted in *tropes* passed down through time, recounting forbearers' sorrows on days of tragedy like *Tisha B'Av*, or remembering celebrations of freedom on *Passover*, when Jews recall the Israelite's "*Song at the Sea*," as the waters of freedom parted."

On his Jewish music CDs, Saul Kaye takes the Jewish experience and blends it with the African one, much like his own journey. He takes Jewish stories and puts them to African-based blues. He adds in characters from Torah and The Prophets. Saul stirs Biblical narratives into the gumbo of African American blues and serves it up as a kind of cross cultural stew, known as Jewish Blues.

http://SaulKaye.CreatingCalmNetworkPublishingGroup.com

The Whole Magilla in Pop Culture

Frank Sinatra brought a Hebrew word into common usage when he sang the phrase, "the whole magilla" in 1963 in *Come Blow Your Horn*:

The taller the tree is — the sweeter the peach
I'll give you the whole magilla — in a one word speech
— reach.

The lyrics are saying that he will condense a long and drawn out explanation into a single word.

The more correct spelling is *megillah*, a Hebrew word for a scroll. In particular, it refers to one of five books of the Old Testament: Song of Songs, Ruth, Lamentations, Ecclesiastes, and Esther.

The most common reference is to the Book of Esther, which is read in its entirety at the feast of Purim. The story wanders at great length through vast amounts of detail, hence the term "the whole *Megillah*." In Yiddish "*gantse Megillah*" came to mean an overly extended explanation or story.

Ki Imanu Eil, God is With Us
Eric Komar

Rabbi Abraham Joshua Heschel is credited with saying, "When a Jew is sad, he cries. When he's even sadder than that, he's silent. But when he's even sadder than that? He sings." With that in mind, I wish to share two instances when tragedy led me to prayer through music.

Purim, 2002

The subway train emerged onto the Manhattan Bridge toward Brooklyn. It was only six months since 9/11 and the wounds were still fresh. Regardless of what subway riders were engaged in, all activity came to a halt as the newly scarred Lower Manhattan skyline came into view. Everyone knew why; we were all thinking about the same thing. The sorrow, the anger, and the resolve were palpable. Such was every subway ride since that horrific event.

During that particular March afternoon commute, I was reviewing music to teach for the upcoming holiday of Purim. As the train began to traverse the East River and that eerie, somber mood came over the train, I found myself staring at the traditional setting of "*Utzu Eitzah*": They can plan their plans and scheme their schemes, but they will fail, for God is with us.

How fitting were those words to Americans in the wake of the 9/11. The attacks seemed to strengthen the solidarity between Americans and Jews, who had been victims of terrorism countless times before. It also occurred to me that Purim wasn't the only time that Jews

219

were persecuted and then ultimately saved by the hand of God. Virtually every holiday celebrated by Jews around the year sprang from a time of oppression by a greater enemy. As the joke goes: They tried to destroy us. We won. Let's eat. I began to jot down a chronology of Jewish tribulations à la Billy Joel's "We Didn't Start the Fire," beginning with Israelite slavery in ancient Egypt.

The train steadily rumbling on the track set the tempo of the song that began to take shape. I chose a 7/8 meter to reflect the precarious, uncomfortable incompleteness being sensed worldwide, switching to a cathartic 4/4 for other parts, particularly the last line of the refrain—*ki imanu Eil* (for God is with us).

Throughout history
our people suffered through hard times:
Victims of injustice, persecution, and harsh crimes.
In Egypt Pharaoh kept us bound in slavery,
Till *Adonai* had Moses lead us 'cross the Sea.
Wicked Haman swore to rid *Shushan* of all the Jews
But Mordechai and Esther made sure he would lose.
And when Antiochus forced upon us
idols and false gods,
God gave the Maccabees the strength to beat the odds.

U-tzu ei-tzah v'-tu-far …
Dab-ru da-var v'-lo ya-kum …
Ki i-ma-nu, ki i-ma-nu Eil …

They can try to plan their plans
and scheme their schemes,
Attempt to realize their maniacal dreams
But no matter what they try, they will surely fail

'Cause God's with us and
we'll always be left to tell the tale.

To be the Chosen People means to have a cross to bear,
To leave our treasured homeland
and to scatter everywhere.
But no matter where we fled or
where our children had to hide,
We still believed with perfect faith
God always was on our side.

The Inquisition, the pogroms under the czar,
They couldn't stop us from remaining who we are.
The darkness took away six million precious lives,
But then our homeland was reborn, and still survives.

We've seen all kinds of threats and stood up to them all,
With the Refuseniks, watched the Iron Curtain fall.
Today new terror keeps appearing at our door,
But I believe God's with us and
one day they too shall be no more.

While not a prayer in the strictest sense, "Utzu
Eitzah" is rather an affirmation of peoplehood, a rallying
cry by those who had had enough and decided to fight
back. It is also a declaration of faith: no matter how great
a threat to Jewish existence is, it will fail because we
always have God on our side, and always will. At many
periods of adversity, it has helped me remember God's
eternal protection over the Jewish people.

Eil Malei Rachamim, God Full of Mercy

Meghan was a sixteen year-old who had it all: She was smart, kind, pretty, talented, and athletic. Then, at the start of her junior year of high school, she was diagnosed with an aggressive brain tumor. In two lightning-quick months, she was gone.

It was clear Meghan was well-liked at school and at our synagogue, where I had served as the music teacher for years. The sanctuary was as packed for her funeral as it was for High Holy Days. The officiating rabbi, who visited her many times in the hospital while she deteriorated, later described the devastating ordeal as one of those times his own faith was challenged.

That first week of November, 2004, was particularly difficult. Not only did Meghan tragically leave us but my aunt, a habitual smoker for decades, succumbed to lung cancer at age 55. We also said good-bye to my wife's grandfather who a few weeks prior reached his century milestone. Even while mourning the loss of these relatives, I could not take my mind off my young student and the grieving parents of their only child, and how just six months earlier in that same sanctuary they were proudly celebrating her confirmation.

Three times that week the words of the Eil Malei Rachamim (God full of mercy) filled my ears and my mind. Not since the loss of my own father nine years earlier did I really focus on the words of this petitionary prayer. It is a prayer recited at moments when the pain of loss leaves us truly helpless, vulnerable, and desperate. As we mourn, we are left with nothing but this humble request that God raise our loved ones into heaven and watch over them forever.

It was at these intensely sorrowful moments that my musical ideas for this prayer began to take root. I had never before even thought of composing a setting to funeral liturgy. Most of my Jewishly-themed compositions were celebratory and uplifting in nature. This one, I realized, was going to be a challenge, and in the end, proved extremely therapeutic. In a few weeks both the lyrics and music were complete. *"God Full of Mercy"* was released in 2007 on my second CD:

They say that life is a journey,
and death a destination.
But when the road ends much too soon,
can there be an explanation?
We foolishly question events we can't control,
Searching for an answer to once again feel whole.

You were an angel loved and admired,
a gift to everyone you'd known.
There must have been a good reason why
you were so early called back home.
We desperately try to accept what we can't change,
Cry out in the darkness in hopes to end the pain.

Eil malei rachamim,
God full of mercy, hear our plea.
Grant perfect rest under Your wings,
As our dear one enters into eternity.
May she rest in peace,
May she rest in peace,
Finding relief in the shadow of Your wings.

We still can take comfort in how you touched our hearts.
And if we remember, you'll never be too far.
They say that life is a journey,
and death a destination ...

When I contacted Meghan's mother for permission to write on this topic, she thanked me for writing "*God Full of Mercy*" and admitted it was only very recently that she was able to listen to it for the first time. It was gratifying that finally hearing it was therapeutic for her, just as writing it was for me ten years ago.

Eric Komar

For two decades singer- songwriter Eric Komar has shared his unique brand of jazz-tinged Jewish rock at synagogues, JCCs, camps, Hillels, and conventions nationwide. His vast performance experience runs the gamut, from preschoolers to retirees, and his advanced guitar skills are recognized among the most prominent musicians in the field.

Eric's music has been described as refreshing, superb and hip sounding, having a sophisticated pop sensibility, and compelling and truly Jewish. His debut CD, *Notes from the Underground* (2003) is noted for a rock n' roll "*Mi Chamochah*" and power-ballad for peace "*Lo Yisa Goi.*" His second effort, *Two Life* (2007) features special guests Peter Alland and Ellen Allard and includes social action anthem "*Justice, Justice.*" He ushered in 2011 with *Ripples,* containing the High Holiday hit "*Return*" and a contemporary setting of "*Dayenu.*" His long-awaited kid's album, *Todah Torah,* showcasing the talents of his students, was released in the Fall of 2013. Several of Eric's pieces can be found in publications from URJ/Transcontinental Music, as well as Craig Taubman's Craig n' Co.

Eric lives in New Jersey with his wife and two children. He currently serves as a synagogue music specialist, does music transcription and typesetting, and teaches guitar.

http://EricKomar.CreatingCalmNetworkPublishingGroup.com

Growing Your Spiritual Community

1. When do you most feel that God is with you?
2. Do you associate the events of 9/11 in the United States with the tragedies Jews have endured? Why or why not?
3. Do you see yourself as a victim for any reason? Do you think Jewish liturgy might help or hurt in this regard?
4. When do you most feel God's mercy?
5. What brings you comfort and hope in the face of cancer, death or tragedy?
6. Is there any particular pray or song that is therapeutic or healing for you?

God is ...

Often how we perceive God has to do with what we are and who we are. This section explores who we are in relationship to God.

The Baal Shem Tov said, "*The world is new to us every morning—this is God's gift; and every man should believe he is reborn each day.*"

About a nearby river he also said, "*That water was waiting from the beginning of time for someone to come and make a blessing over it and drink it.*"

Look around. Where do you recognize God?

The Expansive Duality of *G'vurot* and Our Power

Life and death
on either side of a thin sword
summer and winter
circling through the days
dew and rain
refreshing the growth

Death and life
building from each other
falling and healing
hope for future change
captive and freedom
experiencing one, appreciating the other

Action and receiving
understanding the gifts of both
mighty and in the image
seeing the oneness
holy returning
always returning with gratitude

Mastering and excelling
trying my best
connecting
going the distance between
fertile valley and the soaring pinnacle
grace and beauty
within the multiple aspects of all

—**Kimberly Burnham**

Growing Your Spiritual Community

1. What is your favorite aspect of the Jewish year?
2. Do you sometimes feel mixed feelings as you celebrate a holiday with your community?
3. How would you describe the subtle shifts in your relationship to God or the universe through the seasonal changes and cycles of life?

Gevurot

"*Gevurot* roughly translated, means "mighty deeds". This calls God a source of blessing, supporter of the fallen, author of freedom, and our hope in death as in life. In the context of many persecutions and disasters, this prayer has no doubt provided comfort through every Jewish generation."

—**TempleNashville.org**

Ata Gibur Le'olam Adonai mechayey hakol ata rav lehoshiah. Mechalkel chayim bechesed, mechayey hakol berachamim rabim. Somech noflim verofe cholim umatir asurim umekayem emunato lisheney afar. Mi chamocha ba'al gevurot umi dome lach, melech memit umeychaye umatzmiya yeshua. Vene'eman ata lehachayot hacol. Baruch ata Adonai Mechayey Hakol.

—**Rabbi Jamie Korngold**, Youtu.be/bzqAiHxlmOk

Romemu

Inspire
praise
laud
acclaim
applaud
uplift
honor
extol
pay tribute to
sing the praises of
worship
reverence

respect
adore
exalt
Romemu
so many ways
to share
many experiences
to tell
be grateful!

—Kimberly Burnham

Growing Your Spiritual Community

1. What do you exalt in your spiritual practice and in
your life? How many different ways can you think of to
express gratitude?
2. How do you envision God as you express gratitude?

The Power of Song
Rami Shapiro

We Jews call ourselves *Yisrael* (*Genesis* 32:29), and understand this as one who wrestles (*yisra*) with God (*El*). Given the fluidity with which Hebrew can be read, *yisra El* can also be read as *yashir El*, not one who wrestles with God but one who sings God. The two readings could not be more distinct.

A wrestler has opponents; a singer has partners. A wrestler wins by pinning the other down; a singer "wins" by lifting the other up. A wrestler overpowers the other; a singer harmonizes with the other. Sadly it is the image of God–Wrestler alone that has defined us. It is time to reclaim and celebrate God–Singer as well.

The Universe as Song

Torah tells us that God spoke the world into existence (Genesis 1:3). Before that moment, the breath of God vibrated, trilled if you like, over the waters (Genesis 1:2). From this trilling God shaped words, and from these words came forth the world that you and I know. The world wasn't spoken into being, but sung into being. This is why we don't read Torah, we chant Torah. This is why we don't read our liturgy, but chant it. The cantillation and chanting is not only an aid to memory, it is a reminder that the universe is a song we are called to sing and not a thing we are called to master.

The power of any religious service is in its music. To test this theory, compare the energy generated when a community sings to when it reads responsively. Rarely do the latter come close to the former.

Sermons, too, should sing. Listen to those of Martin Luther King Jr. Listen to his breathing. He is singing, not reading. I periodically attend an African American Episcopal Church not far from my home, and marvel as the pastor "sings" his sermons, and how the congregation becomes a chorus responding to his words. Indeed, as the sermon comes to a close there is often a refrain picked up by the band and carried by the choir until the entire congregation is on its feet completing the sermon with him. He has taken them somewhere—body, heart, mind, and soul. How many rabbis can do that?

Elohai Neshama

I have only one intention when leading a service or teaching a class—to help set people free. My guide is God's call to Avram and Sarai: *Lech lecha*! Walk to your Self, the Self (*neshamah*) that is *t'hora*, pure—free from the conditioning of nationality, ethnicity, parental bias, as well as religion, race, gender, and anything else that keeps us from being free. And in that place to grow strong, and become a blessing to all the families of the earth—human and otherwise (*Genesis* 12:1–3).

There is only one way to take this journey, and that is through the body, especially the breath. And the best way to work with the breath is through silence and song. My "services" are a blending of both, with our singing arising out of silence and the needs of the breath, rather than following the dictate of the script and the tyranny of the printed page.

I find traditional Jewish liturgy too wordy. It is as if we are seeking to hide from reality under an ever–growing pile of words. And, to make matters worse, I

231

find that most of those words no longer speak to me, or uplift me, or invite me into the song of creation. I cannot believe in a cosmic king who judges, chooses, writes books, or dabbles in real estate. My God is reality itself: the nondual source and substance of all that was, is, and will ever be. I don't pray to this deity as if God were other, I seek to awake in it, as it, because it is all there is.

So I cull the liturgy for those short lines—sometimes even single words—that do speak to me, and offer them as chants to be repeated rather than as prayers to be recited. I look at these texts as a means to walking Self-ward. Thankfully I have guides in this culling: Rabbi Shefa Gold and Yofiyah to name but two.

Carrying the Intention

We sing and chant because there is no higher expression of joy, and no more powerful expression of sorrow. When something wonderful and unexpected happens to us, what do we do? We shout with joy. When something horrible and unexpected happens to us, what do we do? We cry with anguish. Shouting and crying are a kind of unformed singing.

The power of song and chant come from our capacity to shape our primal screams in ways that lead us to equally primal wisdom. Shaping the primal is the work of the cantor, chant leader, or music director. And because this is so, she or he must be at home with the primal. A cantor who is trained in *trope* and yet knows nothing of ecstasy and despair may be a fine performer, but cannot be a God–Singer.

A performer entertains, a God–Singer transforms. A performer keeps the congregation at a distance; a God–

Singer draws them near. A performer leads them through a script; a God–Singer leads them to themselves. A God–Singer embraces the congregation in an aural web of compassion. She creates a safe place to do the dangerous work of liberation. She weaves a web of love that invites the congregation to drop the snare of words, and tap the heart of life, both its joys and its sorrows.

And to do this, the God–Singer has to be open to this heart as well. The God–Singer must be the least defended person in the room, the most naked to the hope and horror of just being alive. She must be the most vulnerable and, because she is, she is the most strong as well. It is through her strength that we find ourselves surrendered to truth. She must sing out of her own pain and her own joy. She must work through her own story and make room for the dozens of stories she will carry during the service. Her intention is vital. And if her intention is anything other than liberation, she is a danger to us all.

The Intention of the Congregant

I am less concerned with the intention of the congregant than I am with the intention of the leader. Few of us walk into *shul* prepared to be stripped naked; prepared to be torn open; prepared to meet God in, with, and as ourselves and our neighbors. We come with the week's stories, triumphs, and tragedies, and may have no intention of dropping them. We don't come in order to be free. We must be coaxed toward liberation, and it is the music that does this.

And yet there is nothing so harrowing to a God–Singer as a congregation weighed down in stony silence or self–conscious mumbling. There is little chance of anything transformative happening. Worse, there is all too strong a chance that the God–Singer will despair and take on the role of performer instead.

What should we do in such situations?

First let me suggest what not to do: don't opt for coerced noise. I have seen too many song leaders harangue a congregation into clapping hands and singing loudly. People comply outwardly, but the shallowness of their experience only makes authentic God–Singing all the more difficult.

Too many of us have been taught to equate *shul* with camp; to believe that loud equals deep, and hand clapping equals soul opening. We have been fed a faux ecstasy, a cheap grace, a false sense of community, and even more false sense of freedom. *Davvenen* is not a matter of losing oneself in the mob and of having one's voice drowned out by mere noise.

Davvenen or praying is being enticed by God into a state of unity. *Davvenen* is sensual, erotic: a polymorphous liberation of body, heart, mind, and soul that is far too dangerous for kids. *Davvenen* cannot be faked, or turned on and off at the command of a leader, no matter how charismatic.

So what should we do when we are met with silence and mumbling?

This is what I do: I stop chanting and start sharing. I talk with the congregation about their fears. I speak with them about *lech lecha* and liberation, and inquire into what it is that may be blocking them. I turn their blocks into meditations, and I invite them explore their fears and shatter their blocks though simple melodies and soft probing lyrics.

It doesn't always work, and I have to be honest enough to admit defeat and give people what they want. But this is rare. The yearning for awakening and freedom is just beneath the fear that hides it from us. We should be trained to work with this yearning rather than play to the fear.

My Favorite Chant

My daily spiritual practice is rooted in chanting, and every workshop I lead or lecture I give begins and ends with chanting. I know several and use those that I sense speak to the needs of the community. But one stands out from the rest, *Elohai neshamah sheh natatabi t'hora he*; "My God, the Self You place within me is pure."

Remember, my goal is liberation, walking toward the Self unconditioned by nationality, ethnicity, parental bias, religion, gender, etc. We are not creating this Self, but reclaiming it as our truest Self. And the chant that does this best is *Elohai neshamah*.

Elohai neshamah is an exercise in awakening to Self through the feminine, *neshamah*.

The way of the feminine is the way of *Chochmah*, wisdom. Not the wisdom of the *Kabbalistic* Tree that places her on the side of the masculine, but Lady Wisdom who reveals herself to us in *Proverbs 8:22*. She is God manifesting; she is *Shekhinah*, God present in and as all creation. She is the way of God in, with, and as creation. She is the play of nature who delights in humankind (Proverbs 8:31). It is she who manifests in us as *neshamah*, and she is pure (*t'hora*).

Purity here doesn't mean without sin or stain, but pure as in transparent, the way water is pure; the way air

235

is pure. When we awaken to her as us we become transparent as well; without the distortions of a conditioned mind and heart we see the world as it is— God manifesting.

Power of Chant

I am making some very big claims about the power of chant, and everything I say is rooted in my own experience. Let me share one quick example.

My favorite kind of chanting is *kirtan*, call and response. I once attended an evening of Sufi, Jewish, and Hindu kirtan at the Center for Spiritual Enlightenment in San Jose, CA. Our host, Rev. Ellen Grace O'Brian, warned us not to rush home after the event because we would be in a state of ecstasy and driving under the influence of ecstasy was a very bad idea. I knew what she meant. I had been chanting for years, and had often felt the dropping away of the static "I" of "Rami," and the awakening of the dynamic *Ehyeh* of God. But I was not prepared for the element of *ain od* or nothing but God (Deuteronomy 4:35) that was the gift of that evening.

The chanting went on for hours, and the shifting between chanters and traditions was seamless. The quality of the singers, the power of the chanting, and the willingness of those gathered to become a beloved community led us into that state we Jews call *mochin d'gadlut*, spacious mind. This is a state where all I's are God's I: *Ani Adonai Elohechem*: where "The I of the Ineffable One is the only I" (*Ve'ahavta*). This is the state of *kadosh* (holiness) where we perceive "the whole world permeated with divine glory" (Isaiah 6:3).

When the program ended not only couldn't I drive, I couldn't even walk. I was drunk on the divine.

I'm not saying we should strive for this every *Shabbos*, but I am saying that if we did, our *shuls* would be full week after week.

Rami Shapiro

An award winning author, Rabbi Rami Shapiro has written over two dozen books on religion and spirituality. He received rabbinical ordination from the Hebrew Union College–Jewish Institute of Religion, and holds a PhD from Union Graduate School. A congregational rabbi for 20 years, Rabbi Rami currently co–directs One River Wisdom School. He blogs at Rabbirami.blogspot.com, writes a regular column for Spirituality and Health magazine called *Roadside Assistance for the Spiritual Traveler*, and hosts the weekly Internet radio show, *How to be a Holy Rascal* on Unity On-line Radio. His newest book is *Perennial Wisdom for the Spiritually Independent* (SkyLight Paths).

http://RamiShapiro.CreatingCalmNetworkPublishingGroup.com

Growing Your Spiritual Community

1. Which translation do you prefer "one who wrestles with God" or "one who sings God?"
2. How do you focus on your breath as you pray or sing?
3. What does this quote mean to you: "She must sing out of her own pain and her own joy. She must work through her own story and make room for the dozens of stories

she will carry during the service. Her intention is vital. And if her intention is anything other than liberation, she is a danger to us all?"

4. How do you think of your responsibility as a member in light of this quote? "There is nothing so harrowing to a God–Singer as a congregation weighed down in stony silence or self–conscious mumbling. There is little chance of anything transformative happening. Worse, there is all too strong a chance that the God–Singer will despair and take on the role of performer instead."

5. How do you think of your journey to self?

6. Have you experienced Kirtan chanting in a Jewish setting?

Ashrei: Visioning Happiness with a Grieving Soul
Elizabeth W. Goldstein

Ashrei Yoshvei Vaytecha ōd yehallulucha Selah

Happy is the one who Dwells in your House
Happy is the one whose Praises are yours
Happy is the one who reaches for you
Happy is the one who calls out your name

Ashrei Yoshvei Vaytecha ōd yehallulucha Selah

Silent Meditation

V'anachnu Nevarech Yah, Mayatah V'ad Olam

Halleluyah Halleluyah
Halleluyah Halleluyah

Hal-ley-lu-yah
Hal-ley-lu-yah

    I composed this chant, based loosely on the Renewal *ashrei* chant, while on my bicycle towards the end of the summer of 2013. I rode almost every day. Beginning in March 2013, I took my bike out in the snow and ice. I was determined to ride to *shul* one Shabbat morning and ended up carrying or walking my bike much of the way.

    As the weather warmed, and the days grew longer, I rode more often. Some weekend days, I would be gone five to six hours at a time. I was training for the Hazon Cross USA ride. Although only planning to traverse the state—Seattle to Spokane (Week one of nine)—I had no idea I was preparing for a much longer journey. I was riding the journey of the soul. I was riding away from the only home I knew—my life with her. And although I successfully rode the 300 plus miles, I never really came home.

I was riding all of those miles toward myself, all of those miles to discover that something was gravely wrong. I was married to my best friend in the whole world, I had four spectacular children and I was broken. My brokenness had been for a long time. Hiding deep within me, the hours of biking alone shook that consciousness loose.

When I said goodbye to the last of my new biking friends, I rode from the synagogue to my house in Spokane. I opened the door, hugged my children, sat down at the kitchen table, and I cried for reasons unclear to myself.

I had made it across the state, making new friends and nourished by what Hazon does best, creating vibrant, dynamic, spiritually diverse Jewish communal experiences. But the last day of the ride, my heart was heavy. I didn't want to come home. I had been a racehorse for much of the week, but the last day, the Friday into Spokane, I dragged. And then my tire hit a nail so hard that it ripped a hole straight through my gatorskin tire, forcing me into the van for the eight miles to REI. The tire repaired, I rode the last few miles up the hill to Temple Beth Shalom. She was waiting for me with our children. I had made it but something was wrong.

Something had changed within me but I didn't know what. Did I regret becoming a mother? Did I regret taking a job so far away from a large Jewish community?

It wasn't Spokane or the children or my job. It was us. We weren't in love anymore. I knew it was over and wished it was not. Yet I couldn't go back. Sadness, fear, even terror washed over me as I prepared to walk away from everything I had known for the last 19 years toward a new life.

I walked away from her in a daze and I have only just begun to rebuild myself.

Happy is the one who Dwells in your House
Happy is the one whose Praises are yours

I sang my *ashrei* chant on my bike, in Taize meditation and chant, in the empty Catholic chapel at my university.

I love it because it is mine. I love it because it is meditative and real. I taught the congregation the chant at High Holy Days and as they joined in, something seemed off. My friend said, "it's a nice chant but sort of ironic because it is so obvious that *you* are not happy."

It didn't occur to me that we should only sing *Ashrei* when we are happy. Traditionally, Jews pray the *ashrei* three times a day. I was trying to invoke happiness. I wanted happiness and I could foresee it ahead, but I couldn't touch it. I believe in happiness and that one day I would feel it again.

I was happy to be given the chance to start again, although I was scared to death.

Happy is the one who Dwells in your House

I was content in *shul* and on my bike. I often pray on my bike, especially in the early morning. It is harder to cry on my bike, easier in *shul*. I always associate her with *shul* since that was a major part of the life we shared. Finding my own identity in *shul* and as a rabbi is an ongoing process. In new ways, I strive to integrate God, community, and Torah.

Happy is the one whose Praises are yours

With praise, I try to let God hold my pain. Biblical tradition associates praise with animal sacrifice. It is not enough to feel gratitude. People have to offer something in return for good fortune. We have to face real truths about our failings and strive to be a better version of ourselves. I own my wrongs. With God's help, I pray that in a new relationship I will be better.

Happy is the one who reaches for you

In cycling we lean forward towards the road ahead. Even on a loop well traveled, we begin again, hoping for better time, better weather, sharpened consciousness, more peace, relief from anxiety and a renewed love of self. I walked away from my life with her, but towards myself and towards God. Still it haunts me: How do we know when it's ok to go? How can we make that impossible choice?

Happy is the one who calls out your name

I keep chanting. I call upon the Eternal One—The One who calls to me from the depths of my soul. The One who releases me from narrow places and sets me, vulnerably, back at the beginning.

Over a year later I embrace the struggle to rebuild myself. I direct my best efforts toward being a caring and attentive mother, an excellent professor and rabbi, and a provocative writer. I am full of gratitude and yet still hold pain.

V'anachnu Nevarech Yah, Mayatah V'ad Olam
Therefore let us bless Yah, From now until all time.

Halleluyah, Halleluyah
Halleluyah, Halleluyah

Elizabeth W. Goldstein

Co-Editor of *Music, Carrier of Intention in 49 Jewish Prayers*, Rabbi Elizabeth W. Goldstein, PhD is a professor in the Department of Religious Studies at Gonzaga University and teaches Hebrew Bible, Judaism, and Hebrew. She completed her rabbinic studies at Hebrew Union College-Jewish Institute of Religion in New York in 2001. Her PhD in Ancient Jewish History focuses on Hebrew Bible and particularly its intersection with Gender Studies. Goldstein completed her doctoral work in 2010 from the University of California at San Diego, CA. She is a contributor to several books including: *The Women's Haftarah Commentary: New Insights from Women Rabbis on the 54 Weekly Haforah Portions, the Five Megillot and the Special Shabbatot* (Ed, by Elyse Goldstein, Jewish Lights, 2004); *Jewish Blood: Reality and Metaphor in History, Religion, and Culture* (Ed, by Mitchell B. Hart, Routledge, 2009); and *Embroidered Garments: Priests and Gender in Biblical Israel* (Ed, by Deborah W. Rooke, Shefield Phoenix, 2009). She also contributed two central commentaries to the award winning, *The Torah: A Woman's Commentary* (Ed, by Andrea Weiss and Tamara Eskenazi, URJ Press, 2007) Her upcoming book *Impurity and Gender in the Hebrew Bible* (Lexington Books) explores the role of female blood in the Hebrew Bible. She considers its theological implications for future understandings of purity and impurity in the Jewish religion. Elizabeth still bicycles, writes music and walks on the bluff with her children before tucking them into bed.

http://ElizabethGoldstein.CreatingCalmNetworkPublishingGroup.com

Growing Your Spiritual Community

1. What turning points have you experienced?
2. Have you had experiences where you do not feel the way you think you should or the way others expect you to feel?
3. Have you ever felt like you had to choose between your responsibility to yourself, to your own happiness and success and that of your family or community?
4. "In cycling we lean forward towards the road ahead." What do you lean towards metaphorically? Where in your life are you looking for a better time, more strength, and more happiness?
5. Have you ever felt compelled to do something for your own happiness, your family or community that made it difficult to look some people in the eyes, knowing you did what you had to do?
6. Are you happy?
7. Are you connected to a force greater than yourself?

All in the Zimrahh of Yahh
Shira Kline

Prayer, whether we are laying our head on a rock to dream or sitting upright in the pews of a classical reform cathedral, is a highly intentional act weaved into the storyline of our lives. There is the story of our heart, mind and soul's journey, there is the story of internal desire for connection and sense of Home, and there is the physiological story of our body as it aligns with rhythm and flow of breath and sound. Music is like the lightning rod that interfaces with and conducts the intention of the one that prays.

Infinite Possibilities in Sacred Circle

The experience of leading a service and entering into a relationship with the music, begins for me with how I set up the space, engaging the *Makom* (meaning "place" and also a name for the Divine). Many years ago I studied with Jean-Guy Lecat, the Spatial Designer for sacred theatre innovator and director Peter Brook. Jean-Guy taught me the power of the sacred circle, the most common and simple shape in nature. The circle has the power of unity and wholeness, equality and inclusivity, and most of all infinite possibility in its open space. He taught me to find the circle in every space; walking it out, if necessary transforming the space, until I could feel the shape of circle. I've always connected this notion to the concept of "*Makom*," Jacob's intuitive revelation of God's presence in space and place (Genesis 28:16). And just as Jacob discovers that God is in this place and he did not know it, *Makom* is also one of my favorite names for the

Divine, helping me to experience that everything is God. Once I have found the circle in the space either in the actual set up of the chairs or by walking the space, I like to imagine that I can wrap my arms around it like a big hug. When I am with a community of young children, I imagine the circle as a garden where all things grow. The circle I construct is a field for creation and participation, a space to activate and elevate the imagination. My hope is to provide a safe and accessible place for participants to open heart and mind, to connect to, process, and grow within his or her story. All of this guided by music and song and the space in between the notes.

Before participants enter the space. I wrap myself in my *tallit* (prayer shawl) and take a private moment to ask the Divine to open my channels: to sing through me, to guide my lips that I may articulate and carry Her words, that I may have the presence to shine Her meaning and provide the open space for all to find their way to connection with the Source of Life and Creation.

Toning

Simple opening music invites the participants into the circle, easing the transition from the outside busy world of our eclectic daily lives to the intentional open space of prayer. I think of this initial singing as "toning." Accessible to everyone, toning is a way to massage body, mind and spirit from the inside out. It is a way of synchronizing the vibrations in the room, an open invitation regardless of how each person has entered. Toning may be on a single note or vowel or it may be the opening song of the service. The intention is to welcome, to open up the space for participation, and to prepare us for the moment when we move from a "me" to a "we."

Making music together is a unique way to be in community as it simultaneously engages both the individual voice and the harmony of voices together. The action of singing is a powerful language, different than speaking. Bypassing the intellect, the song for both listener and singer helps us to access our creative soul. This takes us to the place where we are challenged fiercely by our emotions to be present in our needs, hopes, dreams, gratitude and difficulties.

Space Between the Notes

Often, I find that it is in the space between the musical notes - when the singer takes a breath, in the pauses of a piece, when the music concludes - where prayer happens. In some ways, the song teaches the singer how to breathe. It's worth exploring the different elements of the action of singing. We open our mouths and take in a breath, this is where intention is gathered. We pause at the top of the breath and this is where intention is established and set. With the out breath, we let the vocal chords begin to buzz, joining intention with palpable sound vibration. We then pause at the bottom of the breath and this is where intention sinks into the body, heart, mind and soul. This vibration aligns with other vibrations in the space creating harmony and balance. The high frequency vibration of these music notes harmonizes much more than just the circle of fifths!

With the slightest bit of focus, participants are brought together by the sheer nature of this feeling in the room. The conclusion of a prayer is often in the moments after the song or chant, the beats of non-singing that may last a few breaths or a few minutes. This is perhaps when the *ikar* (essence) of the intention sinks into the soul.

I understand that when participants walk in the door, they've chosen to "show up" and in exactly the way they are capable in that moment. Every person enters with their own shadows, needs and availability. I am not interested in getting into their headspace in order to push or pull them to where I want them to be. I trust in the nature of communal singing and gathering. Rather my work is to craft a worship experience through the flow of music and intention in which hopefully all will find their place.

Throughout a service, I pay close attention to my sense of the room and the participants' alignment with the music. I may adjust in any given moment to ensure that everyone feels the invitation to the experience whether they enter through singing or through silence. I hope that all members of the leadership team including instrumentalists share this intention, which every member of the team sees themselves as *shlichei tzibur* (prayer leaders, literally "public emissaries") whose role it is to activate their voices, be it violin, percussion or text, and radiate light for the *kahal* (community) to step into.

A Siddur Full of Stories

As we move through the worship experience, the *siddur* (prayer book) or the leader's guiding words offer us the possibility of different intentions to explore, each with its own *ikar* (essence). There are stories to tell and my role is to choose one to reveal and offer to the *kahal* (community). I may or may not express this in a guided *kavanah* or spoken intention before the song, but I will choose the musical setting for the prayer that tells a particular story. For example, the *"Modeh Ani"* is a morning prayer recited upon waking that offers thanks to the Source of Life for returning one's soul and for having great faith. This may be the story of transition from sleep to wakefulness in which case the setting may be a low and grounded chant that expresses the grumbling and mumbling of the body as it stirs from one consciousness to another. Maybe the story is one of *"Modeh"* (gratitude), where I choose a setting that opens up a space in between the musical notes for personal notes of thanks to arise.

Maybe the story is of *"Ani l'fanecha,"* (I Stand Before You) supported by strong melody to uplift and inspire the soul to stand before its Creator. Or maybe the story is of *"Rabah emunatecha,"* (great faith) with music that soars, expressing the incredibly positive and healthy notion that the Source of Life has great faith in us.

Zemer of Yah

Being a worship leader and engaging in the power of song has also allowed me to explore the meaning of my own story. At different times in my life I have delved deeply into particular texts that I needed to explore through music. About a year ago, the text *"Ozi v'zimrat Yah vay'hi li lishuah* (from Shirat Hayam, Exodus 15:2 and again in Psalm 118:14) popped out of a Conservative prayer book one Shabbat morning and challenged every cell in my body. A loose translation may be "My strength and the melody of God will be my salvation." At first I wanted to understand the word *"Y'shuah"* (salvation). I spoke with many people including Southern Baptists, Kabbalah teachers, Torah scholars, and Zen Buddhist priests. I learned about the many complex stories of salvation and their implications. I understood that this word has to do with life and death, being saved, understanding freedom, being fully aware of one's purpose, and finding balance within the complexities of life.

So the essential question that I had to ask myself was, what in the world is the *Zemer* (the melody, from the Hebrew Zimrat) of *Yah* (Source of Life, breath, salvation)? What does it sound like? What does it feel like? Is there One *Zemer* that everything can hear? Or does every living thing have its own *zemer*? As I learned from Rabbi Arthur Waskow, the "Yahhhhh" is like my out breath and so I knew that whatever this *zemer* was, it had to be something that expressed the very breath and heartbeat of me and of the world.

My exploration of the *Zemer* began with listening from the ground up. When the earth sings, what is its song? How does each sound —the deep soil, the cool stones and the river flow? What happens when the *rakia*, the expanse, mingles with the mountains, oceans, and all growing things? Is it a harmony or an echo? From here I flew on high to listen to the angel's song, light and airy. Finally, I explored my place in it. I found myself sitting by a waterfall and listening to the powerful flow of water as it poured down and danced around every in and out of the pebbles over which it flowed. I listened carefully to this song of the vertical, Jacob's Ladder stretching from heaven to earth. And four parts of a song were born, each one singing a different dimension of the *Zemer* of *Yah*.

Ikar, The Essence of Prayer

With any story to be told, I believe that music is an action that is meant to be felt and experienced. I choose a piece of music to paint, design, construct, tell, whisper, shout out, and express: To really BE the *ikar*, the essence of the prayer. I do feel that the success of the musical moment has to do with the focus of the prayer leader to set the intention. I also believe that the spiritual experience is as wide as the imagination. If the heart of the musical prayer leader flies, the *kahal* (community) will fly. In order for this to work I feel that the sacred circle must truly be an open space for growth and exploration. I do not want to fill in the space for the participant but rather I am comfortable in the knowledge that an open space makes it possible for anything to happen and is the only way for new experience to occur. In this way, the music cannot be an end to itself but is a vehicle in which the hearts of the prayers fly. Every person present is part of *Makom* and no matter what the diverse levels of scholarship or musical aptitude are in the space, there is no hierarchy of prayer when we sing together. Sometimes I imagine that I am building a flying machine and once all are aboard, we fly together. Imagine the machine: you need safety and invitation, doorways and entryways, solid structure and foundation, sparks of magic, wings, expanse, and sometimes the dare of the challenge. You also need landing gear and a nice long runway for coming back home. All in a day's work for a song. And all within the *Zimrahh of Yahh*.

Shira Kline

Named as one of the "New re-engineers of Jewish Life," Shira Kline enlivens rituals and holiday celebrations and inspires a love for Jewish life and prayer with children and adults alike. Shira—"ShirLaLa"—is an internationally recognized, award-winning performer, educator and artist. She tours extensively throughout the United States and internationally with performances in Canada, England, Italy, Israel, Australia and New Zealand. Her popular *ShirLaLa Jewish Kiddie Rock* CDs (ShirLaLa.com) are played in over 25,000 homes, classrooms and communities. She also publishes *"Blog Sameach,"* an online teacher and parent resource center.

Shira serves on the faculty of the HUC-JIR Debbie Friedman School of Sacred Music and the URJ's Hava Nashira Music Institute. Shira Kline is a co-founder of Lab/Shul (LabShul.org) and Storahtelling, "an everybody-friendly, artist driven experimental community for sacred Jewish gatherings" where she currently serves as worship leader, trainer and musical director.

http://ShiraKline.CreatingCalmNetworkPublishingGroup.com

Growing Your Spiritual Community

1. What is the space like in the place or places of your spiritual practice? What shape best describes it? Can you find the circle? Talk about how this statement feels to you, "When I am with a community of young children, I imagine the circle as a garden where all things grow. The

circle I construct is a field for creation and participation, a space to activate and elevate the imagination."

2. How does your spiritual practice start? Is music used to welcome and engage people at the very beginning?

3. Does your practice or community use silence or a period of time after the singing or music? What do you feel and do during the silences?

4. Do you think of the songs in the *siddur* as stories? If so, what is your favorite story from the prayer book?

5. Have you ever listened to the sounds of the earth or nature? What have you heard? Have they ever been a distraction?

6. Consider this statement from Shira Kline, "I close the piece with the words Zimrahh of Yahh (spelled this way specifically) to remind the reader of the breath-nature of the word Yahhhh."

Synagogue Music and Kavannah
George Henschel

Music stirs the soul. I can't explain exactly how, but it does. There's something about setting texts to melodies that transforms them. It's as if the song takes the words and spins them around and around until the words and the music are one. And amazingly enough, one doesn't even need words to experience this effect. A simple *"yai-dai-dai"* or *"ai-ai-ai"* can weave the same spell---sometimes an even greater one. And when it comes to setting a prayerful mood, or expressing one's greatest urges towards spiritual oneness, there's nothing like music.

Being a Cantor in today's synagogue involves more than singing with operatic talent and deep passion to inspire one's congregants. If that were the case, with my pleasant but less than opera-quality voice, I would not be a good choice for Cantor. From my experience, while most congregants today do appreciate an occasional venture into *hazzanut* and vocal fireworks, they seek a more balanced approach to their synagogue music, an approach that engages them and calls for their active participation. As I often say, there are many ways for a person to "participate" in music, and one of these involves listening and not singing. As anyone who has attended a Yom Kippur evening service can attest, listening to the Cantor chant the *Kol Nidre* three times, each one rising higher and higher, is truly a participatory event. But congregants today want to sing, and the liturgical melodies that I write are generally designed for unison or call-and-response singing with the Cantor. When I lead congregational singing, my intention, the

254

direction of my heart--my *kavannah*-- provides the framework for my congregants to establish their own.

Become A Cantor

As a young man, the thought of becoming a cantor never occurred to me. My family moved from Brooklyn, NY, to Franconia, New Hampshire—true culture shock-- about nine months before my Bar Mitzvah. I studied my Torah and *Haftarah* with a large, reel-to-reel Wollensak tape recorder (remember them?). And then my active involvement in Jewish life essentially ceased until I was in my late twenties. I was married and living in Northern Virginia, and when my first daughter was old enough for preschool, we began looking for a synagogue. We joined a small congregation that called itself "progressive conservative," and when they started a choir, I became a member. This was the beginning of my involvement in synagogue music. In my "real life," as I called it, I practiced law at the U. S. Department of Labor. Today I jokingly refer to myself as a "recovering lawyer."

While I had sung in choral groups since my elementary school days, I had never experienced the emotional connection that comes from actually leading a congregation in song. And when I finally had that experience for the first time, it came with some heavy baggage. Our choir had been preparing for the High Holy Days, with one of our members, our friend, Joel, serving as the congregation's cantorial soloist, as he had for several years. About a month before *Rosh Hashana*, we received the shocking news that Joel had died.

Obviously, our congregation needed to deal with the pain and sadness of losing Joel, and it was a difficult time. But there was also the practical issue: someone needed to step forward to help the Rabbi with the music for the approaching Holy Days. And since I was a long-time member of the choir, sometimes as a soloist, several other members approached me and asked if I could handle the task. After all, I could sing fairly well, and I could sight-read music quite effectively. I remember thinking that my folks didn't raise me to do this! Nonetheless, given the situation, I agreed to give it a try.

At the time, it was difficult for a layman to obtain High Holy Day music; the cantorial schools held their collections closely and tightly to restrict access only to their students, not to people like me. But I persevered and was able to obtain a copy of Israel Alter's book of High Holy Day music. Alter's collection was pretty complete, but it was filled with seemingly endless runs up and down the scale and ornamentation that boggled my mind. Nothing like starting at the top, I thought. But I managed to simplify it enough for my purposes, and I was able to cobble together a quite-workable set of services for *Rosh Hashana* and *Yom Kippur*. The congregation definitely appreciated my hard work, and I was rather amazed at how deeply the entire experience touched me: I seemed to inhabit a special space in which I connected the congregation with the Divine Presence.

After that first High Holy Day experience, I began studying on my own to learn music for the various Festivals and other services, as well as life cycle events. And for the next 20 years, I essentially became my congregation's "lay cantor". I never called myself "the Cantor," because I had not gone to cantorial school, and I felt I had not earned the title. But I will admit that it bothered me when our Rabbi would introduce me or thank me for "serving as Cantor."

With all of that as preface: about 10 years ago, I decided that I wanted to take the steps necessary to remove that "serving as" from the title of Cantor. So I enrolled at a small transdenominational seminary in Baldwin, New York. Several years later, after studying with many wonderful cantors, including the great Sol Zim, I received my cantorial certification. I was finally a Cantor! And I was fortunate enough to begin my cantorial career with a small but growing Reconstructionist synagogue in Baltimore, Kol HaLev. I helped conduct the congregation's first High Holy Day services that year, and this fall will mark the beginning of my eighth year there. It has been a warm and wonderful relationship, and I am most grateful for the congregation and the people that I have met there. And one element that I treasure is the willingness of Rabbi Geoff Basik and the congregation to allow me to write music for the liturgy and to share it with them.

Writing Melodies

Before becoming a Cantor, I had only written one piece of liturgical music in my life: a setting for *Avinu Shebashamayim*, the Prayer for Israel that appears in the Conservative Siddur *Sim Shalom*. It was a melody that had actually bounced around in my head on the flight back from Israel one summer. I jotted down some notation for the melody on the plane, and when I got home, I realized that the melody fit the prayer exceptionally well. The choir director in my former synagogue wrote a lovely four-part harmony for my melody, and I understand that the choir still sings it even though I am long gone.

I probably have developed a rather unusual method of choosing which pieces of liturgy are in need of my musical talents. Like so many other Jewish songwriters, I have written my share of music for the "old favorites" such as *V'Sham'ru* and *Oseh Shalom*. But one of the joys of the Reconstructionist siddur, *Kol Haneshama*, is the variety of different readings, texts, and other pieces of liturgy that I've encountered for the first time. And most of these additions or insertions have never been set to music, to the best of my knowledge. I often refer to these texts as "orphan liturgy," because they have not had the opportunity to experience how wonderful it is to be embraced and sung by a congregation. And when liturgy is sung to a melody that inhabits and enhances that text, it gains special power--- whether it is expressing praise or gratitude or wonder, or any combination.

Orphan Liturgy

In the past year, I have written musical settings for several of these pieces of "orphan liturgy." One of these settings is particularly close to my heart. I call it the "*Shacharit Kavannah*." In the *P'sukei D'zimrah*, the introductory part of the Shabbat morning service, *Siddur Kol Haneshama* includes an affirmation that addresses the union of *HaKadosh Baruch Hu* with the *Shechinah*—often referred to as the masculine and feminine sides of the Eternal One. This *kavannah* was originally introduced by the *kabbalists of Safed*, as an introduction to the *Birkat Hashachar*, the Morning Blessings, And in this affirmation, each of us states that we stand here, ready in body and mind, for the sake of the Blessed Holy.

Mitzvah

One with the *Shechinah*, to take upon ourselves the following Mitzvah: *V'ahavta l'reiacha kamocha*---"You shall love your fellow human being as yourself." And only by this affirmation are we given the right to come before G-d in worship, to open our mouths in prayer. It is a striking, stunning moment in the service. As Arthur Green explains in his commentary, "Only by accepting upon ourselves the obligation to love others as ourselves are we allowed to enter the human community of prayer." So instead of merely standing and beginning to recite the morning blessings, we must first take stock of ourselves. Before we bless the Creator for all the things for which we are grateful, we must assert our acceptance of the need to take these blessings to the human level, where we have the power to extend their reach. And we need to focus the mind and the intention on this assertion before we can continue with the morning blessings.

In writing my musical setting for this *kavannah*, I attempted to give voice to the solemnity and importance of what it asks of us. Although the *kavannah* is written in first person singular, we are making our affirmations both individually and as part of a community. Hence, the melody needs to enable us to find our own cores and link them with our fellow congregants. And don't we all hope that our community shares the focus of the *kavannah* with us? What better way is there for us to share the commitment than to sing it together with true intention?

In this way, the music connects us with the prayer, with our own hearts, and with each other.

Kavannah

The word *kavannah* is usually thought of as an individual quality. As an individual, no matter how strong my *kavannah* might be, there is no way to guarantee that yours is just as strong as mine at a given moment. The reverse is also true. If you are truly "in the moment," you cannot be sure that I am, too. But that is truly why we need to use music to connect us. We all know how easy it is for some small disturbance to break our mood and our concentration, regardless of where we are. But when the desired *kavannah* is carried and reinforced by music---be it music that is sung together, or music that is done in a call-and-response manner, or music that is sung by the Cantor alone---it is less likely to be easily interrupted. It is as if our combined attention to the music strengthens the *kavannah* and protects against disturbances.

I have found over the years that *kavannah* is often more about melody than about text or liturgy. When the music captures the mood and the meaning of the moment, it can establish and maintain the requisite *kavannah* whether or not everyone understands the words being sung. The converse is rarely true; the words alone—the *keva*--will not often find their *kavannah* if they do not have a musical vehicle to carry them. But when the melody and the text are well-integrated, they provide the perfect vehicle: a blending of *keva* and *kavannah* that elevate the body and the soul.

George Henschel

Cantor George Henschel began his journey through Jewish music as a choir member and cantorial soloist in Northern Virginia for nearly 20 years. A "recovering attorney," he retired from legal practice in 2003 and enrolled at the American Seminary for Contemporary Judaism, receiving his Cantorial Certification in May, 2007. He has been the Cantor at Kol HaLev, a small Reconstructionist congregation in Baltimore, MD, for nearly seven years.

Cantor George has composed musical settings for various liturgical texts. He feels that music is a necessary element of our connections with the Eternal, with our community, and with each other. To Cantor George, the music carries our thoughts, our fears, our hopes, and our love---music with words, music without words. Congregational singing is a uniquely spiritual experience.

Cantor George is also a skilled calligrapher, specializing in certificates for baby namings and B'nei Mitzvah. He also writes an occasional blog for Kol HaLev, and teaches classes on various aspects of Jewish music.

In his spare time, Cantor George is a dedicated hockey fan, as well as a skilled cruciverbalist (crossword puzzle aficionado) who has finished as high as second in the American Crossword Puzzle Tournament.

http://GeorgeHenschel.CreatingCalmNetworkPublishingGroup.com

Growing Your Spiritual Community

1. If you attend synagogue services, are there musical parts of the service that you look forward to hearing or singing? What is it about those sections that affect you the most?

2. Do you ever find yourself closing your eyes during the singing? How would you envision using the music to enhance your kavannah or intention?

3. Imagine the life of a cantor in your place of worship. Has it changed in the last 50 years?

4. Have you had a bat or bar mitzvah? Compare or contrast your experience of Judaism in the year before your bar or bat mitzvah and the year after.

5. Have you ever been surprised by your ability to stretch into a new role when asked?

6. Have you wanted to sing or pray from the Reconstructionist prayer book, Kol Haneshama?

7. Do you know a text which you think of as an "orphan liturgy" or a piece of text which touches you but has not been set to music?

8. Does singing and praying in a group improve your mood and concentration? Does it help you to avoid disturbances in your thoughts and emotions?

9. Do you agree with these ideas: "When the music captures the mood and the meaning of the moment, it can establish and maintain the requisite *kavannah* whether or not everyone understands the words being sung. The converse is rarely true; the words alone—the *keva*--will not often find their *kavannah* if they do not have a musical vehicle to carry them?"

What Chanting a Prayer Might Just Do For You
Diane J. Schmidt

The *Sh'ma* prayer, "Here O Israel, the Lord our God, the Lord is One," came to me, but only in a rote way, when I was a twenty-seven-year-old photojournalist in El Salvador being tailed by a death squad. It was the only prayer I could remember from my early Jewish education. Now three decades later I finally am beginning to understand why it came to me when it did, in a life-threatening situation, what the *Sh'ma* means, and what it means to me today.

I now am learning more in the Jewish Renewal community in New Mexico. And because for the first time in many years I now stand together with other Jews reciting or chanting the *Sh'ma* and feel a surge of identification and belonging, and because after spending so many years exposed to Navajo spirituality, my understanding is greatly enhanced in the light of that exposure—and I see no difference in speaking of the Spirit in different languages.

Darkening of the Light (excerpt from my unpublished political memoir)

May 14, 1981 El Salvador – In the village I found the justice of the peace in a one-room blue adobe building with the door and window shutters opened. On the left sat a woman at a typewriter. Spaced along the back were two men at desks. When I walked in I knew it was the man there on the left; when he saw me come in he stiffened. I sat down to wait.

When he was free the judge motioned to me and we went out to the back porch. The conversation that day was with a man who was, for all intents and purposes, dead. When I asked him his name, he whispered it. He told me he had months earlier been promised political asylum by the US Embassy and asked for my help. I promised I would do what I could for him.

On the way back to the capital, along the winding mountainous roads, as the taxi driver rounded a certain bend he again half-heartedly asked if I wanted to stop for a swim, something he had seemed particularly anxious for me to do as we passed this place earlier that day. As we slowed, I glanced in the rear view mirror. We were being closely followed by a dark Jeep Wagoneer with wood paneling and tinted windows and a rifle was poking out the back window.

I slowly curled down into the back seat and prayed to every name of God I could think of. The one prayer I knew came back to me from childhood – the *Sh'ma*. I repeated it until we got back into the city, *Sh'ma Yisrael, Adonai Elohaynu, Adonai Echad*; Hear O Israel, the Lord our God, the Lord is One.

Asking Questions

My interest in Judaism would remain dormant. Twenty years later, I moved out west from Chicago to Tucson and began working at the University of Arizona. Soon after I arrived, I visited the Navajo reservation and Monument Valley for a freelance travel story for the *Chicago Tribune*. In the early morning darkness a voice came to me in a dream saying, "Keep asking questions."

Back in Tucson, I volunteered in the Yaqui community's youth arts program initiated by Arts Genesis Director Carol S. Kestler, a member of Jewish Renewal, although at the time I didn't know what that was. Unfolding events led me to meeting my future life partner Frank Morgan, Navajo philosopher, cultural linguist, and educator. I moved to New Mexico, where my exposure to Navajo culture and spirituality developed over many years. As my sense of connection to the spiritual grew, so finally did my interest in learning more about Judaism. At this point I encountered Rabbi Gershon Winkler, whose interest in Native American teachings opened the door to my renewed interest in Judaism, and I probably am now a *NavaJew*.

Grounded in Spirit

The part that had tripped me up, that part about 'the Lord is One'— which I had associated with the word 'monotheism' and an anthropomorphic God, and which had always presented a block to me, I now see as a misunderstanding born of a matter of translation into American and Christian culture: the English words simply don't do justice to Judaism.

As a child, somewhere I had picked up this idea of God as a sort of Santa Claus, who kept an eye on my drives and desires, which of course never really made much sense. My only connection to the spiritual in Judaism as a child, to something that spoke to my higher self, was in an outdoor evening prayer service at Camp Union Institute in Oconomowoc, Wisconsin. We sat on wooden benches in the darkness and as the fireflies came out, I reached out with my senses to feel the trees, the night, the stars. That experience probably comes closer to what I believe is meant in the Sh'ma, and yet at best to speak of God and of knowing what God is presents a paradox.

The best in Judaism—its ethics, its pluralism, and its flexibility—originates, I think, in its awareness of the sacred in everything. I now understand, most importantly, that in Judaism "the Lord is One" in the *Sh'ma* does not especially or even necessarily refer to an anthropomorphic God on high. As learned Jewish scholar Arthur Kurzweil writes in *Kabbalah for Dummies* (I highly recommend all his books, and they are not for 'dummies'): "The prayer is rich with meaning, every word having layers of significance. But the essence of the prayer is a meditation on the oneness of the universe: God is One, everything is God, and everything is One." Very simple!

That of course is not to say things cannot get out of balance. They can and do and harmony must be restored—in Navajo cosmology, patterned after the sacred pattern of the natural world—and upon occasion I have been privileged to attend all-night sings.

That *Kabbalistic* approach feels akin to what in English we have mislabeled Native American traditions, denoting something inadequate: as "animism" or "pantheism" or "nature-worship." A deeply unfortunate misconception underlying that is the presumption that Native Americans do not have an over-arching concept of God – they do. As my Navajo partner said over coffee one morning, "Everything is divine, everything is sacred—The Great Spirit—that's the way he placed everything." They just don't go around *naming* God – hmm, sound familiar? They also don't have a word for "religion," since that would be oxymoronic, separating the spiritual from life.

Coming Full Circle

I wonder what the big deal is, really, that causes so many of the world's religions to insist that theirs is the only one true way, that they are the only ones who've got it right, and not only that, to kill one another over bad translations!

I was also surprised to hear the word *Shima* spoken in Navajo, pronounced like Sh'ma, and which in Navajo means "my mother." Rather than Navajos insisting they are the keepers of the one true spiritual path, Frank explained their teaching, "They say that each ethnic group was given its own ways." The way I understand that is that just as bluebirds and robins and crows each have been given their own songs, customs and plumage, each grouping of humanity has been given its own songs, language, and prayers, its own way to give voice to the spiritual. One way is not "better" than another.

Recently I asked Rabbi Min Kantrowitz, Director of Shutafim, to meet me for lunch to help me understand the *Sh'ma*. At the last minute I asked Frank to join us and so we convened in an informal cross-cultural dialogue over pad Thai in a restaurant on Central Avenue in Albuquerque. Rabbi Kantrowitz re-translated the standard English translation of "Here O Israel, The Lord our God" by translating from the Hebrew "*Sh'ma Yisrael, Adonai Elohaynu.*" She explained that *Sh'ma* means, "Pay Attention, listen with your ears," and *Yisrael*, the name Jacob was given after wrestling with the angel, is "You

267

who wrestle with God, who struggles with trying to understand what God is," and that *Adonai Elohaynu* refers to the unpronounceable name of God, the Tetragrammaton "[YHVH]." The conversation opened up and Frank talked at length about the Navajo transcendent concept of God, which led Rabbi Min to exclaim in an almost child-like voice of wonder, "That's exactly my God concept!"

In Judaism, the *Sh'ma* is recited twice a day, in the morning and in the evening. In one sense it is recited to provide protection. Another, more obscure, Jewish teaching is that the *Sh'ma* is recited every day to make sure that it may be on your lips when you die. Things come full circle when you least expect them to. Suddenly I realized how appropriate it was that this one prayer drummed into me as a child, the one prayer I knew, had come into my head as a talisman, a protection, in a frozen slow-motion hour when I was faced with death.

I'm not a cantor or a rabbi, nor am I a very diligent student of Torah, and I still struggle with the concept of prayer. I'm a writer and sometimes a reporter, so these are explorations for me. The good news that I have to report is that a minute, an hour, a night of spiritually focused singing or chanting can definitely raise your spirits and bring you out of dark places, such as the places that those memories from El Salvador would hold me in. I recommend it.

You never know what chanting a prayer might do, or might have done for you, or where it might lead you. I remember the voice that came to me in the dream I had when I first visited Monument Valley, "Keep asking questions," and how indeed, by doing so, unwittingly I have become "one who wrestles with God."

Diane J. Schmidt

Diane J. Schmidt is a writer, photographer, educator and public speaker. Her work addresses both the seen and the unseen worlds. She covers social and environmental issues in the Southwest and enjoys giving talks with her photos that document coincidence and spirituality in dangerous situations.

Her national awards include a National Endowment for the Arts Visual Arts Fellowship for her photo essays on the city at night published in the *Chicago Tribune Sunday Magazine*, and more recently 1st Place for enterprise reporting from the National Federation of Press Women, a Robert R. McCormick Fellowship to the Poynter Institute for journalism, and 1st place for news reporting from the Native American Journalist Association.

Memorable projects include the art photo book "The Chicago Exhibition," her memoir as a photojournalist covering the civil war in El Salvador, and producing health education materials and seminars for the Navajo Nation. She has a BA from Prescott College in Arizona, a BFA in photography from the Rhode Island School of Design, and an MA in the creative writing program from the University of New Mexico. She and her husband live in New Mexico.

http://DianeJSchmidt.CreatingCalmNetworkPublishingGroup.com

Growing Your Spiritual Community

1. What is your personal connection to the *Sh'ma*? Do you have a particular memory or event you associate it with?

2. How do you or your community embody Judaism with, "its ethics, its pluralism, and its flexibility?"

3. Do you consider yourself "one who wrestles with God"?

4. What is your concept of God? Is your concept of God informed by several different spiritual traditions?

5. What kind of experiences have you had that originated from a Native American tradition?

Speak To Me
Ruth Anne Faust

Have you ever had a "knock your socks off" prayer experience? I have the *"chutzpah"* [audacity] to expect prayer to speak to me, to engross me, to uplift me, and to expand my portals. Engaging study can do this for me. The spark in a smile, a laugh, the gasp of beauty, the wonder of love, and the joy of a little one in discovery ... these all elevate me. Deep expressions or experiences of emotions and amazement exalt me. A stunning sunrise or sunset, spectacular mountains peaking into the deep blue sky with expressive clouds: these capture me in astonishment and awe-filled expansion. But prayer? What do I know of prayer and how can the words of another touch the cells of my soul to speak to me?

Someone Else's Words

Ah. The first problem I encounter is expecting that someone else's words might speak to ME. Our Jewish traditions have set down a massive offering of liturgy that we share with a community that is to guide us to God—whether Orthodox, Conservative, Reform, Reconstructionist, Renewal, or some other form. Such a challenge! Prescribed words are to speak to an entire community so that we, as individuals, might come together and help one another be elevated to the One as One.

The words in the *Siddur* [prayerbook] often feel constricting to me. Years of repetition, however, brings me comfort and familiarity in the presence of others. But the words often elude me and confound my desire to

271

connect to the One beyond me, to Whom I so yearn to connect. Sometimes it is because I don't fully understand the Hebrew and feel trapped by inadequate English translations. Sometimes I allow the drone of a disconnected cantor and/or congregation, and the distractions of activity and conversation to disengage me from the *avodah* [divine service, creation, worship] of bringing prayer into my heart.

What transforms this for me are certain experiences of music, especially when I am "invited" into a chant or song. There is a rapture that comes with melodies that somehow link the deepest core of my being, engaging my very essence to expand into a world beyond words. It can take me to a place where there are no material boundaries or distractions. It can release me from my worries. I can be transported to a place beyond mind, intellect, and thinking.

I struggle with many physical challenges and limitations. It is so easy to get caught in a downward spiral of fear and reactivity or pain and hopelessness. My work is to elevate and separate these intense struggles from my spirit of joy and vitality, love and wonder, appreciation and well-being. Music, the music of chant that speaks to me, does this. It can uplift me and allow me to offer myself compassion and support while reframing my darkness and disappointment, expectation and impatience. It can help me know that there is more than my physical being. It can offer me a path to The Divine, "the Power of the Universe", the Source of All, The One I long to connect to: *Adonai* – MY GOD! What hubris—I want a personal connection to The Divine!

The Words

The particular phrase and example I'd like to share is one I never thought I'd be able to bond with and, quite honestly, was off-putting. The power of connecting to a chant speaks of the transformational potential of encountering and fully taking in a poignant melody:

Yi'h'yu l'ratzon im-ray fee
v'heg'yon lee-bee l'fah-neh-cha
Adonai tzuree v'go-a-lee

This is usually translated as:
May the words of my mouth and
the meditations of my heart
be acceptable to You, my Rock and my Redeemer.

It is traditionally found in the prayerbook at the end of the *Amidah*, "standing prayer", taken from Psalm 19:15 and attributed to King David.

This used to be a prayer that stopped me cold: "Oh no, another opportunity to feel 'not good enough'. Where do those feelings come from and how do I get past them to allow this prayer to speak to me, through me, to elevate me and release me?

At an enchanting retreat of the Women's Cantors' Network (WCN), Robin Anne Joseph introduced us to a chant for this prayer that 'knocked my socks off,' speaking to me in ways that liberated me from the worry of not being acceptable and inviting me to encounter my heart's desires.

A Jewish educator, not a trained cantor, I found myself in the midst of 90 women whose passion in life is to freely and openly share their love of Judaism through their music with barely an ego present!. Robin's melody released me from my constrictions and transported me to a place of yearning and searching.

I have always loved to sing and found song to be a pathway into connecting to my heart space In recent years I had learned to use American Sign Language to connect more deeply with prayer as I worked with special needs students. The melody Robin offered sent me soaring. I returned home with the tune embedded in my cells and began to personalize the translation.

While I can't offer you the tune here, I'd like to offer the English versions that I created for myself, intertwining these phrases with the two-part melody of Robin's. I imagine you joining me in the midst of the harmonies of magnificent voices that always capture me and bring tears not only to my eyes, but also to my parched heart and soul. I began by retranslating the Hebrew relatively closely to the traditional understanding of this prayer. Then I found myself being moved to beyond the actual Hebrew:

Yi'h'yu l'ratzon im-ray fee
v'heg'yon lee-bee l'fah-neh-cha
Adonai tzuree v'go-a-lee

"May the longing of my words and
the yearning in my heart
be worthy of Your love, my Source and my deep Hope."

Yi'h'yu l'ratzon im-ray fee
v'heg'yon lee-bee l'fah-neh-cha
Adonai tzuree v'go-a-lee

"May the searching of my heart and
this hunger in my soul
open me to be restored as I surrender here to You."

Yi'h'yu l'ratzon im-ray fee
v'heg'yon lee-bee l'fah-neh-cha
Adonai tzuree v'go-a-lee

"I long to sense You near,
may Your Presence be right here
as I open up to You, may I find myself anew."

Yi'h'yu l'ratzon im-ray fee
v'heg'yon lee-bee l'fah-neh-cha
Adonai tzuree v'go-a-lee

"May this fear that dwells within and
the pain I hold so deep
find expression in Your love and offer me release."

Yi'h'yu l'ratzon im-ray fee
v'heg'yon lee-bee l'fah-neh-cha
Adonai tzuree v'go-a-lee

"May I find solace in Your love,
accepting Your Will as it will be done
awakening my soul to feel its Source and
expand into The One."

Yi'h'yu l'ratzon im-ray fee
v'heg'yon lee-bee l'fah-neh-cha
Adonai tzuree v'go-a-lee

"May the weaknesses in my bones and
the weary struggle I expose to You
be cradled in Your wings and
eased by your Essence True."

Yi'h'yu l'ratzon im-ray fee
v'heg'yon lee-bee l'fah-neh-cha
Adonai tzuree v'go-a-lee

"May the doubts within my mind and
the fears deep within my heart
find comfort in You, my God, as
my soul is one with You."

Yi'h'yu l'ratzon im-ray fee
v'heg'yon lee-bee l'fah-neh-cha
Adonai tzuree v'go-a-lee

"May this deep, dark hole within…raw and
crying out in pain
be filled with Your Light and Love,
in this life-soul I try to regain."

Yi'h'yu l'ratzon im-ray fee
v'heg'yon lee-bee l'fah-neh-cha
Adonai tzuree v'go-a-lee

"May the darkness in my heart and
the yearning for Your Light
find acceptance deep within my soul and
be transformed unto Your Might."

Yi'h'yu l'ratzon im-ray fee

v'heg'yon lee-bee l'fah-neh-cha
Adonai tzuree v'go-a-lee

May Your Presence so concealed be opened and
revealed as I search for The Divine and
make it truly mine.

Yi'h'yu l'ratzon im-ray fee
v'heg'yon lee-bee l'fah-neh-cha
Adonai tzuree v'go-a-lee

   This experience has opened a world of possibilities
for connection. The melody is not so much haunting as
totally immersing; it electrifies every cell and challenges
every part of my being—my heart to harmonize in
concert with The One. It was the chant itself that allowed
me, encouraged me, and instructed me to redefine and
retranslate a traditional prayer that had never spoken to
me before. These words have brought me to a felt-sense
of harmony through the music of an angel.
   Beyond words, I thank Robin Anne Joseph as well
as the many other amazing creators I have been blessed
with as teachers and mentors: Shefa Gold, Debbie
Friedman, Joseph Ness, Andrea Cohen-Kiener, Hanna
Tiferet Siegel, Sam Glaser, Craig Taubman, Beged Kefet,
Julie Silver and too many amazing cantors and educators
from WCN to properly identify. Each one has inspired
me and continues to feed my soul. I've drawn from these
artists and encourage you to find the music they offer us
all. Each one, in their own way, leads me out of my
stuckness and offers me the "friendship" and compassion
of expansion, opening, understanding. Through their
musical artistry and passion for sharing their love-

connection to The Divine Source they fill me with music that sends me soaring, helping me to discover what is in my heart, to know of my longings, and to give expression to my yearnings for a personal connection to The Divine.

Ruth Anne Faust

Growing up in Anchorage, Alaska in a devoted, but secular Jewish family, Ruth Anne Faust is thankful to modern orthodox grandparents who shared their passion and love for their Judaism, she was always enticed to learn more.

When Ruth Anne married, she—in the midst of a hectic schedule doing an intense International Montessori educational year—and her husband, Halley—in medical school, on an even busier schedule—decided to set aside Shabbat to insure time together. That opened up a world of Jewish observance and sensibility. Her wise grandparents encouraged her to become kosher so they could come to visit and that was the beginning of more extensive physical connections to Jewish observance. In the process, a deepening relationship to spiritual-soul aspects became paramount.

As Ruth Anne moved from Montessori teacher, to mom of two boys, to providing programming at her synagogues (family, meditation, healing, children's and special needs services), both during Shabbat and mid-week, to working with special needs children in preparation for their Bar/Bat Mitzvah her Jewish studies and explorations of the worlds of wonder, appreciation and *kabbalah* began to round out her sense of self.

Music has always been a pathway into Ruth Anne's heart. Learning chanting over many years with many wonderful teachers (Shefa Gold, Andrea Cohen-Keiner, Karen Drucker, and amazing cantors at the Women's Cantors' Network) created an ongoing, powerful support through challenging times as well as during easier, exultant celebrations. Ruth Anne has found compassion, ease and renewal through music.

Today, Ruth Anne lives with her husband in Santa Fe, New Mexico, appreciating the vistas, gardening, refreshing air, amazing hiking and community. They both spend significant amounts of time enjoying and helping with granddaughters in the East, along with their sons and daughter-in-law. She visits her Alaska family each summer and spends more and more time in celebration and wonder.

http://RuthAnnFaust.CreatingCalmNetworkPublishingGroup.com

Growing Your Spiritual Community

1. What do you expect from prayer and the prayer book?
2. If you look around yourself, what elevates you? Have you ever had a "knock your socks off" prayer experience?
3. As you sing, chant, or pray, do you think about who wrote the words? Do the words come from a similar tradition as your own? How is your current spiritual practice different or the same as the writer of the music or words?
4. Do you connect to the words in both Hebrew and English or better in one or the other or some other language?
5. How does music, singing, praying change how you see your physical challenges?

6. Are you confident? Are you doing your best? Where do you go when you hear or say the words:

Yi'h'yu l'ratzon im-ray fee
v'heg'yon lee-bee l'fah-neh-cha
Adonai tzuree v'go-a-lee

May the words of my mouth
and the meditations of my heart
be acceptable to You,
my Rock and my Redeemer.

As I Intended

Summer 2013,
I intended
to bicycle 3300 miles
across the US
raising money and awareness
for Hazon,
for sustainability,
for healing,
for this
amazing planet

I intended
to keep kosher,
eat healthy,
lose weight,
drink lots of water
sing and pray
more connecting within
in 20 Jewish communities
as I rode East
from Seattle to Washington, DC.
through the very heart of a country

I intended to get enough sleep,
stay dry,
bask in the sunlight,
notice the beauty around me,
listen to the birds,
and ride like the wind
to push myself physically,
mentally, emotionally, spiritually

to stay in one piece, *Shalem*
to find my inner peace, *Shalom*

I intended to learn how to be a Jew,
a little more Hebrew,
to know myself better
to know God
the God of the people around me
the God of patterned fractals
and the natural world
the God of Oneness

I intended to create a bridge
from West to East
between us and them
from this space where I am
to all of whom I can be
to find the narrow places
once explored leading to a bend
in the fabric of reality
where I could reach through
the unknown
and know

I succeeded in many ways
achieving my intended goals
as I rode and sang and prayed
most of all my intentions changed me
changed my relationships
changed the communities around me
all the ones I touched
changed
and I will never be the same

as I intended all along
with this journey

—**Kimberly Burnham**, from the upcoming book of poetry, *The Journey Home*

Growing Your Spiritual Community

1. Have you challenged yourself physically, emotionally or spiritually with a big goal? How old were you?
2. Do you have a vision board or specific goals that you have written or drawn out? Do you make lists of your goals?

Adamah V'shamayim, The Illusion
Between Sound and Silence
Kimberly Burnham

Adamah V'shamayim, is forever lashed to my bicycle, the lightweight baby blue Trek, I rode 3000 across the very heart of America on Hazon's 2013 Cross USA ride for sustainable agriculture, food justice and our legacy to the next generation.

Heat of Fire

Heat of fire,
drop of water,
I can feel it in my body,
in my spirit
and in my soul.

The words of Shimon Suissa, a 20th century poet connects us to our senses and to our environment. These words, from the song, *Adamah V'shamayim*, connect earth—*adamah* and sky—*shamayim*.

Like the land, music and songs are passed from one generation to the next. Like the land, music is changed by the hands and hearts that touch it and are touched by it. There are people, like the song catcher, who try to capture the songs, the melodies, the words, the intentions, and the feelings of the songs and preserve them for us all.

But like language, melodies and lyrics are fluid. They are changed by the lips that utter them and the minds that contemplate them. The languages we learn and use transform us. When we see others' responses to our words we are also changed.

If I sing off key, I see the looks on the faces around me and I adjust my behavior. If I sing the wrong word or forget the melody, I hear the discord with those around me. I am changed, not only by the words and by the melody of my song, but by the responses, be it subtle or exaggerated, of those around me. I am in relationship to others as I sing—and to the natural world—the wind, the water ...

Strong wind,
deep water,
tall trees,
warm fire,
I can feel it in my body,
I can feel it in my soul.

—The Israeli group, Bayit Chadash's version of *Adamah V'shamayim.*

The Sound I Am Making

One of my teachers, sound healer, Jill Purce says, *"It is more important to listen to the sound you are making than to make the sound you are listening to."*

There is something that happens to us when we hear ourselves, truly hear what we are saying, singing, praising, and being. As I bicycled across the land, I had so much time to think, to listen, and to feel. I thought about the land. I thought about the wind, the sun, and the rain. I listened to the birds—snow white pelicans, red winged black birds, blue jays, and cardinals. I listened for the different voices that told me the abundant variety of birds in the fields, lakes and forests around me.

The wind sounds different when it is hitting you full in the face as you ride as compared to when it is pushing you, easing your way, helping you from behind. It is almost silent as it blows from behind a bicyclist. Like a tornado whooshing, it sounds, when it blows straight into your face, as you bump up against reality. The world is changed when you encounter the physical vibrations of this world. Some might even say you bring your reality into existence as you bump up against the environment.

Adamah and *shamayim* meeting at the horizon all around you evokes thinking about what is important. Why am I here crossing the land, riding forward towards the Eastern horizon? It was always ahead, the horizon, that thin line between up and down, between earth and sky. A goal, it is nonetheless—an illusion. Beautiful, sometimes it is seems so real, that winding line between the top of the lush green mountains and the purple red clouds at sunset. But look closely. Where is it—where the dirt meets the air? What do you see?

Precious

What is precious to you? Where is the line between the red earth, full of iron, carbon, nitrogen, hydrogen, potassium, calcium, sodium, silica, and oxygen and the abundant air full of nitrogen and oxygen? They are not the same—earth and sky but where exactly is the line separating them, and then separating them and us. Where is the line between the nitrogen and oxygen of the earth and those same elements of the sky? Look closely and you will see the illusion.

So it is with sound and silence. Where is the line in between? Where do the molecules of sound end and the elements of silence begin? What touches your heart more deeply, the sound or the silence, the earth or the sky? The line between is just a delusion.

Sometimes that line is a battle line: Is it evolving? Who created it? Who owns it? Is it God-inspired, or is it scientific? Is it one or the other as we sit in the duality of life? Where is the line between the unity of the universe?

When camping with a thin tent between you and the wind, the rain, and the sound, the illusion of separation is less real. When you look for a soft flat spot to pitch your tent, you feel the earth and you look at the sky. You wonder what the night will bring. And you know the separation between light and dark is not real. And you hope for "dry earth and warm fire" and sometimes you get, "cold wind and deep water."

Music that touches us deeply is complex. It is not one or the other. There is no duality. It is not yours or mine. It is not good or bad. It simply touches us. Touch is that sensation that goes both ways. When I touch you, I feel something and you feel something. It is not the same, what each of us feels but we both experience something. So it is with sound drumming on my eardrums. I feel something, as does the being creating the sound. It might be a person, an animal or the elements of this earth and sky.

Sometimes there are no words but simply sounds and rhythms that reach inside and draw the very best from each of us. "*Heya... heya ... heya ... heya ... heya ... heya ... heya ... ho,* " wrote, Shimon Lev-Tahor Suissa, he set the words to a folk tune, said to be from a New Zealand Maori refrain which also connects us to the land and to the past.

Vision of the Land

Hazon—Vision in Hebrew—the largest Jewish environmental, food justice and sustainable agriculture organization has adopted this song, *Adamah V'shamayim*, almost like an anthem. It is a reminder to "*love the earth, love the sky.*"

For me, the melody and words of the song trigger memories of days in the sun, of rainstorms, of love and laughter, of touching the earth, riding towards the horizon and reaching for the sky. And I wonder what is it about this particular arrangements of notes laced with memories that draws me into the invisible realm of spirit that can't be seen but can be heard and felt.

This particular pattern of sounds and letters familiar now is irrevocable linked with a life changing experience tied to this amazing land. I rode to raise awareness of the preciousness of our environment and I rode intimately connected to the land and the elements. I bicycled to help the world and the children of generations to come but it was I that grew and felt and learned the most. With the connection to earth, sky and people, despair's flock lifted from my body like a cloud of geese. Emotions danced at the edge where the water meets the land. Sensations like an abstract painting until we see them, and recognize the beauty with gratitude for all there is for us to experience, if we just look.

Up close, the river is a blur of motion like an impressionist painting. Blobs of paint on the life's canvas come into focus as we gain some distance. The land is like poetry in motion; a second look gives a stronger impression.

Aki Cosmos

Each community has a way of ordering their universe. In the Ojibwa tradition, Aki, they tell the story of a land where once was no pollution and springs flowed still clearly through the heart of mother earth; where flocks of eagles soared in the sky, whitefish abounded in the lakes and countless deer roamed the woods in herds. "Traditionally, the People of the Anishinaabeg and the land are one. They are one complete thing. All life forms are considered animated and inter-related "persons" or "relatives" possessing a consciousness, rationale, and a will of their own. Thus, taken in the widest sense, Aki not only means "earth" or "country" but also "cosmos." The sacred web of life can be traced back to one cosmic source." —Zhaawano Guzhik in *The Universe of the Ojibwe / Anishnaabeg*.

Mountains

As I moved between here and there, as if climbing this mountain brings me to a different place, any more than singing this song transports me into a different reality; it is I who move and is moved. Time and space and sound change me, ordering my life in a new and more beautiful way.

The mountain and the *parsha* or Torah passage, *Behar Sinai* begins with an explanation of the *shmita* year. How will this year be different from the last seven or from the last 49? *Shmita* is a Shabbat or rest for the land with a prohibition on planting and harvesting your land. It is an opportunity to look at how we eat. On Shabbat or the *shmita* year will you change how you travel or donate money? I recently had a chance to help someone in debt to make a fresh start. It was someone I love and for whom I would do anything. It broke my heart when I learned of her debt and of her struggle. I felt like I should have known; I should have done something sooner but we can each only do what we see.

Some of our connection to the land and community is about how we live our lives, how we plan the future and how we feel about ourselves. *"Be kind, for everyone you meet is fighting a hard battle."* Ian Maclaren attributes this quote to the philosopher, Plato.

Hazon's Nigel Savages asks us to consider the future, the next *Shmita*: "Where will you be in September 2022? How will your *shul*, school or home be different? You could decide to plant fruit and nut trees that will come to fruition by then. You could spend time discussing as a community how to establish an integrated food policy in your institution—covering not only *kashrut*, but what food you serve, where it comes from, whether you grow any of it yourself, and learning about food justice."

Adamah V'shamayim sings us the image of connection between earth and sky, between us and them. It also brings contrast and a way to experience the world. We understand the physical reality of our world through duality. We understand hot because of cold.

Yet, is safe the absence of danger any more than earth is the absence of sky? What reality are we singing through the earth and sky to our world as we birthing our lives each day?

In one of the paradoxes of life, we seek oneness or connection and yet, in this human body, we understand our physical reality through duality and contrast. *Adamah V'shamayim* reminds us that we are connected.

Kimberly Burnham

To this work, Kimberly Burnham, PhD brings 12 years of finding meaning in Jewish Renewal and music in Colorado (*Neve Kodesh*) and Connecticut (*P'nai Or* and *Shir Hamakom*). In 2013, she bicycled with Hazon, raising awareness and money for sustainable agriculture and food justice. An award winning poet, she won Sage USA's contest with a poem about her nine-week Hazon Cross USA journey as she enjoyed the beauty of words, songs and diversity in more than 20 Jewish communities.

A graduate of Brigham Young University in Provo, Utah, Kimberly made official her conversion to Judaism in 2014.

Kimberly founded the Creating Calm Publishing Group with Ann J. White. She uses her social media expertise to help authors, poets, musicians and artists share their gifts more widely. She contributes to the monthly edition of *Year of the Poet* from the Inner Child Press Poetry Posse.

An integrative medicine practitioner, Kimberly specializes in helping people with brain and nervous system disorders like Parkinson's, Multiple Sclerosis, Huntington's, and memory issues as well as chronic joint pain or diabetic neuropathy. Helping clients, she brings not only her training in alternative medicine but also her own story of eyesight recovery after being diagnosed with a genetic eye condition. You can hear more of her story on the Creating Calm Network.

http://KimberlyBurnham.CreatingCalmNetworkPublishingGroup.com

Growing Your Spiritual Community

1. What do you try to capture when listen to a song—a connection, a memory, an emotion? What are you captured by when you listen?

2. Think about the quote: "It is more important to listen to the sound you are making than to make the sound you are listening to." What does it mean?

3. How are you affected by the medicine wheel elements of Air, Water, Fire, and Earth? Are you drawn to heat of fire and to gardening in the earth?

4. What does how you treat your piece of the earth and sky say about you? What does it say about your family, your community and all those boundaries where you touch your neighbor?

5. If you consider your diet, are there more perennial fruits, nuts or seeds or more annual fruits, vegetables or wheat, soy and corn? What is the impact of your diet on the environment?

6. Have you shared a struggle with someone who could support you financially, emotionally, or with a kind word?

7. Where will you be in September 2022? How will your *shul*, your school or home be different than it is now?

Dancing With God
Ann J. White

As the flicker of hope drew dim in the second century BCE, a miracle happened. The Jews were victorious in their revolt against the Seleucid monarchy, and the small vial of oil burned for eight days.

And they could sing, *"I extol You, O Lord, for you have lifted me up and not let my enemies rejoice over me (Psalm 30:1),"* according to Miriyam Glazer in *Psalms of the Jewish Literacy, A Guide to their Beauty, Power and Meaning* (New York, Aviv Press, 2009, p. 49; All translations of the Psalm are from *Tanach*, Philadelphia, PA, The Jewish Publication Society, 2000).

Throughout the course of our history, we have been challenged, attacked, and oppressed. We have fallen and we have been lifted up. Psalm 30 is a celebration of our lifting up—our survival.

Known as *Mizmor Shir Hanukat Habayit*, "a song for the dedication of the house," we can ask ourselves, "which house?" since the Temple in Jerusalem was not yet built. Is it an actual structure, a gathering of like-minded believers, or is it the house of our spirit—our own human body? The beauty of this psalm is that it holds all of these ideas and more. It is a celebration of being healed from a physical illness, a broken heart, a human frailty, or an actual war between nations. Every breath of this psalm is a salve from God for our human spirit.

Personal Healing

This psalm resonates so powerfully with me because I see it as a song of collective and community uplifting as well as personal healing. It is a song celebrating the survival of our faith, our dreams, and our people. In June of 1967 when Israel went from despair to triumph, in 2006 when the Hezbollah rockets terrorized Haifa, says Miriyam Glazer in *Psalms of the Jewish Literacy* and now in the summer of 2014 as rockets light up Gaza shedding Israeli blood. From the darkest times in our history, we get hope, strength, and sustenance knowing God will lift us up and we will dance in the streets once again.

Dancing

The Jewish spirit is one of survival–Israelis love to dance in the streets. Israel is often plagued by bombs and blasts and war, yet for Jews, it is life nevertheless— *l'hayim!* And life is always celebrated. This psalm celebrates how God can *"turn our lament into dancing."*(Psalm 30:12).

A powerful image that I have is being in Jerusalem in September of 2001, days after 9/11, when the world was on edge, yet the Israelis still danced in the streets. I asked a woman in the street, "Aren't you afraid?" And was told, "If we stayed home every time we were scared, at every bombing, every explosion, what kind of life would that be? It is our spirit to live and to live with passion. So we dance in the street!"

Personally, I call upon this psalm in my own life— as I stumble and fall, as life deals me tragedy, as I get in my own way—yet my God lifts me up, shines light on the path, turns my tears into dancing, and yes, *"turns my grief into dancing."* (Glazer, pg. 49.)

Part of the human condition is the management of the ego. We celebrate our own success as though we created it ourselves in a vacuum—we salute our wins, yet sadly, often blame our losses and failures on others. Spiritual growth enlightens and teaches us that God is with us as we succeed and as we fail—we are not alone in either case.

"When I was untroubled, I thought, 'I shall never be shaken," for You, O Lord, when You were pleased, made (me) firm as a mighty mountain.

When You hid Your face, I was terrified. I called to You, O Lord; to my Lord I made appeal..." (Psalm 30:7-9)

And God is always there when we are.

Turning Our Darkest Times into Light

Stories of imploring God to turn our lament into dancing, and our darkness into light are found in the Holocaust literature. Consider these thoughts of Victor Frankl in *Man's Search for Meaning* (New York: Washington Square Books, 1984) where he shares:

"A thought transfixed me: for the first time in my life l saw the truth as it is set into song by so many poets, proclaimed as the final wisdom by so many thinkers. The truth—that love is the ultimate and the highest goal to which man can aspire. Then I grasped the meaning of the greatest secret that human poetry and human thought and belief have to impart: The salvation of man is through love and in love. I understood how a man who has nothing left in this world still may know bliss, be it only for a brief moment, in the

contemplation of his beloved. In a position of utter desolation, when man cannot express himself in positive action, when his only achievement may consist in enduring his sufferings in the right way—an honorable way—in such a position man can, through loving contemplation of the image he carries of his beloved, achieve fulfillment. For the first time in my life I was able to understand the meaning of the words, 'The angels are lost in perpetual contemplation of an infinite glory.'

Just as we ask, "What house?" we can ask, "Who is our beloved?" God is, or can certainly be, our beloved. And as we carry the image of God in our hearts, in the forefront of our thoughts, we can turn to the words in Psalm 30 to ask for God to uplift us and turn our suffering into peace, if not dancing. Viktor Frankl carried the image of his beloved wife in his heart, yet he admits to believing in a Super Being that we could call God.

Who did he turn to for deliverance? To whom did he cry out for salvation? A power other than himself—a beloved to heal, uplift and turn his sorrow into light.

Another of my favorite thoughts during this time of darkness comes from the old soul, Ann Frank in *The Diary of a Young Girl*. She wrote, *"The best remedy for those who are afraid, lonely or unhappy is to go outside, somewhere where they can be quiet, alone with the heavens, nature and God. Because only then does one feel that all is as it should be."*

I read this as dancing with God, dancing with God in nature, hidden in attics, in our hearts, "because only then does one feel that all is as it should be." Only then can God turn our grief, our sorrow, our lament into peace, light or dancing. Sometimes, as with Ann Frank and with many I have counseled as a trauma chaplain, that light, that dancing, comes as we transition to the other side and dance with the angels.

Unveiling God At Will

In the trauma unit, repeatedly, I heard, "I have turned away from God, He won't help me now." Or, "I don't have a connection with God." How soothing it is to assure someone that God never turns away from us. The hiding of "God's face" is the veil of our own making. We are free to lift that veil any time we need sustenance, support, or healing.

I often used this prayer in my chaplaincy work. It is comforting to know that *one may lie down weeping at nightfall; but at dawn there are shouts for joy,"*(Psalm 30:6). Or as contemporary poet, David Rosenberg expressed, *"...cry yourself to sleep but when you awake light is all around you..."* (*The Poets' Book of Psalms: The Complete Psalter as Rendered by Twenty-five Poets from the 16th to the 20th Centuries;* Laurence Weider, Ed., New York. Oxford House, 1995, p. 40).

Life can look scary when we believe we are alone. How frightening it is at night when fear erupts in our hearts—when things seem beyond hope—when we weep in despair over a tragic event, a sick child, a broken heart, a loss of a loved one, a marriage or a job. We grieve, we moan, we cry rivers of tears in our solitude.

Who hasn't felt abandoned at some point in their life?
Who hasn't trembled in fear?
Or felt the anguish of despair or heartbreak or failure?
To be human is to feel these emotions.
Yet how comforting it is to call out to God and "be healed."

To have our lament, our grief, our sorrow turned into joyful lightness—a passion for life and survival that leads us to dance in our rooms, in the rain, in the night, in the streets—to celebrate our human spirit!

Inspired by the Psalm, as God rips off *"our sackcloth and girds us in joy"*—imagine the feeling of shedding our sorrow, tossing off our mourning clothes and being free to sing out in celebration!

Psalm 30 is a celebration of our human condition—from illness to health, from darkness to light, from despair to dancing—but more, it is a celebration of our relationship with the divine. For when we open ourselves up to God and allow God's Divine Light to flow through us, to uplift us, when we surrender to this Divine Light, we do more than survive—we thrive—we become the light, the light for another, the light unto the nations.

Dear God, thank you for turning my grief into dancing. Dear God, I shall surrender to the beauty of Your Light and Dance with You in my life.

Ann J. White

Rabbi Ann White, JD, MSJS is a rabbi, interfaith chaplain and certified grief counselor. She is the founder of The Creating Calm Network, a global broadcast group dedicated to inspiring, educating and motivating others to live holistic lives in heart-centered communities and on a sustainable planet. She often interviews change agents and hosts shows to shine CCN's light on uplifting projects (CreatingCalmNetwork.com).

Along with Kimberly Burnham, PhD she co-owns The Creating Calm Network Publishing Group dedicated to working with authors from their idea, through publishing and then their launch.

She lives in the magical area of Sheboygan, Wisconsin where, along with her Creating Calm Network Broadcast company work, she officiates at weddings and funerals, writes books, and shares her home with an old dog and new puppy.

http://AnnWhite.CreatingCalmNetworkPublishingGroup.com

Growing Your Spiritual Community

1. What house do you think this passage is referring to? "A song for the dedication of the house."
2. What has happened in your life that you feel is "miraculous"? What kind of place were you in, before you saw the "miracle" in the experience?
3. What healing have you experienced in yourself, your family or your community? Did you feel the power of God orchestrating this experience?
4. How do you feel about God being called "Beloved"? What does "beloved" mean to you?
5. What do you think about this idea? "We are free to lift that veil any time we need sustenance, support, or healing."
6. How do you feel about the duality of life? About the fact that as humans, we experience pain, suffering and grief as well as joy, celebration and dancing? I once asked my congregation if they would like to live forever and the majority said that knowing life was finite gave greater meaning to each day, greater purpose. Do you agree?

Creating Safe Space

Speaking our hearts
we recite
morning creating
meaning behind words
ritually mindful
attuned to the universe
seeing God's face turned towards

Psalms 30 Mizmor Shir
dedication, praise
establishing a safe space
You have raised me up
my enemies have nothing
to celebrate acknowledging
I feel safe
no success for things that bring me
down to succeed

My God, lifted me
from the pits of despair
morning is beginning to break
cracking through the darkness of night
still all around me
I am calm
together we over turn my sadness

—**Kimberly Burnham,** Also see Rabbi Menachem
Creditor Youtu.be/hP5C636zPk8

Halleluyah – A Simple Song About Jewish Worship and Wrestling with God
Aaron H. Tornberg

Benches stand in for pews in this congregation. Fans and water bottles dot the benches next to uncomfortable campers and staff. I stand before them charged with singing the song that will remove them from this earthbound plane and take them to a place where music will distract from the conditions in the room. The familiar—beginning verse and then the ever-present and easy to sing refrain of *Halleluyah* keeps coming back and bringing our minds out of the present. We are in the realm of prayer and joy.

I heard there was a secret chord,
That David played and it pleased the Lord,
But you don't really care for music, do you?
It goes like this:
The fourth, the fifth,
The minor fall, and the major lift,
The baffled king composing Halleluyah.
- Leonard Cohen

Thank You Shrek

Leonard Cohen's song *Halleluyah* is a fantastic piece leading into a deeply felt worship experience. Moved, I felt the need to share it as a camp song leader, as thanks to the popular movie, Shrek (Dreamworks, 2001), I believed the song would become a favorite of both kids and staff. (give me an example of how it became a favorite of one camper) Singing *Halleluyah* is incredibly rewarding and has deep meaning for me. My introduction of the song into a worship context stems from my own difficulty at reaching a prayerful state. Music is my gateway to Jewish prayer. This song is one that truly makes me feel like God is present.

Cohen's Judaism

Though the song is universal, it is strongly Jewish, both in its authorship and in the topics it brings up for discussion. A line from Cohen's song *The Future* states, "I am the little Jew who wrote the Bible." Cohen identifies himself as a Jew and a part of the Jewish people. We are the People of the Book. We are the people who wrote the Bible. Cohen owns this and in *Halleluyah*, identifies the problems with the Bible and our interpretation of it. As Jews, we sometimes doubt God, argue with God, plead with God and try to reach a state of prayer within which we can say, "*Halleluyah!*"

Jewish Songs in Pop Culture

I first heard the song, *Halleluyah* in the movie *Shrek*. For some reason, the song (as sung by Rufus Wainwright) was part of the soundtrack. I was never sure why this was included in the movie, but it seemed to fit with the tone of the narrative. I then heard the song many times working at Barnes and Noble during graduate school. The song seemed to be on repeat throughout many of my days working there. While not initially one of my favorites; like the slow integration of the song into the popular consciousness, it grew to be an important part of my life. While Rufus Wainwright has a low, thin voice, it seemed appropriate for the song, given the type voice and style of the original composer, Leonard Cohen. For those who are unfamiliar with Leonard Cohen, he has a soft and gravelly voice that has become his trademark. My first exposure to him was through a *Best of Leonard Cohen* album, one of the few my mother kept from her college albums. I first heard songs such as *Suzanne, Hey That's No Way to Say Goodbye,* and *So Long Marianne* - all classics to the initiated. That particular Cohen album did not include *Halleluyah*. In fact, the songs in that compilation were more likely to mention Jesus as a poetical, lyrical metaphor than songs from Cohen's own Jewish tradition. The songs were great as folk music, but not something I would normally use in a Jewish context such as worship services.

As Cohen grew as an artist, he began to write more cynical, biting, satirical poetry, including the song I chose for use in worship, *Halleluyah*. I learned about the song in more detail in the fascinating book, *The Holy and the Broken: Leonard Cohen, Jeff Buckley, and the Unlikely Ascent of "Hallelujah"* by Alan Light (2013). As I delved into this book, I began to see the incredible beauty of the song and the extremely Jewish struggle with God that Cohen wrote about in the few simple verses and chorus. Light writes "in even the most superficial reading that the verses undercut any sense of simple blind faith." (Light, 217) Cohen's *Halleluyah* is for praying with a feeling of faith, but faith rooted in knowledge, and an understanding of Jewish identity and all that goes with it. Cohen's struggle with God is clearly outlined in the song and teaches Jewish ideals. After all, the *Tanakh* (Jewish Publication Society, (1985), *The Jewish Bible: Tanakh: The Holy Scriptures*) tells of Moses and Abraham both arguing with God, presumably as a precedent for God to be a fallible being with whom all Jews may struggle at one time or another.

Wrestling with God

Yet, the struggle with God in Cohen's characterization is extremely complex. The goal of the song's narrator is to say "*Halleluyah*!" - in one English translation, "Praise be to God!" As Cohen describes his journey to saying "*Halleluyah*," he is critical of several characters and stories found in Jewish tradition. The person of David is paramount in the song as his is the first image painted for us.

Cohen plays with the idea of David's "secret chord" as if Cohen might just have found the answer to that mysterious and holy set of notes. Yet, he teases us by saying that "we don't really care of music," and he gives us some fairly normal chords that might equal this secret to divine music, "the fourth, the fifth, the minor fall, the major lift." We are set up for the song's philosophical structure. Cohen refers to the "baffled king composing *Halleluyah*." The structure set up here moves the songwriter's internal narrative from bafflement to understanding that despite God's contradictions, somehow, the "*Halleluyah*" comes to pass.

The song sticks in my brain like a comforting mantra. The simple melody, combined with the meditative repetition of the word *Halleluyah* can be appreciated by virtually any audience. But even beyond this repetitive chorus (almost a song without words, a *nigun*) the struggle is always tied to text. I feel, Cohen trying to balance his own struggle with these questionable ideals and his strong devotion to Jewish tradition. According to an interview with Cohen (1993 Interview by Arthur Kurzweil for the Jewish Book Club), he comes from well entrenched Jewish leaders. Both his grandfathers were rabbis. One was a scholar of Hebrew Grammar and called "*Sar HaDikduki*" or Prince of Grammarians." The other was the founder of the Jewish Colonization Association.

Text Study

As I studied this song, I treated each line like a text study and tried to figure out why Cohen would use these particular examples. He mentions:
David's music
David's obsession with Bat-Sheva
Delilah's seduction of Samson and subsequent removal of his greatest power – his hair
The connection between a loving God and a God who needs the love of people
The personal internal struggle that it is hard to say *Halleluyah* to God when we don't truly know His name.

These concepts and connections to Jewish tradition seemed like they were ripe for unpacking when I was working at a Jewish summer camp. I was writing a new songbook and determined that Cohen's *Halleluyah* would be very successful due to its familiarity to the campers (again thank you *Shrek*) and its great potential for Judaic discussion. After some discussion about the appropriateness of one particular verse, the version chosen included the topics listed above.

It was very important to me that the song perform two functions. First, I wanted to use this song as a teaching tool to open up discussion about Jewish music, Jewish composers, using the Bible in everyday life, and how we can reconcile the problematic parts of Judaism with our own lives.

I tried and succeeded to make *Halleluyah* not only part of the camp musical lexicon, but also encouraged the campers to really think about why we sing these Jewish songs. Once established as part of my music curriculum, I discussed making the song a normal opening to Saturday morning Shabbat services. We began using this song to help get in a prayerful mood every week.

Vivid Illustrations

With vivid illustrations, the song is ripe for introspection in the context of Jewish worship. Introduced early in the camp season, *Halleluyah* was a great success both in Camper/Staff enthusiasm and integration of Judaic content. It was determined by some unknown rubric to be the "song of the summer."

The final line of each verse leads the listener to feel the journey of the songwriter:
... *The baffled king composing Halleluyah.*
... *And from your lips she drew the Halleluyah.*
... *It's a cold and it's a broken Halleluyah.*
... *The holy or the broken Halleluyah.*
... *With nothing on my tongue but Halleluyah.*

Within these five lines, Halleluyah is reached only after one is baffled, forced, grudging, doubtful and finally, at a loss for anything but Halleluyah.

A Choice of 80 Verses

Cohen originally wrote around 80 verses in composing *Halleluyah*. He gave all 80 to Jeff Buckley to go through and choose which verses to use in his recording of the song. Rufus Wainwright sings his own selection, and Cohen varies the verses he uses. One can only imagine what lines of Cohen's will never be used in determining how to reach the elusive praise to God. What follows are the verses I chose in using the song specifically for my context – Jewish worship services with campers and adults. I believe the song to be valuable in teaching important lessons to us all.

In our struggle with God, we reaffirm his presence in the midst of our congregation. On a miserably hot and humid day, dressed in Shabbat Blue and White, singing this song picks everyone up a bit. We sing of Cohen's struggle as we struggle with our own discomfort in the ritual of prayer. *Halleluyah* indeed became the "song of the summer" as described by some counselors. It also provided campers with vibrant discussions of the text associated with the song. I became even more convinced that this song is a great worship song. As Jews, we can struggle with God and still sing a joyous *Halleluyah*, knowing that we are not perfect, God is not perfect, but we reaffirm Jewish life again and again.

Aaron Tornberg

Currently working freelance as a computer consultant, Aaron Tornberg is a guitar instructor and teacher of after school programs. He brings creative and engaging educational experiences to students throughout the Boston area.

Aaron lives in Salem, New Hampshire with his wife, Kim, his son, Benjamin and his dog Shayna. He also works at North Shore Community College campuses in the Kids-to-College program as well as non-credit community education courses mostly in the field of Web Design.

Throughout his career, Aaron has been known to record music with David Goldblatt and others. Those recordings can be found on this blog under the Music and Jewish Music tabs.

Recently, Aaron has worked as Head of Shira at Camp Tevya in New Hampshire. He is also working during the year as a music teacher in Temple Beth Abraham Religious School.

http://AaronTornberg.CreatingCalmNetworkPublishingGroup.com

Growing Your Spiritual Community

1. Are you familiar with the song, *Halleluyah* in the Dreamworks' children's movie, *Shrek*?
2. Are there any other "Jewish" songs that you are familiar with in pop culture?
3. Did you or do children in your spiritual community go to camps that have a specific spiritual focus?
4. Are you a fan of Leonard Cohen? To learn more about Leonard Cohen you can read his 1993 interview by Arthur Kurzweil for the Jewish Book Club upon publication of Cohen's book of poetry, lyrics, and writings. Leonardcohenfiles.com/arthurkurzweil.pdf

Seek Peace, a Brit Shalom

"If I am not for me, who is for me; and if I am (only) for myself, what am I. And if not now, when?" —Hillel, *Ethics of the Fathers*, 1:14

People's Climate March

Y'hi shalom becheilech shalvah be'arm'notaich.
Let there be peace in your borders, tranquility in your castles...

"Last Sunday, I had one of the most transformative experiences of my lifetime. Together with the incomparable Josh Nelson, I performed at the People's Climate March in New York City, offering music and prayers for the healing of our planet to over 400,000 people of all faiths. It was the most extraordinary gathering—more positive energy and love than I've ever witnessed. Since I was a little girl I've heard stories of the redemption and what it would feel like for humanity to come together in love. Singing at the People's Climate March was my first real taste of that possibility. I am forever changed."

—Neshama Carlebach and Josh Nelson Release a Powerful Musical Video Offering a *Heartfelt Prayer for Peace* Against Searing Images from Israel and Gaza. In the Midst of a Summer of Bloodshed and Strife, The Duo Performs Shlomo Carlebach's Iconic Song, September 24, 2014.

Esa Einai – Finding the Music in Prayer
Arnie Davidson

Torah speaks to our literal mind with words, but ancient wisdom recognized that the message is driven deeper with hypnotic *trope* (traditional ancient chanting). This vibration musically dances the letters and phrases in a rhythmic end run around logic, direct to the inner home of understanding—our hearts.

Our liturgy also speaks with words culled from centuries of life experience. Just as *trope* acts as the message bearer of *Torah* to our subconscious, melody ignites and delivers prayers to our hearts. We each vibrate with the unique expression of self, which is both heat seeking and torch bearing. We are warmed by the hypnotic, contagious flames of communal prayer, just as our attention fuels the fire.

For me, music is a carrier of meaning—an inviting buffet of word moods. Song or meaningful sound invites community participation—lending variety and magnifying the source—through the diversity and collective experience of a room full of listeners. It forms a sound mosaic with the unlimited potential of a kaleidoscope

The same melody can drill through the communal and find its mark in one heart, resonating and calling up a melody moment, strike a nerve, uncover a buried memory, or energize one's whole being into joyous movement and song.

New Channels of Receptivity

The purpose and intent of my music is to open up a new channel of receptivity by selectively focusing and restricting/opening sensory pathways. There is subconscious receptivity to familiar states and to common secular music and tonality, contrasted with possible discomfort, distance, and even alienation to unfamiliar Eastern European based scales and modalities.

I remember being encouraged to write worship music as a teenager when I was part of a youth group. My early work was not noteworthy, but it opened my mind to the idea that the ancient words of our liturgy were not in a monogamous relationship with one spousal melody. The words are free. They are free agents, living expressions that are always receptive to revealing timeless meaning through new sound highways. *Torah* is a living book. Similarly, the words of our *Siddur* (prayerbook), vetted through centuries of diverse life experience, have been passed down to us for generations, *L'dor Vador*, prequalified, fine-tuned and finely distilled by our ancestors and elders.

The trick, I believe, is to find the right carrier, the perfect conduit for words of meaning in past context to be rediscovered and celebrated in the context of our lives today.

Our Commonality

We have much in common with those of past generations. We walk in similar bodies; embracing the same fundamental moral compass of *Torah*. We fall in love, and we feel the same pain of loss or separation. We yearn for the health and success of our family. We care for our young, and we care for our elders. We hurt from misfortune and we aspire to more and better in the future. At our core, we share the same heart and spirit as those before us.

Yet today, we are different. We've lost some of the sense of peace and rest and comfort that slower times offered. I believe that we feel less connected than our elders – less connected and embraced by the Oneness of Judaism; less connected to the support of a coherent and powerful community; and less connected to the invisible word of intuition and our common link to the vibration of all life, beyond the limits of our five senses.

The Piano Philosopher

I play piano. During the past 15 years or so, I've found a home as an accompanist at a Reform synagogue near Hartford, Connecticut, US, playing for *B'nai Mitzvah* ceremonies at Shabbat morning services. At last count, I have done these more than 225 times. The first four or five times, I had to learn the music and service order, but for the next few hundred times, I got to both play music and watch faces. So the mini philosopher in me came up with a few insights after watching 10,000 worshipers.

I observed that many people in this community often didn't have training in, or a clue about Hebrew, either pronouncing it well or understanding it, but they often wanted to sing it really badly. So, hastily transliterated sounds spontaneously emerged with the best intention. It's like the Hebrew version of those misheard song lyrics, "You make me feel like a rash on a woman", instead of "You make me feel like a natural woman (Carole King).

Despite the unfamiliarity, most worshipers did try to get a return on investment for their time in the sanctuary; a few hours of rest and retreat and reflection, away from the busy expectations of the world outside the four walls of the sanctuary. It is here that I noticed unexpected moments, with their exterior firewall down, when they let in the words and the sound of prayers with centuries of experience of purpose connecting an open spirit with our ancient heritage.

Those were the moments that I looked for, just a small convergence of rhythmic relaxation and melodic receptivity that would carry the potent payload of the words to find their mark. So, I began the process of blending my own highly melodic song preferences with prayer phrases from the original text and, in English, according to my own interpretation.

My first attempts at this were musical gifts to my children on the occasion of their Bar and Bat Mitzvah. Although conceived as single-use prayer offerings, these prayer melodies were rapidly recruited as part of the regular worship service at my congregation. Encouraged by this, I've written about 25 prayer settings in this same manner.

Sim Shalom Musical Peace

One of my fondest current experiences is a workshop that I lead called "Finding the Music in Prayer". Participants study the original text and history of a prayer. We learn the perspective and the phrasing, and attempt to place it in its proper historical context. We next begin a discussion of how these words and ideas might resonate in today's world. We record our thoughts, ideas and phrases. Finally, we select the most relevant word elements, both from original text and from our interpretation, and we create a song.

An example of this process is my setting of *Sim Shalom*. Our discussions at a Limmud, United Kingdom workshop began with studying the original text, which describes us, the Children of Israel, asking our Parent, the Source of Peace, to grant and spread peace over us. Our discussion evolved to the topic of children and peace, and ultimately turned toward the observation that we learn peace in the playground as children, but somehow forget it as adults. The prayer song evolved with English verses, reflecting on the simplicity and necessity of peace between children, and a Hebrew English chorus:

> "*Sim Shalom, Shalom*, it seems so long in coming.
> Please *Avinu*, help us open up our hearts,
> To see *Shalom, Sim Shalom, Shalom*."

Esa Einai

And this leads to my setting of *Esa Einai, Psalm 121*, known best for its opening line of majesty and comfort.

> *"I lift up my eyes to the mountains*
> *Where does my help come from*
> *from the Maker of heaven and earth."*

This is truly a beautiful Psalm of reassurance, affirming that we are never alone, always protected and watched over as we go and as we come, by our Keeper who never sleeps. Sometimes, in our lowest moments, we cannot even find or access any of our own strength, and the journey toward empowerment begins, at a primal level, with the knowledge that we are not alone. These are beautiful poetic words.

Coincidentally, there are two aspects to this prayer, two perspectives that the listener might assume in drinking in these flowing poetic words. These are suggestive of the two contexts, liturgically, that *Esa Einai* occupies in the Jewish worship space: on Yom Kippur in the context of atonement, and in mourning for comfort.

This Psalm, which speaks of the majesty of God, can be both diminutive and supportive. As we reflect on the scope of all of nature, and focus on the towering mountain tops, we are diminished and feel small. This context plays perfectly into the imagery of repentance, atonement and return of *Yom Kippur*, where we are reduced to a dependent flock of sheep tended by a kind and loving, but all powerful Creator, who writes and seals our fate for the coming year.

This context has a flip side however, one from which we can derive great comfort. And it is in this context, that *Esa Einai* has forged its way into familiarity. At the times of our greatest grief, when we, through our own faltering resources, feel weak and small, we invoke and summon and affirm our partnership with the Source, Creator of Life, and Sculptor of the majestic mountain. Who better to guide us through times of uncertainty and doubt? When life comes to bully us, it is easier to face this event with an imposingly powerful partner.

Worshipers of many religions turn to this Psalm for comfort. Unfortunately, I experienced it in a situation where it seemed hauntingly inappropriate, rather than consoling.

I was attending a funeral for a cousin of mine, the first to pass of his generation in my family. He died of cancer, and he had more than his share of suffering, but he was a man filled with love. He was not particularly religious, a secular Jew, but his life, ethics and love of life reflected all of the highest values that we know. The chapel was overflowing with family and friends, and his life and gentle personality was remembered and captured in words from clergy and family. And then, a cantor sang *Esa Einai* a cappella. Ouch. It really didn't fit, or comfort or console. It just seemed removed from the real life reality of celebrating a man's life, a man who did real world things up until 2003. It felt like bringing in a kazoo to a symphony. I knew that the words were beautiful and meaningful, but the delivery system didn't work for me. More important, it interrupted the flow of a beautiful ceremony for those in the room.

One of my mentors, Josh Nelson, a brilliant musician and contemporary Jewish songwriter, defined one of his missions as being the production of worship music that inspired and engaged the senses and captured the vibe of our secular music ear. To have Jewish music live right next to your favorite popular music on your iPod, without apology. I had his words in mind when I set out to create a carrier melody for *Esa Einai.*

I chose to retain the original Hebrew for the chorus, and use my interpretive English translation for the three verses. My challenge was to have a simple but interesting, engaging and maybe a bit haunting chorus melody that offered enough repetition to engage listeners to participate, despite unfamiliar but simple Hebrew. I used a repetition of words to encourage this. After all, we learn songs through repetition, and the chorus *of Esa Einai* presents, then repeats several words. The words and phrases are simple, and many words are familiar from other prayers.

Esa Einai el heharim.
Meayin yaavoh
Yaavoh ezri
Ezri Adonai
Oseh Shamyim Vaaretz.

Here are the verses, in our native language of English, which roughly correlate with a translation of the Psalm, with a bit of poetic songwriter's license. Based on my funeral experience where this Psalm was sung down on us from the pulpit, I wanted to use more casual language, giving permission to the listener to find and explore their own personal relationship with the melody, the prayer and ultimately, with God. I also referenced *Shechina*, the feminine aspect of God, to call upon the nurturing, nourishing qualities that comfort. It ends with a single Hebrew phrase, rhymed with the preceding English: *Me-atah v'ad olam* (from now until the end of time). I love this image of enduring comfort.

I lift up my eyes to the mountains so tall
And call for your help, send comfort for all
Maker of heaven, Creator of life,
Source of our strength, Adonai

Keep me from falling, steady my feet
Shechina, who never will slumber or sleep

317

God is my Keeper, Protector and Shade
From harm, in the night and the day.

Protect me from evil, shield me from wrong
Guardian of Israel, my spirit be strong.
Watch over us as we go and we come
Me-atah v'ad olam.

    Esa Einai is one of my favorite song children, as I call them, and there is a contagious simplicity to the melody that seems to invite listeners to become participants, and to find their way into the comforting and timeless words of this Psalm.

    In the end, that is my purpose. I am not looking to rewrite the liturgy, or to make a statement about a prayer, but merely to open a door of interest and awareness where there may not have been one. Certainly, I don't have the capacity or interest to replace some of the beautiful liturgical melodies of our past. I do want the music to jump down from the *Bimah* (pulpit), though, and find a vehicle and medium to invite worshipers to discover the rich liturgy of our heritage and to open their mouths and hearts to discover the music in this prayer.

    There is continued precedent for taking original text and setting it in the familiar music of the day, interpreted in the language of the worshiper. Great cantorial pieces that have endured for over a century often had their roots in the music of the day. Today it sounds classic, but it once was new, and was probably even initially rejected in favor of the tried and true standards that came before.

Entraining With The Earth

I began by speaking of music as vibration. The words of *Torah* and liturgy speak to our literal logical mind, but their poetic rhythm and inflection engage us in a deeper place. Worship music has the added characteristic of drawing us in through melody and rhythm, promoting familiarity, engaging us in through primal, subconscious vibration. When we are empowered and free of stress, our brain and the vibrations of earth and our surroundings synchronize, as we entrain, synchronize, normalize and calm our mind frequency to the heartbeat of raw sound.

To drink in the relaxing, reassuring pleasure of vibration and sound, we need to leave behind the fear and stress that immobilize us and hijack our senses. The words of prayer, the music in prayer and the resonance of community in a sacred space all invite us to open our hearts. It is my feeling that familiar contemporary music, coupled with evocative lyrics in our native English language, also invites the spirit to relax, rejoice and revel in the message of our ancient texts, as well as the miracles within everyday moments.

I envision contemporary Jewish music as a bridge, cracking open a doorway to receptivity, welcoming familiarity and promoting comprehension. It encourages us to receive and attune to the timeless vibration and sound of Torah. In the comfort of those time honored words, we are welcomed, warmed and we find spiritual Home.

Arnie Davidson

A contemporary Jewish music singer/songwriter, international performer and worship leader, Arnie Davidson is the founder of *Shir Hamakom*, a music worship community based in Glastonbury, Connecticut USA. He has released four albums of worship music and he leads worship with music partner, Shelly Aronson. He is best known for his interactive workshops at synagogues, conferences and with youth groups, "Finding the Music in Prayer", where participants are guided to discover new meaning in ancient text by creating new music and original lyrics.

"Too much of our liturgy is locked away in a vault of tired melodies and rote recitation. There is an amazing discovery process that occurs when these words see the light of the present day, reflected through the lens of familiar contemporary melodies, instruments and modern language. I'm not looking to replace beautiful traditional melodies, but rather to open a new door of access and understanding to a generation of worshipers; seekers of Jewish spirituality and connection in a secular world. My goal is to create new worship music that inspires and invites, but also shuffles on your iPod without apology."

Shir Hamakom, Arnie's Jewish worship music community is a growing example of creating a worship experience from the worshiper up, rather than from the *bimah* (pulpit) down. "Shelly (Aronson) and I are truly worship leaders rather than performers. Our unique *siddur* (prayerbook) welcomes Shabbat with 60 minutes of wall to wall music, traversing the ebb and flow of the service in an interconnection of song moments, uninterrupted by sermons. It's a focused spiritual twist on that Top 40 radio adage of 'More Music, Less Talk'." By disengaging the logical mind, we are free to let in the power and vibration of a roomful of voices on a common mission. We let the music do the heavy lifting, subtly drawing in the comfort of community, exhaling the baggage of the work week."

Arnie's signature music blends original Hebrew text with interpretive English lyrics, carried by contagious melody, served on a bed of warm and familiar contemporary music. It is new and welcoming. It is Shabbat music that lasts all week long.

http://ArnieDavidson.CreatingCalmNetworkPublishingGroup.com

Growing Your Spiritual Community

1. Are you familiar with the idea of entrainment? What are you entrained with?
2. What do you think of this quote, "... the idea that the ancient words of our liturgy were not in a monogamous relationship with one spousal melody. The words are free. They are free agents, living expressions that are always receptive to revealing timeless meaning through new sound highways."
3. In what ways do you see your life as similar or different from your ancestors a hundred or two hundred years ago?
4. How old is the oldest person in your community or in your family? What have you learned from them lately?
5. Have you ever done as Arnie Davidson has done, "In songwriting, I sought to dissect and disassemble each

prayer into its component phrases and ideas. I then reassembled it, taking some liberal liberty with words, to retain the original text and underlying spirit of the prayer in an accessible and welcoming new melody."

6. What do you think of the rhyming in different languages? "It ends with a single Hebrew phrase, rhymed with the preceding English."

"Watch over us as we go and we come
Me-atah v'ad olam."

Psalm 121

A song for ascents. I shall raise my eyes to the mountains, from where will my help come?
My help is from the Lord, the Maker of heaven and earth.
He will not allow your foot to falter; Your Guardian will not slumber.
Behold the Guardian of Israel will neither slumber nor sleep.
The Lord is your Guardian; the Lord is your shadow; [He is] by your right hand.
By day, the sun will not smite you, nor will the moon at night.
The Lord will guard you from all evil; He will guard your soul.
The Lord will guard your going out and your coming in from now and to eternity.

—Chabad.org

Esa Einai Psalm 121 Arnie Davidson - Beth Schafer - Shelly Aronson

Youtu.be/YHyTNfg7LhE

Tefilat HaDerech

"Y'hi ratzon milfanekha Adonai Eloheinu
velohei avoteinu shetolikhenu l'shalom
v'tatz'idenu l'shalom v'tadrikhenu l'shalom,
v'tagi'enu limhoz heftzenu
l'hayim ul-simha ul-shalom.
V'tatzilenu mi-kaf kol oyev v'orev
v'listim v'hayot ra'ot ba-derekh,
u-mi-kol minei pur'aniyot
ha-mitrag'shot la-vo la-olam.
V'tishlah b'rakha b'khol ma'a'se yadeinu
v'tit'nenu l'hen ul-hesed ul-rahamim
b'einekha uv-einei khol ro'einu.
V'tishma kol tahanuneinu
ki E-l sho'me'a t'fila v'tahanun ata.
Barukh ata A-donai sho'me'a t'fila."
—Tefilat HaDerech, The Traveler's Prayer

Shalom on the Journey

Shalom
shalem
fashioned from
here to there one
piece of mystical fabric
a magical carpet
protecting oneness

peace
shalom
salaam

three requests
sought in the East
and in the West

a whole
universe
of blessings and fear
traveling full of wonder
beauty
compassion

finding peace
within
with ...

—Kimberly Burnham

Growing Your Spiritual Community

1. Do you connect with something greater than yourself
differently when you are at home compared to on a
journey or vacation?
2. Do you have any ritual or special activity that you do
at the beginning of a journey?

Experiencing Melodic Peace
Rebecca Schwartz

Intention is experiencing the moment; not looking back, not looking forward, but truly being there. Music brings passion to my life by awakening my body and soul, and gives me a sense of peace. Music has the ability to put everyone on the same playing field. Regardless of whether they're young or old, rich or poor, humans are moved by music. Race and religion don't come into play. We are all equals, and music unites us.

What is your "why" for coming to synagogue? Some people attend for *Shabbat*, High Holy Days, *Havdalah*, and that has meaning for them. Others enjoy the social aspect; the *kehillah* (community). Some are in pain (physical or emotional) and long to ease that pain. Music can send the mind and soul into a different state.

The Moment

My intentionality while singing is to draw you into that moment, no matter what the reason you are here. Joy can be greater, family can be closer, and friends can share together. Have you ever watched children sing? They smile, dance, hug, and really experience the songs. As we get older, we often forget how to do this. We become self-conscious around others. My goal is to get people back to feeling the freedom we can feel when we sing. Music and singing can help us forget about our physical or emotional pain. Music can act as an anesthetic, allowing our minds to forget worry and pain, even if just for a short time. Music can be aerobic exercise for the brain, allowing our minds to wander and wonder.

Shalom

Oseh shalom bimrovav, hu ya-aseh shalom aleinu v'al kol Yisrael, (v'al kol yoshvei teivel).

May the One who makes peace in the high heavens make peace for us, and all Israel, (and all who inhabit the earth).

Peace. It's something we all talk about. It's something we all dream about. Is it possible to have a world without turmoil? What would happen if we rose up in song instead of rising up with weapons? What if children were taught at an early age to sing a song of peace and love to one another?

The Intention of Music

It was very interesting to actually think about intention in my music. This is something that has always just felt natural to me. Whenever I sing, I feel the music within me and it pours out automatically filled with emotion. I've just never known any other way. This project has really made me think about what I do when I share my music with others. I feel like I'm a part of something bigger than myself, and this gives my life true purpose. I can't say it's been easy to express intention but it's pretty cool!

I believe in the power of prayer through music. Its intention is to engage our minds and lift our spirits, but music can also calm our inner turmoil. My role is to be a musical messenger through Jewish text. Music is a gift that allows us to connect with one another and God in a different dimension. When I sing, I'm opening up my soul to others. I'm sharing a part of me, and my hope is that they will share a part of themselves with me as well.

The singing draws all of us toward light and away from darkness. This "light" can be a sense of peace, well-being, holiness, wholeness, and more. My intention is to have those around me not only "see the light", but feel that light shining on them and feel the warmth. They can feel God's presence (if they believe in God), or just BE present—be aware. Feel alive.

Many of my congregants come to services for the music. It's a huge part of what my temple is all about, and I'm grateful to be a part of such a warm and loving community. I never want to see anyone "checking out" emotionally during a service. Music should envelop people and carry them to higher heights. If I'm not feeling well or something is bothering me, I do my best to hide it as it affects not only my mood, but my congregation's mood. I give prayer my all, and together we are lifted to a higher place. Also, even if I'm not feeling well, I often feel better during and after a service. I'm hopeful that everyone around me feels the same way.

We're one huge voice that brings warmth and holiness that's hard to beat. Music is a bond that I've witnessed in both congregational and camp settings. Spontaneous harmonies often occur during a service. The more voices, the stronger that bond becomes. People are less afraid to step outside their comfort zones, and this can really be empowering.

Vision

Eye contact is extremely important to me. While there are times I close my eyes to feel a specific moment of prayer, such as the beginning of the *Amidah* (standing prayer) so I can make my own connection to God, my intention is to make those same connections with those around me. We may smile or not, but people rarely look away once we have engaged in eye contact. They don't seem to feel uncomfortable by my reaching out to them, but rather, it seems to help them focus on being in that prayerful moment.

The music used in a prayer can bring back memories, and feelings emerge that we may not have felt in years. In writing new melodies for familiar prayers, I try to consider how I want people to feel. How do you want to feel? My goal is to create melodies that are easy to sing, easy to teach, true to the text, and can be spiritual steppingstones for the soul.

Various melodies can create a range of feelings. A slower melody may create calm, while a more spirited melody may be uplifting. Both can create that sense of inner peace. Songs sung within communities make their way into other communities, are often translated into different languages, and become universal anthems of peace. One example of that is *"From a Distance"* by Julie Gold. Another example is the plethora of melodies for *"Oseh Shalom"* that are sung around the globe. Slow, fast, major and minor keys, some for adults, some for kids, but all are moving us to think about striving for a peaceful planet.

Prayer Landscapes

Using a term coined by my friend Rabbi Howard Bogot to describe my music, I try to create a "landscape for prayer". Imagine a blank canvas, and each prayer becomes a new color on that canvas. My intention is to paint a picture in the minds of those around me. Just as someone can lose him or herself in physical exertion of the body, music can be a mental stimulant or relaxant. The colors on the canvas can be bright or muted, and each person can use his or her palate to paint a unique picture.

My music comes from a mysterious place in my soul. I feel like I was given a musical gift when I was born. My parents certainly nurtured that gift, and I've done the same for my children who are both musically gifted. While I wrote a lot when I was in my teens and twenties, I had not written music in about twenty years. I missed it, but didn't dwell on it. When I started writing music again, it was to Jewish prayers. Once I started, I couldn't stop. It was as if there was divine intervention, and I was completely blown away when I came up for air. I'd written sixteen songs in just a couple of weeks.

These songs completely changed my life. That was the point when I realized that it was my job to share this gift with others to help lift them spiritually, just as I had been lifted. The music brought me joy, and I began a journey I had never imagined I'd be taking, leading up to where I am today. My belief in God has always been strong, but this feeling of complete and total peace washed over me, and this is what I try to share with those around me when singing.

Music is an integral part of the worship experience. Many people don't read Hebrew or have trouble following along, even with transliteration.

Imagine a ball game where someone reads the Star-Spangled Banner. Do you think the crowd would get totally psyched at the end, if not for the singing of the song that helps get them there? The same can be said about melodies for prayer. The intention of the music is to raise us up and get us there. The melodies make the prayers come to life.

Prayers of peace have been a theme I've written about most often because I think the lack of peace within and around us is what creates the most amount of stress.

I've written three melodies for *Oseh Shalom* and one for *Sim Shalom*, as well as some English-based songs. These prayers and melodies continue to bring a warm, fuzzy feeling to me whenever they're sung. My congregants often close their eyes and truly focus on these prayers and songs, and the melody helps them find that focus, calm their minds, and achieve a sense of peace.

Only a Matter of Time (with both original English text and the Hebrew for *Oseh Shalom*) was written for my children in the hope that they'll see world peace in their lifetimes. It continues to be an anthem I've used with both children and adults to help them feel my hope, especially when something truly awful is happening in the world. My intention is to help lift people up when they're down, and in so doing, I lift myself up. I often feel helpless during sad times, and my writing helps lift me from this fog.

Healing Music

My gift of music has also helped me overcome my own health issues. While music can be a major stress-reliever, my job in the music field can also be stressful. Singers need to constantly take care of their bodies and voices, and when we get sick, we often have to continue to perform. I had vocal problems on and off a couple of years ago, and developed a vocal hemorrhage that was finally diagnosed between *Rosh Hashanah* and *Yom Kippur*. Busy season! I was placed on vocal rest for a few days. For someone who is so vocal, this seemed like it would be impossible. What I learned during this time was that silence is golden, and I used this time to hear the music within me, even if I couldn't let it out. This kept me strong, focused, and aware that my physical suffering could be overcome with a positive attitude and concentration on the prayers I was singing inside me. I learned true patience and resolve, became more aware of those suffering physically or mentally, and sought to draw them in even closer. After about a month of vocal rest, my hemorrhage was completely healed. I continue to be aware of the gift of my voice whenever I sing.

May music continue to lift us up, keep us from falling, heal our wounded bodies and souls, and enlighten us as we go on our way. May the One who makes peace in the high heavens make peace for us, all Israel, and all who inhabit the earth, and let us say: Amen.

Rebecca Schwartz

A professional singer, guitarist, and award-winning songwriter, Rebecca Schwartz has written and co-produced five albums (four spiritual and one secular), two songbooks of her spiritual music, and has written and recorded songs to help teach autistic children.

Rebecca serves as Cantorial Soloist and Music Director at Congregation Kol Ami in Elkins Park, Pennsylvania. She specializes in worship experiences, engaging people in the power of prayer through music.

Rebecca also teaches guitar and mentors Jewish song leaders in community and camp settings, helping them to share their musical gifts.

Rebecca sings at private *b'nei mitzvah* and wedding ceremonies, and travels for special artist-in-residence events and weekends. She has performed and presented musical workshops in the United States, Canada, Israel, and The Netherlands. Rebecca has received musical awards from *Shalshelet's First International Festival of New Jewish Liturgical Music* and *Just Plain Folks*. She has been published in a number of Jewish songbooks and publications.

Rebecca is married and has two sons. A song of peace and hope she wrote for them can be heard on YouTube and at Rebeccasongs.com.

http://RebeccaSchwartz.CreatingCalmNetworkPublishingGroup.com

Growing Your Spiritual Community

1. What helps you be in the moment?
2. What is your "why" for going to synagogue?
3. Is it possible to have a world without turmoil? Is it naive to ask, "What if children were taught at an early age to sing a song of peace and love to each other?"
4. Do you find your peaceful place more easily with your eyes open or your eyes closed?
5. Have you ever had a healing experience, either physically or emotionally involving music? Have you shared this experience with others and would you feel comfortable talking about this in your spiritual community?

Gift of Peace - Hu Eloheinu
Shelly Aronson

When I was about four and a half years old, which according to my kids was before the earth cooled, I remember going to *shul* for the first time with my grandfather. I can still feel the sense of delight and magic in sitting next to him, mesmerized by the melodic chanting of prayers. Prayers that I came to learn were chanted by my rabbinic ancestors: my great grandfathers and great uncles. Even now, I can still feel that sense of spiritual connection when I attend services; that feeling of being one with those who came before, and those, who at that very same moment throughout the world, are intoning the same ancient prayers.

What I never imagined then, as that very young, impressionable girl, was that one day I would be the one at services offering a melodic chanting of prayers. A musical seed was planted in me in those days, oh so long ago, and it has been growing ever since.

The Feeling of Sound

I believe in my heart that '*music is what feelings sound like,*' and that belief is what lies at the core of my musical intention. When I sing, for me it's not about singing notes and saying words; my intention is for the listener to *experience the music* rather than just hear it. I try to get in touch with what touches me in order for me to touch others; to tap into my own experiences, be they joyful or painful, so I can convey the meaning of the prayer-song to the listener. The challenge often lies in putting aside my own emotions, so that in the moment, I not only project, but convey, those very feelings without being overcome by them. I try to find the light in myself, so I can reflect it to others.

As I grew, and the musical seed within me began to take root, it was nurtured by the unique empowerment of women taking place within the Reform movement—and by the Women of Reform Judaism (WRJ) in particular.

Sisterhood

Nearly eleven years ago, as Sisterhood President of my congregation, I attended the Biennial in Boston and had the privilege of writing in a *Torah* scroll commissioned by the Women of Reform Judaism. This unique experience of honoring my children and grandchildren, as well as a dear friend who was terminally ill, etched an indelible *'handprint on my heart.'* There, I placed my hand atop the scribe's, and together, quill in the now one hand, we wrote the ancient letters that would be kept alive throughout generations. I then took part in a *Siyum* ceremony, which was led by Debbie Friedman (z"l), legendary composer, singer, and songwriter credited with creating a new genre of contemporary Jewish music. The *Siyum* ceremony is the completion of any unit of Torah study, followed by a celebration in honor of a mitzvah. Hundreds of women gathered to celebrate the completion of the *Torah*. Women read from the new *Torah*. We embraced one another and swayed together in song. It was a defining moment. It was the moment that I heard the ancient voice within me, encouraging me to listen to my own heart song and add formal knowledge to my spiritual connection. It was the moment where I chose to become a *Bat Mitzvah.*

I never had a formal Jewish education before preparing for my Bat Mitzvah, so I understand that not everyone knows what the Hebrew words mean during services. In offering songs and prayers to our worship community, my co-worship leader, Arnie Davidson, and I, begin with the words, then add the music, the voices, the spirit, the inspiration and the emotions—both tears and giggles. It's as if we take a thousand puzzle pieces and put them together in a way that creates a surprise, a beautiful image, and what we hope will become for listeners, a spiritual soul-soothing picture.

Magical Musical Moments

People attend services for so many reasons. Some are alone and want to feel part of something. Some have partners who want to connect, and music can provide that connection. Some are filled with joy, overflowing with their own spirit and are able to share, while others are depleted from the work week and just need a nesting place to find a peaceful moment. And some arrive filled with pain. Music can both soothe and mask pain. Life can sometimes seem dark and hopeless; but, at least for a moment in time — a magical, musical moment — all is peaceful inside. Then, the outside world, or whatever is stirring inside each person, can just be background noise.

I am always touched when I notice the *small* moments during our service, when someone may look up in wonder or surprise after having experienced an unexpected spiritual connection. That person may get teary, as if moved by a word, phrase, note or intonation, and it is then when I realize that even if only one person is moved, or inspired, or soothed…all else *is commentary.*

When I think about my own *small* moments at services, the *Aleinu* prayer comes to mind. Even when I was a child, that prayer has always been my favorite. Yes, it signifies the impending end of the service, but more than that, the words and the beautiful melody have always nestled deep inside me creating a feeling of being cared for, watched over—and safe. When the service evolves to the *Shehu Noteh Shamayim*, the traditional, disparate melody seems to break the spell for me, as it always seems out of sync.

Where Songs Come From

My gifted music partner and composer, Arnie Davidson, often tells a story about those two prayers. He heard it shared by Debbie Friedman at a music workshop in Connecticut, and it related to the text following *Aleinu: Shehu Noteh Shamayim.* Debbie spoke of leading a *Kabbalat* Shabbat service at a large Reform congregation, where she noticed a family of three occupying the front row: two young parents and their toddler son. The family was equipped with kid amusements to keep him occupied— juice boxes, crackers, matchbox cars, coloring books, and the works. Best of all, the strategy worked; the young boy was occupied until…the *Shehu Noteh Shamayim.* When the congregation joined in, the boy stood up, faced the worship leaders on the *bimah,* and compliantly began weaving his fingers in and out to the familiar tune of the "itsy bitsy spider," the *traditional* melody that the prayer was apparently derived from. Debbie summed up her story by admonishing those present that the *sacred* and familiar melodies of our worship sometimes have dubious roots. She issued the challenge for someone, *please*, to accept the charge to rewrite this prayer melody without it being derived from a nursery rhyme. A few years later, Arnie composed an original version of *Hu Eloheinu* in response to Debbie's invitation. His soulful melody weaves itself into a tapestry that began with the *Aleinu* that then becomes a warm blanket we can spiritually wrap around ourselves.

Why We Are Here

A dear friend shared some beautiful words with me many years ago, just before my daughter's wedding: *"The decision to have children is to decide to forever have your heart walk around outside your body."* From those early days sitting beside my grandfather through to my adulthood, I have come to see sharing music with others in the same light. We're only on this earth for a moment in time—to make a difference, to be remembered for what we have accomplished, whatever that might be, and to make someone's life a little better because they knew us—to leave a legacy. Prayer-songs, and the emotions they stir, the peace they instill within, can last forever. Prayer-songs can be our legacy, our gift of peace, our heart forever walking around outside our body— comforting, awakening and soothing others—maybe, just maybe, inspiring others to hear their own heart songs.

Shelly Aronson

Co-worship leader Shelly Aronson is a strong spiritual voice at *Shir Hamakom*, a Jewish music worship community based in Glastonbury, Connecticut, USA. Along with songwriter, Arnie Davidson, she helped conceive the unique and contagious contemporary Jewish music that defines this community. Using a melodic blend of original Hebrew text and interpretive English lyrics, Shelly delivers a warm, heartfelt, and welcoming invitation to participate in worship using her rich, breathtakingly resonant voice.

Although Shelly is trained in nonprofit community organization and development, and business, her Jewish music journey is experiential rather than academic. What began as casual participation in worship music has evolved into a personal Jewish musical journey that engages us, empowering our native impulse to celebrate life with song.

Later in life, Shelly discovered the power of melody and voice to carry words of prayer and inspiration to community through, what she calls, soul-soothing music. Music soothes, comforts and stirs people. She says, "I feel so privileged to help make that happen. Song and melodies rejuvenate and validate our connection to one another, yet awaken the spark of holiness within."

Shelly's rich gift is her warm, resonant voice coupled with an intuitive interpretive talent that uses sound to disarm the logical mind, rushing directly to the heart, nourishing the spirit.

http://ShellyAronson.CreatingCalmNetworkPublishingGroup.com

Growing Your Spiritual Community

1. What are your first memories of a religious or spiritual practice?

2. Have you had a Bat Mitzvah, Bar Mitzvah or other coming of age ritual? Why did you do it or not do it? How did it change you?

3. Have you had formal Jewish or religious training? What value have you found there?

4. How does this quote touch you, "The decision to have children is to decide to forever have your heart walk around outside your body?"

Reaching Peace Through Music in Prayer
Steve Dropkin

It is a supreme and awesome responsibility to write music to our sacred liturgy and texts. For most people worship is a private matter. Even in the context of congregational worship we pray alone or silently for a good portion of the service. But when music is introduced and the congregation joins in and sings together, a singular voice is created that is indeed powerful and profound.

All too often congregants come to me with a misconception about the music in worship. They will comment to me, "I liked the song you sang tonight." This is a huge misunderstanding about the role of the music that is sung in our worship service—that the prayers are songs. Prayers are *illuminated* by music. Music truly "lifts" our liturgical text, and hopefully to a higher place.

I never cease to be amazed at how powerful the prayers become when the music is well written and meaningful. When this happens the intention of the musician is felt as well as heard. This has always been a goal of mine as a writer and composer.

Urgency

There are two places in the worship liturgy that have always captivated me. There is a transitory ebb in the service that comes after *Mi Chamocha* and is captured in the *Hashkiveinu*, and again as the *T'fillah* is concluded with *Oseh Shalom*. These two prayers, though not specifically connected, transmit a certain sense of urgency in their intention and that, to me, is wonderful and purposeful.

In Judaism the commitment to the concept of peace is, and always has been, a cornerstone of our people. In the world today most people would translate and equate the meaning of the word 'peace' as something that would be the opposite of war. "If we could just put down the guns and agree on our differences, then we could have peace." While this may be true, it falls far short of how Jews feel and interpret peace. For us, the meaning is much deeper and far more encompassing.

If you examine the Hebrew root of the word *shalom*, which is the word *shalem* (*shin-lamed-mem*), it translates to mean *complete*, as in a circle or something that is never ending. When you apply that meaning to the Jewish interpretation of peace, it now represents something that is indeed much more powerful. Peace will be in a time when there is true tranquility, that will be all pervasive. Not just in the world as we know it and understand it today, but in our own individual lives as well. It will be a time when our own inner-peace and outer-peace will match. When there will be a rich harmony throughout humankind. This, to me, is what we are talking about when we refer to the *Olam Haba-ah*, the world to come.

So, as I look at these two prayers: *Hashkiveinu* and *Oseh Shalom*, I am struck by the meaning of the words themselves, and the specific message in them and the urgency these prayers convey.

Shelter of Peace

As I approached composing music for *Hashkiveinu* there were two ideas I wrestled with in defining how I felt the music should *feel* with respect to the text. In the first section I wanted to *feel* the motion of the liturgy through the music. I wanted to have it move up and down as "we laid down and rose up" each day.

In the bridge section of the piece I was struck by the concept of a "shelter of peace". A shelter is a refuge and a protected place, providing safety and comfort. However a shelter of peace is not only that, but one that has God's loving presence and 'hands' to shield us completely. A shelter is a sturdy and strong dwelling, yet serene and safe. To me this created a musical paradox, and the music needed the same approach. It needed to be strong at first, and then to be gentle, as we transitioned back to the first section of the prayer.

A Tugging Towards Peace

This brings me to a discussion of the musical intentions for *Oseh Shalom*. Having just asked God many times for blessings in our daily lives, I sought to again create urgency in the musical setting of the liturgy. The goal was to have the music gently *tug* at you rather than push or rush the participant. The anthem quality to the piece allows for a crescendo as the culmination of the *T'fillah* and a resolve, both musically and liturgically, in the worship service.

The eternal and universal message of peace is truly embodied in *Oseh Shalom*. Acknowledging that it is God who makes peace (not people) in the heavens, grant us, and Israel peace. Modern linguists (Reconstructionists) are now including the words *yoshvei teivel*, and all the world peace.

My thought was to try to create and construct a melody and a mood the represented that *hope*. The same hope that the prayer holds—a plea for peace and at the same time is peaceful in and of itself.

Strangely, I cannot recall hearing a memorable melody to this text until Nurit Hirsh wrote her version that debuted in the 1968 Chassidic Song Festival. Certainly there must have been earlier renditions, but most people I encounter consider the Hirsh, the *Mi Sinai* melody very special, for sure.

Oseh Shalom and the message it conveys must be quite important because it is included twice in each service! When I realized this, my approach to the musical setting was further influenced. But I say again, and in my opinion, if you sing my melody too fast, you actually lose some of that power.

Musical Kavannah

The musical *Kavannah* that is in the worship experience is for me the key to spiritual experience. The ebb and flow of the music used in the service, when juxtaposed well with the liturgy, is one that allows God to enter our hearts and minds, and provides ongoing moments to "let go" and feel the strength of the words themselves. In the end, the intention of the music raises the liturgy and us with it to an even more powerful place, and to a much deeper and more meaningful overall experience.

Unfortunately, and all too often, worship services are rushed these days it seems to accommodate time schedules. I refer to this as "stop watch" prayer worship. But like a good movie or a good book, if the integrity of the service and the worship leaders are mindful of the rhythm and cadence of the service, then the time issues vanish and no one bothers to even look at their watches. They are engaged and moved by the experience.

The two prayers I have talked about are, for me, essential to the creating of a moving worship experience. They are both reflective in nature and allow the congregant the needed moments to *exhale* and soak in God's intentions and love. I believe these two prayers are vital in creating the magnificent peace we all strive for as Jews. And when the music is connected well to this meaningful liturgy, then transcendent moments occur that lift us all up.

There are no "rights or wrongs" here, only interpretations and stylistic approaches. These are gleanings and understandings, if you will. My role as a congregant and participant is to enjoy them for what they are. To be able to *let go* for a few minutes, or even just a moment. To be touched and blessed with God's grace. Music clearly helps me get there. And through music I stay in God's presence much, much longer...

Steve Dropkin

For well over 40 years, Steve Dropkin has been actively involved in Jewish music. He began his journey by learning song leading skills at the Eisner Camp in Great Barrington, Massachusetts, at age 14. In high school, he became the Regional Song leader for the Jersey

Federation of Temple Youth, a region of NFTY, the national youth organization of the Reform movement. That experience led to his inclusion in three songs on the NFTY Sings albums. Throughout college, and into his adult life Steve continued to song lead at retreat weekends and synagogues.

These experiences finally inspired him to find and share his own "inner message" as he began writing Jewish songs. His knack for writing catchy and accessible melodies has contributed to his success as a composer. Steve's commitment to composing useful and poignant settings to texts and liturgy is the hallmark of his work.

For more than ten years, he has been a regular guest lecturer at the Hebrew Union College—Jewish Institute of Religion's School of Sacred Music in New York. His presentations on contemporary Jewish music have been heard by scores of cantorial students who use his concepts to balance contemporary music with the more traditional Jewish modes. He has also been a guest panelist at the American Conference of Cantors' national convention.

Steve's songs have been heard on in-flight music programming, and his powerful song, *If Not Now, When?*, was chosen as the New Jersey State Anthem for the first World AIDS Day commemoration. He has been a finalist in the American Jewish Song Festival, as well as the Zionist Organization of America Song Contest. His composition *Hashkiveinu* was the winner of the first-ever Shalshelet Choral Festival.

You can find Steve's work in *The Complete Shireinu, The Complete Jewish Songbook, Shabbat Anthology* I, II and VII, and *The Complete Jewish Songbook for Children: Manginot II*. Several of his songs are included on the

Ruach: New Jewish Tunes compilation albums and companion songbooks as well as in the first *Nigun Anthology*. Steve was a contributor to the Torah Alive music curriculum. New arrangements of three of Steve's major liturgical pieces (*Shalom Rav, Oseh Shalom,* and *Hashkiveinu*) have been released by URJ/Transcontinental Music as choral settings for synagogue choir. His music is also included in the American Conference of Cantors' *Chazzan's Life-Cycle Manual.*

http://SteveDropkin.CreatingCalmNetworkPublishingGroup.com

Growing Your Spiritual Community

1. How do you define peace? What are your thoughts on inner peace, community peace and world peace? What helps you create more inner peace?
2. What is your response to this quote from Steve Dropkin, "In truth, I think it would be more accurate to describe music's role as prayers that are *illuminated* by music."
3. Where in your life do you feel an urgency—a desire for change?
4. If you were comparing and contracting these two pieces: *Hashkiveinu* and *Oseh Shalom,* what similarities and differences do you see and feel?

Six Attributes of Peace
Ter Lieberstein

'I can't sing.' How many times have I heard this phrase?—Too many times to count. It's usually the result of some third grade teacher and their misguided instructions: 'Move your lips, dear, but don't let any sound come out.' Or it may result in a family member who criticized you and told you only to sing in the shower. And even—heaven forbid—a music teacher who said that you were hopeless.

I've heard highly trained opera singers who perform arias with every note pitch perfect, but completely bereft of emotion. On the opposite spectrum, I've seen a street saxophone player pour everything he has into his music for a passing dollar, and his sound reaches deep inside with its intensity.

The Universal Language of Music

A profound method of communication, music is a universal language. Music affects our mind, hearts and spirit, opening emotions and facilitating connection and healing. Whatever the melody, there is something about experiencing music in a group that brings people together as a community. The responsibility and goal of the soloist is to create an atmosphere that draws people into that community. But how exactly do we accomplish that? ... With intention.

Many components affect the accessibility of music, including the quality of the composition, the skill of the performer, the acoustics of the venue, and much more.

But nothing is as vital as focus and attention, passion and commitment, all of which comprise musical intention.

There is something deep inside of me that draws me to the joy of the mystical connection that music brings. My intention when I lead services or other programs is to be a mirror for others to recognize their own light. By allowing my transparency and vulnerability to be shared and embraced, others can do the same, opening their hearts to Divine love and healing.

The Journey That Brought Me Back

To actually be the source of the music, to be responsible for calling it forth, is an extraordinary experience and a profound blessing. But without the intention behind the music, there is no connection. I am always aware that I am simply a vehicle for the music to blossom, and that those listening will respond to the experience in their own way. Each individual has his or her own unique spiritual journey, as have I.

Guitar playing cantors didn't exist when I was growing up. I found the services to be remote, boring, and I was completely disconnected. Following my confirmation at 16, I left Judaism to search other paths (like many of my generation): Bu-Jew, Hin-Jew, and various other religious studies. A song brought me back to Judaism. The song was *Listen* by Doug Cotler, who is the Cantor at my brother's congregation. With Doug's generous guidance I launched on a new path as a Cantorial Soloist. I found that the music played in contemporary synagogues was emotionally moving and deeply spiritual, as well as fun and accessible. And guitar-playing cantors have now become the norm in the realm of Jewish music.

As I studied and took classes, I began to have a profound appreciation for the texts and liturgy. The words and prayers of the service took on meaning as I studied them and heard each prayer set to a variety of melodies. As a songwriter, I too became inspired to fashion my own musical interpretations for the liturgy.

When I first set out to write a setting for a liturgical piece, I embrace the texture of the words. I chose a prayer that resonates with me, and tried to find the essence of its meaning in my life. My intention is to communicate through the music how the sentiments and ideas in the text touch my soul.

Grant Us Peace

An example of this process is the prayer *Sim Shalom*, a simple text with deep meaning which is recited as a blessing at the end of the morning *Amidah* (standing prayer). The opening phrase reveals a glimpse into the world of gratitude. A closer examination of each word helps to understand the more intricate content of the prayer.

Sim shalom tovah uv'rachah,
chein vachesed v'rachamim,
aleinu v'al kol Yisrael amecha.

Translation:
Grant us peace, goodness, and blessing, graciousness, kindness compassion, upon us, and all of Israel, Your people.

Sim: Grant

The most common translation for *'Sim'* is to grant. We don't demand, we ask. I see prayer not as a petition, but as a way for us to move more into alignment with our awareness of God's Presence. We have to move into a position of willingness and humility in order to facilitate this closeness.

Shalom: Peace

In biblical Hebrew, the verb *shalem* means to be complete, whole, or sound. As an adjective, *shalem* means complete, safe, full, perfect, or at peace. The noun *shalom* means completeness, soundness, welfare, or peace. The sense of deep serenity, the notion that everything is exactly as it should be, is the fulfillment of shalom, a place we only find in each present moment. *Sim Shalom* places this concept of 'wholeness' as the first quality we ask for. Without that 'centeredness', none of the other qualities can be embraced.

Tovah: Goodness

What does goodness mean in our lives? At first glance, we appear to be asking for good things to come to us. But the deeper meaning asks us to embrace the qualities of goodness in ourselves — virtue, righteousness, moral excellence and integrity. This is a goal to strengthen and strive for in our lives.

Uv'rachah: (and) Blessing

Bracha is related to the Hebrew word *b'raicha,* a pool from where water bubbles forth: a geyser. If you've ever been to Yellowstone (a very magical and spiritual place), you know that when a geyser erupts, the water overflows and sprays upward in an impressive expression of power and grace. That is *bracha:* blessings that overflow, spilling forth to embrace us and those whose lives we touch.

Chein: Graciousness

In the Torah, graciousness is one of the qualities assigned to God. "And the Lord passed before him and proclaimed: Lord, Lord, benevolent God, Who is compassionate and gracious, slow to anger and abundant in loving kindness and truth." — *Exodus 34:6.* We are always attempting to emulate the qualities of God. Graciousness is giving without the expectation of recompense and walking through the world with calm acceptance.

Vachesed: Kindness

Acts of kindness are central to the teachings of the Torah. The quality of being warm-hearted and considerate, humane and sympathetic is represented by many of the *mitzvot* (commandments). These include offering hospitality, visiting and comforting the sick, providing clothing and food to those in need, comforting mourners, and many others. There is no limit to the obligations of practicing loving-kindness, and it is important in every facet of our relationships.

V'rachamim: Compassion

A Talmudic term used for God is the Aramaic *Rahamana*, 'the Compassionate'. Compassion is the emotion of caring concern. True compassion is limitless. It is not an extension of your needs nor is it defined by your limited perspective. In asking for compassion, we invite this quality to develop and blossom within us.

Aleinu: Upon Us

In Judaism, communal prayer is embraced as a part of being connected to the Jewish community. The sense of being bonded through time and space is an essential concept in our tradition, grounding us in mutual values and connecting us to the past, present, and the potential of the future.

V'al kol Yisrael: And All of Israel

Yisrael is a word with various meanings: May God prevail; one who struggles with God; and God perseveres. One of the dilemmas of being human is the ambiguity of life. We struggle with choices and concepts, even with the idea of whether God exists. This questioning is an inherent part of the ongoing process of life. Dwelling on the attributes listed in this prayer helps us to delve into the peace of gratitude and quiet the struggle.

Amecha: Your People

We are reminded that we are God's people, not as an exclusive ('chosen'), but are meant to live our lives as examples of holiness and righteous living in the world.

The six attributes—*shalom, tovah, u'vracha, chein, v'chesed v'rachamim*—help us to acknowledge how much we have to be grateful for. In thinking about these qualities, I wrote English words to my version of *Sim Shalom*, expressing the meaning of the prayer and the importance of peace in our lives.

Peace in our hearts, peace in our minds
Peace in our lives, in our beings
Peace in our breath, peace in the stillness
Peace in the depth of our souls

Peace in this moment, peace in this hour
May we have blessing and mercy
Peace in our time, goodness and life
Peace amongst all living things

The Heart of Inspiration

The assessment of the text is an important intellectual component of building intention to the leading of a prayer. Writing the musical setting comes straight from the heart of inspiration. When I write a melody, it is a co-creation with God.

God makes the grapes; we make the wine.
God makes the wheat; we make the bread.

In the same sense, the music flows through me in a mystical manner that defies coherent explanation. The notes are simply there. Of course, as a musician, I also employ technical skills and rewrites often come fast and furious. But it's all done with the intention of bringing emotional impact to the words we pray. To lift the heart, transport the spirit to an elevated state of awareness—that is my goal.

The last component in the process of creating an intentional prayer is leading a prayer service. I might put great effort into writing or learning a piece, studying the meaning and carefully crafting the musical setting. However, it is all for naught if I don't set my ego aside and focus. I'm not singing for my own gratification or for accolades. I am singing to be a vessel through which others can connect to something deep within themselves. The focus must be on being present in the very moment of each note, each chord, and each expression of God's love.

Am I able to do this in every moment of every prayer? Hardly! Sometimes I'm thinking of the mistake I just made, what comes next or even (I have to admit it) the grocery list. But the Divine Intention is always there, and I do my best to fulfill it.

Music lives at the core of my being. Without it, I simply wouldn't be me. I feel blessed and privileged to have the opportunity to share my heart and love through this amazing form of prayerful gratitude.

Ter Lieberstein

A published singer and songwriter, cantorial soloist, Ter Lieberstein is also a life cycle celebrant and ordained chaplain. With warmth and deep compassion, she has worked with all ages and populations. She officiates at many kinds of life-cycle ceremonies and works with seniors and hospice to provide services, musical programs and spiritual support.

In addition to her work with others, Ter has created a performance series called *"Voices of Women"* that explores the journeys of the women of Torah through song, story, readings, and interactive participation. To learn more about Ter and hear song samples, visit LovingStone.com.

http://TerLieberstein.CreatingCalmNetworkPublishingGroup.com

Growing Your Spiritual Community

1. What do you think of as the responsibility of the soloist? If you were writing a job description for the soloist, the cantor or the rabbi in relationship to music what would you say?
2. What would you add or subtract from this list?
"Components that affect the accessibility of music:
the quality of the composition
the skill of the performer
the acoustics of the venue
focus and attention, passion and commitment, musical intention."
3. How do you define mysticism? Does music add a mystical component for you?
4. Do you examine the words of the prayer you are singing or chanting? What have you found there?

5. Have you written the words or music for a piece from the liturgy? What is your process?

6. What do you think of this quote from Ter Lieberstein, "Writing the musical setting comes straight from the heart of inspiration?"

7. By filling in the blanks apply this thought to your own life, "God makes the grapes; we make the wine. God makes the wheat; we make the bread." God makes _____, I make _____.

Inner Peace: The Dance of Eggs and Stones
Michael Gurian

Everyday we must risk something. Life is a dance between eggs and stones. Things must break, if we are to say, "I've lived!" Arrogant or just dreaming, ignorant or testing the world, our risks break shells before little birds can be born. We are that powerful.

You know this, don't you? You've felt the guilt and shame of your errors. We who carry light in our heads are so smart we often remember people's fragility after we've broken their hearts with our dancing.

What will it take to be a better person—to dance with more grace, to know when my harsh steps are right ones, and wrong ones? If I lie down at night recalling a day for which I should be judged, mustn't I change? The next morning, mustn't I rise up and pray?

I must learn the next piece of choreography God has written for me in covenant. I must work to meet brothers and sisters who will advise me. I must listen to what they say, see what they see, wander toward their wisdom as does the stone from the original mountain, falling toward the nest of eggs below.

If you have been mean or arrogant or ignorant or mistake prone this year, do not use your actions or shames as excuses to stand away from this life. Our goal is not to become stationary in God's eyes.

God made us from both eggs and stones so we can fulfill the eternal commandment of intimacy: repair.

Friends, isn't it wonderful this life is so fragile?

How else would we teach one another how to love?

Michael Gurian

A marriage and family counselor in private practice, Michael Gurian is the New York Times bestselling author of twenty-eight books published in twenty two languages. He originally wrote this piece as a silent Amidah reading for Yom Kippur Morning Service. He is a member of Congregation Emanu-El and Temple Beth Shalom in Spokane, Washington.

He cofounded The Gurian Institute at MichaelGurian.com which conducts research internationally, launches pilot programs and trains professionals. As a social philosopher, Michael has pioneered efforts to bring neuro-biology and brain research into homes, schools, corporations, and public policy.

http://MichaelGurian.CreatingCalmNetworkPublishingGroup.com

Growing Your Spiritual Community

1. Where in your life are you taking risks? Do you see risk taker as a positive attribute?
2. What do you do as an individual or as a community to create repair?
3. How will you use the stories in this book to create peace both inner peace and peace between communities?

What We Make Of The Music

The famous and gifted violinist Itzhak Perlman, who survived polio as a child is credited with saying, "*You know, it is the artist's task to make beautiful music with what you have left.*" —**Jewish Pathways.com**

Forty-Nine

Seven times seven days
beginnings
seven words in Bereishit one
seven times wholeness—completion

Giving direction, purpose, relationship
to my place plus
north, south, east, west,
up and down
presenting points of reference

Seasons of wholeness in a Jewish year
families gathering chanting on
Rosh Hashana, Yom Kippur, Sukkot,
Chanukah, Purim,
Passover to Shavuot
49 days of people, places
and desires accounted for
in the seeking
of relationship to God

Communities praising in seven
notes in the musical scale
circling we dance on Simchat Torah
every day blessings learning
God is ...
in the 49 holy letters—
Sh'ma Yisrael
Hashem Elokeynu, Hashem Echad
Baruch shem kavod
Malchuto le olam vaed

Growing special species in the Land
Israeli wheat and barley,
grapes and pomegranates,
figs, olives, and dates
multiplying seven times seven

Sefirot, traits in service
kindness, strength, and beauty
triumph, splendor and foundation,
complete with kingship
seven emotional states nested
gevurah within chesed
the strength of giving
hod sheba malchut journey the days
until malchut of majesty

Words, songs, and prayers whisper
gematria's Vah Yi Dah Bayr [222]
and words, and He spoke
from Lay Mor, [271]
spoke to, saying
generates math and logic 49
271 minus 222

A Shabbat for the land
seven times seven
leads to a jubilee
a new era of freedom
growing naturally
nourishing the peace, dirt and people
for another set of cycles
round the sun

Celebrating Mystical Mazel Tov
Mem [40] Teit [9] as we enjoy
fractal planes and subplanes
a universe of physical, emotional, mental,
unity, spiritual, divine and
the monadic one

—Kimberly Burnham

Growing Your Spiritual Community

1. What do you know of Kabbalah, Gematria and the power in numbers?
2. Do you connect with a special number?

Aleph Bet in Numbers

aleph or alef 1
bet (& vet) 2
gimel or gimmel 3
dalet 4
hey or heh 5
vav 6
zayinz 7
chet or khet 8
tet 9
yud or yod 10
kaf 20
lamed 30

mem 40
nun 50
samech or samekh 60
ayin 70
pey or peh (& fey) 80
tzadi or tsadi 90
kuf 100
resh 200
shin 300
tav 400

Glossary

Here are translations for some of the words in this book. The words are primarily from Hebrew or Yiddish

Abah—Father

Adamah—Earth

Adonai—God

Aliyot—Ascendings or going up. This refers to the act of being called to the Torah during the morning service. The one who is called recites a special blessing before and after the Torah reader chants a portion of Torah text.

B'nei Mitzvah—daughters or sons of the commandment. Usually referring to the synagogue ceremony of the 12 or 13 year-old.

B'shert—the woman or man who is destined to be your spouse

B'tzelem Elohim—in the image of God (cf. Genesis 1:26-27)

Baal t'fillah—The prayer leader

Baal kriyah—Chanter or literally master of the reading

Baal Korei—Torah reader

Baboker, Vab/voker—and the Morning

Ben—Son; Beni-my son

Bimah—Pulpit or altar

Brachot—Blessings

Bubbie—Grandma

Cantillation—Special musical notes we use to prepare the Torah chanting

Chai—18 prayer, life-giving and life-fulfilling

Chevrutot (also Hevruta)—Partnering or shared Torah study

Chuppah—Wedding canopy

Davening—Reciting the daily prayers

Dumbek— Goblet drum, an instrument

Dvar-torah—Words of Torah (an interpretation, speech, or homily on the weekly Torah portion.

Eilu Devarim—At the beginning of the morning service we study an excerpt from the Mishnah called Eilu D'varim, "these are the things" which reminds us what it means to lead a Jewish life.

Erev—Evening

Hanukkah—The 8 day celebration usually in December - festival of lights.

Hashem—God

Hidush—New insight

Hineni—Here I am

Hoda'ah—Gratitude blessing

Iyunei tefilah—Meditation on prayer

Kabbalah—Mystical Judaism, Receiving the chain of tradition

Kabbalat Shabbat—Service of receiving the Sabbath; usually filled with rich music

Kavannah—Intention

Kehilah—Congregation

Kesher—Connection

Kevah—Fixed prayer

Kol Nidre—Prayer service at the start of Yom Kippur

Kumsitz—Sitting around and share new songs with the group.

L'dor Vador—From generation to generation

Leyn—Yiddish for read; often used to refer to Torah chanting

Lech lecha—"Go forth," a quote from Genesis 12:1. Also the third Torah portion in Genesis.

Midrashic—"Exegetical"--an interpretation
Minhag—Local custom
Minyan—Congregation
Mishkan—Dwelling
Mizrachi style—Middle Eastern
Modim—prayer of gratitude
Mohel—Performs the circumcision
Neshamah—Spirit, Self
Nigun—Wordless tune, also spelled Niggun
Nigunim—Wordless tunes
Nusach—Melody lines for liturgy
Pirkei Avot—Ethics of the Fathers
Piutim—Hymns and acrostic poems
Rosh Hashana—New Year
Sephardi—Western European descent
Shamayim—Sky
Shalem—Wholeness, One Piece
Shali'ach tzibur—Prayer leader
Shalom—Peace
Shechinah—Divine Spirit
Sheliach tzibor-Representative on behalf of my people
Shiur—A lecture or lesson
Shochet—Ritual slaughterer
Shofar—Ram's horn
Shtetl—Village
Shul—Synagogue
Siddur—Prayer book
Smikha—Ordination
Sukkah—Temporary hut, shelter used on the Feast of
        Tabernacles
Tashlich—ceremony of "casting out" bread into water in
        order to symbolize sins on Rosh haHashana-
        Jewish New Year

Tefilah—simply "Prayer" or the standing, silent prayer at
the acme of the morning service

Tehillim—Psalms

Teshuvah—repentance, "returning"

T'hora—Pure

Tikkun Olam—Healing the world

Torah trope—see "Cantillation"

V'tzohorayim— Afternoon.

Vab/voker—Morning

Zimmun—Invitation to bless

Z'mirot—Shabbat songs

Index

Growing Your Spiritual Community—Questions That Started The Book

Each of the forty or so participants, musicians, cantors, author, poets, and singers in this project were asked to respond to these five questions.

1) When you sing in a Jewish prayer context, where do you direct your attention? What do you intend with your song? Towards what does the singing draw you?

2) "Music is the carrier of intention, so the intention and focus of the person leading liturgical songs is vital to the wellbeing of the congregation." Do you agree or disagree with this statement? How do you understand this idea?

3) "The intention and focus of the individual listening to and participating in a Jewish prayer service, influences not only their own wellbeing but that of everyone else around them because the music connects us." Do you agree or disagree with this statement? How do you understand this concept?

4) Is there a piece of music—a prayer, praise or gratitude expressed in music that particularly touches you, why?

5) Would you like to share a story about the power of music in your spiritual, mental or physical life?

Please contact us at the Creating Calm Network Publishing Group if you would like to be involved in Volume Two.

$23.95 Music / Mind & Body / Spirituality

What does a particular liturgical song mean in a community, and in an individual heart?

What is your personal story of connection to music, song, chanting, and spiritual lyrics?

How does music change a life or bring back memories of a time of transformation?

How are new songs, lyrics and music birthed in the Jewish community?

These questions and more are explored by the authors—rabbis, cantors, poets, healers, and musicians, who share their wisdom and delight with you.

Music, Carrier of Intention in 49 Jewish Prayers is a window into the heart and spirit of a profoundly diverse Jewish prayer community.

If you are looking for ways to make your own spiritual practice more engaging or more meaningful, this book can provide a gateway to that journey. Forty plus authors open their hearts to you and share the ways in which music, song, prayer and Judaism have touched each of them. They come to you from diverse backgrounds—East coast to West coast, North America and beyond, Orthodox and Conservative to Reform, Reconstructionist, Jewish Renewal and more.

Each section is a prompt for individual and communal soul searching. It will provide you, your book group or spiritual community with the tools to pray more joyfully and intentionally.

Made in the USA
Middletown, DE
12 November 2014